The God of All Flesh

The God of All Flesh

And Other Essays

WALTER BRUEGGEMANN

edited by K. C. HANSON

CASCADE *Books* · Eugene, Oregon

Other Books by Walter Brueggemann
from Cascade Books

🖎

Praying the Psalms, 2nd ed. (2007)
A Pathway of Interpretation (2008)
Divine Presence amid Violence (2009)
David and His Theologian (2011)
Truth-telling as Subversive Obedience (2011)
Remember You Are Dust (2012)
Embracing the Transformation (2013)
The Practice of Homefulness (2014)
Into Your Hand: Confronting Good Friday (2014)
The Role of Old Testament Theology in Old Testament Interpretation (2015)
Prophetic Imagination toward Social Flourishing (forthcoming)

Cascade Books
An Imprint of Wipf and Stock Publishers
199 W. 8th Ave., Suite 3
Eugene, OR 97401

www.wipfandstock.com

ISBN: 978-1-4982-0644-0

Cataloging-in-Publication data:

Brueggemann, Walter.

The God of all flesh : and other essays / Walter Brueggemann ; edited and with a
Foreword by K. C. Hanson.

xiv + 174 p. ; 23 cm. Includes bibliographic references and indexes.

ISBN: 978-1-4982-0644-0

Note: Essays republished in revised form from Festschriften.

1. Bible. O.T.—Criticism, interpretation, etc. 2. Bible. Old Testament—Theology.
I. Hanson, K. C. (Kenneth Charles). II. Title.

BS1192.5 B78 2015

Manufactured in the USA

CONTENTS

ABBREVIATIONS

AB	Anchor Bible
ATANT	Abhandlungen zur Theologie des Alten und Neuen Testaments
BA	*Biblical Archaeologist*
BASOR	*Bulletin of the American Schools of Oriental Research*
BWANT	Beiträge zur Wissenschaft der Alten und Neuen Testaments
BZAW	Beihefte zur Zeitschrift für die alttestamentliche Wissenschaft
CBQ	*Catholic Biblical Quarterly*
EvTh	*Evangelische Theologie*
FOTL	Forms of the Old Testament Literature
HBT	*Horizons in Biblical Theology*
HTR	*Harvard Theological Review*
HUCA	*Hebrew Union College Annual*
Int	*Interpretation*
IRT	Issues in Religion and Theology
JAAR	*Journal of the American Academy of Religion*
JBL	*Journal of Biblical Literature*
JSOT	*Journal for the Study of the Old Testament*

JSOTSup	Journal for the Study of the Old Testament Supplements
LAI	Library of Ancient Israel
OBT	Overtures to Biblical Theology
OTL	Old Testament Library
SBLDS	Society of Biblical Literature Dissertation Series
SBT	Studies in Biblical Theology
ThBü	Theologische Bücherei
ThTo	*Theology Today*
TLZ	*Theologische Literaturzeitung*
ThBü	Theologische Bücherei
VT	*Vetus Testamentum*
VTSup	Vetus Testamentum Supplements
WMANT	Wissenschaftliche Monographien zum Alten und Neuen Testament
ZAW	*Zeitschrift für die alttestamentliche Wissenschaft*

FOREWORD

This is the second volume of collected essays from Walter Brueggemann originally written for Festschriften; the first was *The Role of Old Testament Theology in Old Testament Interpretation: And Other Essays* (Cascade Books, 2015). These essays demonstrate his discerning analyses of biblical texts. But more than that, they articulate the depth his theological insight, as well as his social analysis.

In his Preface, Brueggemann notes that these essays highlight his enduring interest in the books of Jeremiah and Psalms. I would also point out that a recurring theme here is God's created order. This focus has long been a major theme of Brueggemann's work. His volume *The Land: Place as Gift, Promise, and Challenge in Biblical Faith* (Fortress, 1st ed., 1977; 2nd ed. 2002) was a breakthrough volume for the theological reading of the Old Testament and was the lead volume in the series Overtures to Biblical Theology (for which he was one of the editors). And he has continued to participate in the conversation of how our reading of the Old Testament is a powerful resource for understanding our sense of place, rootedness, and connectedness to the land.

What these essays provide me is a reminder of the imaginative potentialities within the ancient texts. I find new dimensions, new dynamics, new possibilities after reading Brueggemann's essays on texts that I have repeatedly read, translated, studied, and written on. It humbles me, but also energizes me.

K. C. Hanson
Eugene, Oregon

PREFACE

This collection of essays has accumulated over time, so that they are diverse and pluralistic in their subjects and approaches. There is nonetheless a consistency to my work with recurring theme and accents. Several of these essays are a bit more programmatic as I articulate my angle of interpretation. Not least among my concerns is the recognition that the practice of interpretation is an act of imagination that goes beyond "the given," that is, the capacity to entertain and take seriously a "world" other than the one that is in front of us. Thus with reference to "psychological criticism," the human person is indeed a world-maker in the exercise of productive imagination that is not merely reproductive and reiterative, but capacity for fresh initiative.

The more important accent of my work, however, consists not in programmatic interpretive efforts but exposition that is text specific. And while I have done other things as well with my interpretive energy, the recurring focus of my work, as is evident in this collection, concerns the book of Jeremiah and the book of Psalms.

The book of Jeremiah, with its demanding, excruciating, buoyant imagery, is a primal script wherein Israel is, by the poet, walked into its sixth-century displacement and walked out of that displacement in hope for restoration and new historical possibility. It is this two-fold interpretation into that abyss and out of the abyss that gives the book its immense contemporary power for us. In this collection I have included four pieces on Jeremiah, though the essay, "The Creatures Know," does not major in Jeremiah. But it takes up the text from Jer 8:7 on the wisdom of creatures and the contrasting foolishness of Israel. This essay shows the poet utilizing an appeal to "nature" (creation, creatures) as way to illuminate the self-destructive obtuseness of his contemporaries. The accent of that essay is powerfully exposited by Robin Wall Kimmerer in her recent book, *Braiding*

Sweetgrass (Milkweed, 2013). Her subtitle, *Indigenous Wisdom, Scientific Knowledge, and the Teachings of Plants*, exhibits a vigorous awareness, not unlike that of Jeremiah, about the lively and pertinent testimony of the "natural" world. The other Jeremiah essays included here offer empowering images and illuminating metaphors that leap off the page into our contemporary work of faith in a cultural context where we are slowly walking into an abyss with the profound yearning for restoration.

The other recurring interest for me, the book of Psalms, is represented here by two essays, one a close reading of Psalm 37, and the other a notice of the ambiguous pronouns, "we, us" in Psalm 67. The ambiguous interpretive possibilities in both Psalms make clear the immense power of the Psalter to evoke interpretation that both *conforms* to our presuppositions and that alternatively *speaks against* such presuppositions. Thus the Psalms may be read for "us" (Psalm 67) and our possessiveness (Psalm 37) in a narrow self-confirming way, or they may be against that, toward an expansive, inclusive "us" beyond our tribe (Palm 67), and against and assumed entitlement to affirm wisdom of a demanding kind (Psalm 37). When read innocently according to privilege, the Psalms may substantiate "the Dream" of glorified entitlement exposited by Ta-Nehisi Coates, *Between the World and Me* (Spiegel & Grau, 2015). When read with critical alertness, however, the Psalms open that "Dream" for the sake of a better vision of historical reality. Thus readers are invited into the playful crevice of imagination where new life may come and push up against old life that is too much treasured.

I am glad that these essays can be republished, because they were originally published as tribute and thanks to some of the most important and influential scholars in our discipline. For that reason I am grateful to those scholars who originally edited the several honorific volumes and invite me to contribute; their work as editors is characteristically tedious, demanding, and under-appreciated. And I am, as always grateful to K. C. Hanson (along with his colleagues at Cascade Books and Wipf and Stock) for their attentiveness to my work. I will hope that these several probes into the text will invite fresh engagement for readers with these remarkable and demanding biblical texts.

Walter Brueggemann
Columba Theological Seminary
July 30, 2015

one

THE GOD OF ALL FLESH

Of all of Terry Fretheim's remarkable published corpus, I regard his 1991 article, "The Plagues as Ecological Signs of Historical Disaster," as his most remarkable piece and arguably his most important.[1] In that article, Fretheim argues that Exodus 1–15 is grounded in creation theology. He makes his case by careful attention to the rhetorical usage of the inclusive adjective "all" (כל) and by translating ארץ as "earth," not merely "land."

This essay builds upon that article by exploring four Jeremiah passages that reflect the horizon of creation through the recurring phrase "all flesh" (כל בשר). That phrase refers not only to human beings but to all of God's creatures. This analysis advances the well-established understanding that the Jeremiah tradition operates on the horizon of creation.[2] It does so in order to take full account of the "world upheaval" that is coming at the end of the seventh century and to claim that Yahweh will instigate that upheaval through the agency of Babylon. This upheaval impinges upon the theological claims of Jerusalem and the royal-temple ideology that is placed in jeopardy by the upheaval of the sixth century.

1. I am glad to offer this essay in thanks and congratulations to Terry Fretheim. Over the course of my work, no one in the field has been more important for me than Terry; his work and mine have been very much in tandem. I am, moreover, always instructed by his careful but good-spirited critique of my work. I am greatly in his debt.

2. See Fretheim, *God and World in the Old Testament*; and Brueggemann, "Jeremiah: *Creatio in extremis*" (chap. 3 below).

"All Flesh" in the Flood Narrative and in Second Isaiah

Jeremiah's usage of "all flesh" is best understood as flanked by two texts that function theologically with reference to the world upheaval and to the restorative power of Yahweh as creator. First, the phrase "all flesh" occurs prominently in the flood narrative of Genesis 6–9.[3] On the one hand, the rhetoric of the narrative presents the flood in sweeping categories, envisioning the termination of every creature, that is, "all flesh." On the other hand, the narrative celebrates the ark as a device whereby representatives of "all flesh" are rescued and offered new life:

- *all flesh* is corrupt (Gen 6:12)

- *all flesh* is to be destroyed (Gen 6:13, 17; see 7:21)

- representatives of *all flesh* are protected by entering the ark (Gen 6:19; 7:15–16)

- representatives of *all flesh* leave the ark to begin new life (Gen 8:17)

- a promise never again to destroy *all flesh* (Gen 9:11, 15)

- God's covenant with *all flesh* whereby new creation begins (Gen 9:15–17)

The phrase recurs in order to trace the characteristic pattern of Israel's faith that leads *into the abyss* (chaos, flood . . . exile) and that hopes *out of the abyss* into new life.[4] While the flood narrative is articulated in generic, non-Israelite categories, there is no doubt that the pattern of presentation reflects the pattern of Israel's own life (a) *into and out of exile*, or alternatively, (b) *judgment and hope*. Marvelously, though "all flesh" is sentenced to destruction, "all flesh" is rescued and given new life guaranteed by divine promises of fidelity. The usage of "all flesh" refers to every aspect of creation; all creatures die and live by Yahweh's activity.

Second Isaiah employs a double usage of "all flesh" in Isa 40:5–6:

> Then the glory of Yahweh shall be revealed,
>> and **all people** shall see it together,
>> for the mouth of Yahweh has spoken.
> A voice says, "Cry out!"
>> And I said, "What shall I cry?"

3. Fretheim, "The Plagues as Ecological Signs of Historical Disaster," 387 n.7.

4. On the pattern, see Clements, "Patterns in the Prophetic Canon." On the figure of "the abyss," see Brueggemann, "Meditation upon the Abyss."

>*All people* are grass,
>>their constancy is like the flower of the field.

This NRSV rendering of בשר כל as "all people" unfortunately misses the cosmic accent of inclusive creatureliness.

All creatures will witness the dramatic return of Yahweh' s glory to Jerusalem. The return is presented as though it were of significance beyond Israel, a point related to Jerusalem's cosmic significance (see Isa 2:2–4). To be sure, the second in v. 6 tones down the claim of v. 5, because "all flesh" is transient. That qualification, however, does not dim the claim made in v. 5 that "all flesh" shall see the triumphant sovereignty of Yahweh disclosed through the restoration of Judah. It is appropriate to the very creatureliness of "all flesh" to attend to the work of the creator-restorer God, upon whose rule they depend.

While Second Isaiah's usage of "all flesh" is much more limited than that of the flood narrative, reference to the flood in Second Isaiah demonstrates the doxological sweep of the Isaiah passage. Yahweh is indeed "getting glory" by the restoration of Israel, a glory fully visible to the creatures in ways that enhance the creator's splendor (see Exod 14:4, 17; Isa 42:8; 48:11).

Four other uses of the phrase appear in Isaiah. In Isa 49:26, "all flesh" attests that Yahweh is sovereign and savior of Israel. Isaiah 66:16 claims that Yahweh's punishment of Israel's enemies visited upon "all flesh" will cause Jerusalem to rejoice. The phrase is used in a characteristically dual way in Isa 66:23–24. Verse 23 anticipates that "all flesh" will worship Yahweh; but in v. 24 "all flesh" will abhor the deathly scene left byYahweh's judgment. These latter usages reinforce the double usage in the flood narrative. Isaiah 40:5–6 and 49:26 demonstrate that Yahweh's judgment and restoration of Jerusalem are exhibited and available to all creation. While the impact of those actions is directly upon Jerusalem and upon Israel, the reality is the effective operation of Yahweh's total and unfettered, unqualified governance.

"All Flesh" in Jeremiah

The Jeremiah traditions will now be considered in light of these usages. Since Isa 40:5–6 and the final form of the flood narrative are clearly situated in the sixth century, it follows that the Jeremiah tradition that flourished in the same period would similarly employ "all flesh." The events pertaining to Jerusalem at the time of the exile are broadly presented and concern Yahweh' s effective governance of the entire cosmos. Inevitably, interpretation of those events would proceed on a very large scale in order to draw Babylon into the world of Yahweh's rule. We turn to the four usages of "all flesh" in Jeremiah, each of which occurs in a distinct genre and from a separate strand of the tradition.

Jeremiah 32:27–41

This extended divine prose oracle divides into two parts. The chapter appears just after the "Book of Comfort" in chaps. 30–31 and precedes the miscellaneous collection of promise oracles in chap. 33. Thus it occurs in a context of hope but is distinguished by its prose style. Chapter 32 proceeds from the brief narrative account of vv. 1–15, but then is filled out by the prophetic utterance of vv. 16–25 and by the divine oracle that concerns us (vv. 27–41). The first part of the oracle is a conventional prophetic judgment speech concerning Jerusalem (vv. 28–35). Most of this material indicts Jerusalem, but the divine threats concerning its capture by Nebuchadnezzar and the "removal" of the city are direct and unqualified. The judgment speech begins with a divine declaration of punishment (vv. 28–29), followed by an extended indictment detailing Jerusalem's recalcitrance. The declaration of punishment, governed by the divine "I," is crucial:

> Therefore, thus says Yahweh: I am going to give this city into the hands of the Chaldeans and into the hand of King Nebuchadrezzar of Babylon . . . (Jer 32:28a)

In vv. 28b–29, Nebuchadrezzar is the active agent of punishment, so these verses offer a characteristic formulation of double agency. In sum, vv. 28–35 assure that Jerusalem's punishment is justified.

The oracle turns in v. 36 with "and now," followed by "behold" (or "see") in v. 37. Again Yahweh is the subject of a series of first-person verbs: I am gathering, I will bring back, I will give, I will make, I will put, I will rejoice, I will plant (vv. 37–41). This divine assurance is remarkable in light of the reference to Babylon's approach authorized by Yahweh (v. 36); that negative reference, however, is rhetorically overridden immediately by הנה ("see") and the turn to restoration.

The two subunits of the divine oracle, vv. 28–35 on punishment and vv. 36–41 on restoration, summarize the final form of the Jeremiah tradition, a twofold assertion variously voiced through the verb cluster in 1:10. Notably, the God who speaks this double future for Jerusalem is "the God of *all flesh*" (v. 27). The scope of Yahweh's rule is as broad as creation. In the Jeremiah tradition, however, this language suggests that Yahweh is God of Israel, but *also* God of Babylon. This usage of "all flesh" expands Yahweh's sphere beyond the covenant with Israel. Yahweh's sovereignty is not fully comprehended in "they shall be my people and I will be their God" (v. 38), but pertains elsewhere as well. Conversely, the phrase "God of all flesh" de-absolutizes the pretentious ambitions of Babylon and makes imperial power penultimate. Thus, the "creation faith" voiced in this phrase is made to serve the geopolitical horizon of the Jeremiah tradition, allowing for the *Babylonian onslaught* and in turn for the *termination of Babylon* as well; no historical agency is absolute before "the God of all flesh," with the important qualification that with Israel, "the God of all flesh" has made an "everlasting covenant" (v. 40).

Jeremiah 12:7–13

This prophetic judgment speech belongs to the poetic materials usually assigned to the prophet Jeremiah. They follow vv. 5–6, Yahweh's response to the prophetic lament of vv. 1–4.[5] The judgment speech begins with three first-person indictments; Yahweh's conduct toward Israel, however, is not assault; it is rather abandonment to "her enemies." The indictment is briefly given in v. 8c: "She has lifted her voice against me."

The rest of the oracle expresses divine judgment in two different images. The operational word is "enemies." Jerusalem and Judah are now exposed to risks and dangers that YHWH permits against "my heritage." In v. 9, hyenas, birds of prey and wild animals, clearly images of assaulting creation, constitute the threat. By contrast, v. 10 invokes "shepherds," that is, other rulers, no doubt Nebuchadnezzar. The poetry emotively portrays a devastation wrought through the agencies of creation and history.

These divinely permitted assaults upon "my heritage" result in whole-sale desolation. The verdict concerns "the whole land," the same phrase

---

5. The divine response (vv. 5–6) to the lament (vv. 1–4) is surprising. In this genre the divine response is characteristically comfort and assurance; here it appears as a more intense challenge. Fretheim (*God and World*, 174–81) reads Jeremiah 12 as a coherent unity in which vv. 7–17 continue God's response as Yahweh's lament. I agree, but suggest that divine anger accompanies the grief.

that Fretheim renders "the whole earth" (v. 11). The consequence of Israel's recalcitrance and Yahweh's anger is massive. Verse 12 reinforces the picture of devastation. The "spoilers" traverse the landscape with their devastation resulting in "no shalom for all flesh." That is, every creature is jeopardized. NRSV's "no one shall be safe" assumes that "all flesh" refers to human beings, a rather anemic translation. Verse 13 reiterates "the fierce anger of the Lord."

"All flesh" (v. 12) corresponds to "all the land" in v. 11. Two matters require comment. First, Fretheim, with reference to my own work, has often insisted that human agency, not divine agency, works such devastation according to prophetic rhetoric.[6] I believe the matter is more complex. Of course political agents (portrayed as scavenger animals) enact the ruin of Jerusalem. But the act is permitted, if not directed, by Yahweh. Thus, the text affirms double agency. Second, "all flesh" is made more acute by the earlier mention of hyenas, birds of prey, and wild animals, which would be included in "all flesh" and were in the flood narrative. Here, however, they are not included in "all flesh," because for the poet they are the very agents who will jeopardize "all flesh." Such a distinction is only acceptable in poetry that seeks to convey emotive recognition and not precise analysis. The negating energies of the God of "all flesh" are mobilized against the recalcitrant city.

Jeremiah 25:30–31

The peculiar nature of chap. 25 is widely recognized.[7] It testifies to the development of the Jeremiah tradition toward apocalyptic imagination. Once again the assertion that Yahweh wills Nebuchadnezzar's devastation of Jerusalem (25:1–11) and subsequent judgment upon Babylon (25:12–14) are held together. Babylon's judgment is then expanded to include judgment against "all the kingdoms of the world" (vv. 17–26). Verses 27–29 reverse the direction, from judgment of the nations back to judgment upon Jerusalem.

6. Since Fretheim's "relational" hermeneutic emphasizes human agency, direct divine agency is not the first way he reads a prophetic text. In my judgment, Fretheim overstates the difference between us. I agree completely with his conclusion that "[f]or Israel, God is both directly involved and rules and judges through means" (*God and World*, 339 n10).

7. See the essays in *Troubling Jeremiah* by Martin Kessler ("The Function of Chapters 25 and 50–51 in the Book of Jeremiah"), Robert P. Carroll ("Halfway through a Dark Wood"), and John Hill ("The Construction of Time in Jeremiah 25 [MT]").

The two aspects of judgment are nicely juxtaposed in vv. 30–32. All judgment is rooted in the holy habitation of Yahweh, a reference to either heaven or Jerusalem. In v. 30, Yahweh roars against "his fold," paralleling "all the inhabitants of the earth." The following verse emphasizes the nations that stand under Yahweh's threat:

> The clamor will resound to the ends of the earth,
>> for Yahweh has an indictment against the nations;
> he is entering into judgment with all flesh,
>> and the guilty he will put to the sword,
>> says Yahweh. (Jer 25:31)

Here, "all flesh" parallels "the nations" (see v. 32). The last line of v. 31 judges only "the guilty." This suggests that in the day of reckoning, all are tested, but not all are guilty (see Amos 9:9–10). Unlike the wholesale threat of this chapter, this line allows exemptions from judgment. But as no specific indictment is given against the nations, neither is any basis offered for exception or exemption. It is enough to notice that "all flesh" is the scope of judgment, even if there are exemptions, so that the text operates in immense scope, well beyond Jerusalem. These verses need not be regarded as "apocalyptic," but suggest extremely violent judgment still within the historical sphere.

Jeremiah 45:1–5

This narrative report of an oracle to Baruch concludes the so-called "Baruch document." The narrative dates the oracle to 605 BCE, a decisive moment for the Jeremiah tradition, namely, Nebuchadnezzar's rise to power.

The narrative report, after an editorial introduction, begins with a lament from Baruch, who is publicly allied with Jeremiah and so under immense pressure and in serious danger (v. 3; see Jer 36:19, 26, 32). Jeremiah's response falls into two parts, a public oracle concerning the land (v. 4) and a personal address to Baruch (v. 5). The public oracle utilizes the four decisive verbs of 1:10. The usual sequence of the verbs, however—in which the negative verbs, "pluck up and break down," are followed by the positives, "build and plant"—is here reversed. What has been built is to be broken down; what has been planted is to be plucked up. The reversed order radically characterizes the dismantling of Jerusalem, a theme reflected in the poetry of 4:23–26. The scope of the reiterated verbs concerns "the whole land" (כל־הארץ). While v. 5 personally addresses Baruch, the more general negative judgment occurs even here: "I am going to bring disaster (רעה) upon *all flesh*." Thus, the prophet (or the tradition) cannot resist yet one more judgment against the realm, so overriding is that accent even in the midst of personal assurance.

The general oracle of v. 4 is similar to the statement in 25:30–31 wherein the inclusiveness of devastation pertains to "all the inhabitants of the earth . . . to the ends of the earth . . . *all flesh*." It is remarkable that the so-called *apocalyptic* material in chap. 25 and the *scribal* statement in chap. 45 are parallel. Both apocalyptic and scribal statements imagine a divine assault on "all flesh," undoing the order of creation and dismantling the infrastructure of Yahweh's beloved community. The scope of devastation echoes the scale of the flood narrative's destruction of all creation.

Significantly, the oracle of chap. 45 moves beyond the vision of devastation in chap. 25 to a post-devastation possibility. The sanction against "all flesh" is unqualified. In the midst of that devastating verdict, however, there is a ואתה ("and you") addressed singularly to Baruch. Baruch is the subject of a possibility beyond the loss of "all flesh." The rolling corpus of Jeremiah presses toward a scribal remnant that will culminate in the Ezra movement.

Christopher Seitz suggests that Ebedmelech (39:18) and Baruch (45:5), both of whom receive their life "as a prize of war" from Jeremiah, constitute the remnant of the faithful, as do Joshua and Caleb in the land tradition.[8] Only Joshua and Caleb of the older generation make it through the wilderness to the land of promise. Similarly, Seitz suggests that Ebedmelech and Baruch make it through the exile because of their faithfulness to the covenant and Jeremiah. In both traditions only the two faithful ones survive destruction and are granted access to the future. Seitz's insight suggests that in the Jeremiah tradition Baruch and Ebedmelech recall Noah's family on the ark, who are "righteous" and protected for the future. Here, "all flesh" is under severe judgment, but an exception is made of representatives of "all flesh."

"All Flesh" and Creation Theology

The four "all flesh" texts demonstrate, as a footnote to Fretheim's work, that the Jeremiah tradition is grounded in creation theology. I am struck by the

8. Seitz, "The Prophet Moses and the Canonical Shape of Jeremiah"; and Seitz, "The Place of the Reader in Jeremiah."

variation of the four uses from a critical perspective, while concurrently noticing the constancy of the theological affirmation.

Read diachronically, the four texts represent four distinct moments in the development of the Jeremiah tradition:

- **12:12**, "no *shalom* to all flesh," comes from the Jeremiah tradition, perhaps from the prophet himself. Fretheim's own reading of the text connects the usage to the genuine lamentations of Jeremiah. This usage depicts Yahweh's grief and anger at Jerusalem's recalcitrance and anticipates Yahweh's authorization of "shepherds," historical agents, in their devastation. Thus, "all flesh" pertains to judgment by the Lord of all creation against Jerusalem.

- **32:17** is a divine oracle attached to the account of the land purchase at Anathoth. While the purchase narrative is plausibly linked to the prophet, the prayer (vv. 16–25) and the divine oracle (vv. 26–41) are more likely products of the tradition. The appellation of Yahweh as "the God of all flesh" is a summary of our entire study. The formula acknowledges Yahweh' s capacity as creator to reverse field and move from judgment to restoration. While vv. 28–35 articulate divine judgment, the passage surely focuses on the promise of restoration in vv. 36–41. The God of all flesh may cause a radically new beginning exactly as the God of all flesh had done in the post-flood oracle of Gen 9:8–17.[9]

- **25:31** belongs to a development of the Jeremiah tradition toward apocalyptic imagery, though vv. 30–32 themselves are more in line with prophetic rhetoric. These verses anticipate judgment against "his fold," that is, Yahweh' s entire creation. The reference concerns the devastation of the nations—most specifically, Babylon—anticipating complete and unmitigated judgment.

- **45:5** offers an oracle of personal assurance to Baruch amid a general oracle of devastation. As the culmination of the "Baruch document," this text embodies a development beyond the prophet, although such an oracle from the prophet is not unthinkable. The general announcement of the devastation of "all flesh" is the key assertion, and brings this announcement into agreement with 25:30–32. The announcement of assurance to Baruch has no parallel in chap. 25. Thus this

---

9. Note especially the parallel concerning the "everlasting covenant" in Gen 9:16 and Jer 32:40.

THE GOD OF ALL FLESH

oracle is a development of the scribal community that anticipates a surviving remnant of the faithful. The apocalyptic development of chap. 25 is rather odd in the Jeremiah tradition and should perhaps be seen as an extrapolation of the scribal tradition as the uttered poetry moved toward canonical text.[10]

The four texts thus reflect prophetic poetry (12:12), an extrapolated prose oracle of judgment (32:17), an apocalyptic surge of judgment (25:30–32), and a general judgment qualified by a scribal remnant of faithful survivors (45:5). The spectrum of usage indicates the supple, imaginative capacity of the Jeremiah tradition.

Given these differentiations, however, the fourfold use of the term "all flesh" serves on large scale the judgment–restoration theme of the prophetic tradition.[11] Three of these texts concern divine judgment (chaps. 12, 25, 45). In Jer 12:10–12, the concern is Jerusalem's failure and the enactment of divine judgment by human agency. In Jer 25:30–32, the judgment focuses upon the nations over whom the creator God presides. In Jer 45:5, the theme of judgment concerns כל־הארץ ("all the earth"), but the focus of that threat is Jerusalem. All three texts concern divine judgment, sometimes by human agents, some directly by Yahweh, concerning both Jerusalem and the nations. These "all flesh" passages depict divine sovereignty enacted in a variety of ways against recalcitrant creaturely society.

The spectacular function of our phrase in Jer 32:27, however, is different, because it explicitly uses the phrase as a divine appellation and because it moves to restoration (vv. 36–41). If we emphasize this articulation, we notice it voices the culminating theme of the Jeremiah tradition, namely,

---

10. On the defining role of the scribal movement for the shaping of Judaism, see Davies, *Scribes and Schools*.

11. Clements, "Patterns in the Prophetic Canon," 49, 53, comments on the canonical shaping pattern of the prophetic traditions: "In such fashion we can at least come to understand the value and meaning of the way in which distinctive patterns have been imposed upon the prophetic collections of the canon so that warnings of doom and disaster are always followed by promises of hope and restoration . . . We must see that prophecy is a collection of collections, and that ultimately the final result in the prophetic corpus of the canon formed a recognizable unity not entirely dissimilar from that of the Pentateuch. As this was made up from various sources and collections, so also the Former and Latter Prophets, comprising the various preserved prophecies of a whole series of inspired individuals. acquired an overarching thematic unity. This centered on the death and rebirth of Israel, interpreted theologically as acts of divine judgment and salvation."

restoration that coheres with the vision of Second Isaiah, to which Fretheim refers in detail in his discussion of creation in prophetic tradition.[12]

Each of these texts is concerned with historical concreteness—in turn, with the city of Jerusalem, with Babylon, and with other nations. Use of the creation formula, however, renders all such historical concreteness penultimate. Jerusalem is penultimate, notwithstanding its expansive ideology of ultimacy. Babylon is penultimate, in spite of its imperial aggressiveness and pretense. The God of all flesh presides over all creation and, in the end, wills "good." Fretheim would no doubt concur that divine judgment is serious and pervades the tradition of Jeremiah, but is not the last divine word; the last divine word is a promise:

> I will make an everlasting covenant with them, never to draw back from doing good to them; and I will put the fear of me in their hearts, so that they may not turn from me. I will rejoice in doing good to them, and I will plant them in this land in faithfulness, with all my heart and all my soul. (Jer 32:40–41)

The creation theme, so well served by "all flesh," situates all the *destabilization of history* in the context of the *abiding fidelity of the creator* and so the consequent *abiding stability of the creation*. While the prophet articulates the undoing of creation in 4:23–26, the promissory passages assert stability, coherence, and reliability that issue in a fundamental assurance made even to the exilic generation. The constancy of Yahweh's commitment to Israel is as reliable as the creation itself:

> Thus says Yahweh: Only if I had not established my covenant with day and night and the ordinances of heaven and earth, would I reject the offspring of Jacob and of my servant David and not choose any of his descendants as rulers of the offspring of Abraham, Isaac, and Jacob. For I will restore their fortunes, and will have mercy upon them. (Jer 33:25–26; cf. Jer 31:35–36, 37)

This return to creation from the vagaries of history yields two remarkable insights:

1. The stuff of "history" that has long characterized Jeremiah studies in particular and Old Testament studies in general has produced an accent on judgment and an awareness that the historical process inexorably worked to the undoing of Jerusalem and of Israel. A refocus on creation invites an accent on restoration, stability, and well-being. The themes around

---

12. Fretheim, "Creation and Salvation in the Prophets," in *God and World*, 181–98.

which we pose interpretive questions make a huge difference in theological outcomes! Fretheim's refocus on creation provides immense theological potential.

2. Emphasis on stability, coherence, and the reliability of the God of "all flesh" speaks an immediately urgent pastoral word in a society beset by inchoate and massive anxiety. In our society, anxiety covers a spectrum of issues from contested sexuality, to uncertain economy, to terrorist threats in an overly armed world. That pastoral word, even amid smoldering Jerusalem in the sixth century, is that the center will hold. It will hold because the center is not the city, the king, or the temple—nor any of their counterparts in Babylon. The center is the God of all flesh. This God governs, so Fretheim has taught us, not primarily by disruptive actions but by an "abiding" that issues in newness: restoration and well-being. In the end, the God of all flesh reverses the verdict of Jer 12:12 and allows "*shalom* for all flesh," in Jerusalem and perhaps even in Babylon (see 29:7).

Bibliography

Brueggemann, Walter. "Meditation upon the Abyss." *Word & World* 22 (2002) 340–50.

Carroll, Robert P. "Halfway through a Dark Wood: Reflections on Jeremiah 25." In *Troubling Jeremiah*, edited by A. R. Pete Diamond, Kathleen M. O'Connor, and Louis Stulman, 73–86. JSOTSup 260. Sheffield: Sheffield Academic, 1999.

Clements, Ronald E. "Patterns in the Prophetic Canon." In *Canon and Authority: Essays in Old Testament Religion and Theology*, edited by George W. Coats and Burke O. Long, 42–55. Philadelphia: Fortress, 1977.

Davies, Philip R. *Scribes and Schools: The Canonization of the Hebrew Scriptures*. LAI. Louisville: Westminster John Knox, 1998.

Diamond, A. R. Pete, Kathleen M. O'Connor, and Louis Stulman, eds. *Troubling Jeremiah*. JSOTSup 260. Sheffield: Sheffield Academic, 1999.

Fretheim, Terence E. *God and World in the Old Testament: A Relational Theology of Creation*. Nashville: Abingdon, 2005.

———. "The Plagues as Ecological Signs of Historical Disaster." *JBL* 110 (1991) 385–96.

Hill, John. "The Construction of Time in Jeremiah 25 (MT)." In *Troubling Jeremiah*, edited by A. R. Pete Diamond, Kathleen M. O'Connor, and Louis Stulman, 146–60. JSOTSup 260. Sheffield: Sheffield Academic, 1999.

Kessler, Martin. "The Function of Chapters 25 and 50–51 in the Book of Jeremiah." In *Troubling Jeremiah*, edited by A. R. Pete Diamond, Kathleen M. O'Connor, and Louis Stulman, 64–72. JSOTSup 260. Sheffield: Sheffield Academic, 1999.

Seitz, Christopher R. "The Place of the Reader in Jeremiah." In *Reading the Book of Jeremiah: A Search for Coherence*, edited by Martin Kessler, 67–75. Winona Lake, IN: Eisenbrauns, 2004.

———. "The Prophet Moses and the Canonical Shape of Jeremiah." *ZAW* 101 (1989) 3–27.

two

THE CREATURES KNOW

It is by now a truism that "wisdom thinks resolutely within the framework of a theology of creation."[1] That now common assumption among interpreters, however, has not always been obvious. It is, rather, a hard-won consensus that emerged in a season of scholarship preoccupied with "history," in which theological interpretation of the Old Testament was dominated by the programmatic slogan "God acts in history." The connection between wisdom and creation has permitted interpretation to move outside "history" and to challenge the fear of "natural theology" that pertained in Barthian circles of interpretation. Once that consensus judgment was reached about creation and wisdom, however, it has not been at all clear what the creation–wisdom convergence may mean, and it has been treated very much in a reified way, either as a dogmatic claim, or as a method, or as a defense of "natural theology" as distinct from and opposed to a "theology of the word."

In this brief discussion I wish to explore the creation–wisdom convergence in a much more elemental way by considering that God's "creatures," the counterpoint to the "creator"—all of them, nonhuman as well as human—have a wisdom about how to live well, faithfully, and responsively in a world governed by the creator God. From the outset of my formulation of this brief argument, I have intended to consider two texts in particular that evidence the knowing of which nonhuman creatures are capable, Isa 1:2 and Jer 8:7. While I have pondered this writing assignment, I was clear about the argument I wished to present to honor Professor Bergant; I have, however, puzzled for a long time about how to proceed. I finally found my

---

1. Zimmerli, "The Place and Limit of the Wisdom," 316.

way with the suggestions of a playful novel and a whimsical essay that relate loosely to our theme. It occurred to me that because sapiential texts are characteristically "figured" and not straight-forward, the two contemporary texts to which I will appeal, marked by whimsy and playfulness, are appropriate access points for my argument. I imagine that the ancient wisdom teachers who reflected upon the inscrutability of creation might approve such a slightly tongue-in-cheek approach that articulates created reality alternatively, an alternative that nonetheless lives close to the creaturely character of the world.

Leavers and Takers

The playful novel to which I refer and by which I have been given an opening is *Ishmael* by Daniel Quinn.[2] I first learned of the book recently from an e-mail from a West Coast conservationist, whom I do not know, who wrote to ask me about the book. My correspondent reported that the book urges that the narrative of Genesis 4 is the clue to all contemporary social-political, environmental problems. By prompt return, without having seen the book, I expressed my misgiving about that thesis, given that the narrative of Genesis 4 functions in no important way in the remainder of the Hebrew Bible.

But then I read the book. The story-line is that a gorilla, previously named Goliath but now renamed Ishmael, becomes an "instructor" to a human student who has great curiosity. At first the two commnicate by eye contact; but soon the gorilla speaks and leads his human student by sustained Socratic method to a revision of his notion of created reality.

It is the initial assumption of the human student, informed as Ishmael observes, by the story of "Mother Culture," that human beings stand outside the "laws of creation" and are capable and permitted to exercise control over the rest of creation as the exceptional creature with remarkable and absolute entitlements. Indeed, as Ishmael observes, the humanly constructed account of creation (as in Genesis 1–2) is to portray humanity as the ultimate and final creation, after which there will be none other. (It is observed in passing that the creation narrative as told by jellyfish make the same interpretive maneuver, that the goal and final act of creation is the emergence of jellyfish.)

---

2. Quinn, *Ishmael: An Adventure of the Mind and Spirit.*

Over time Ishmael begins to expose the mistaken narrative of human exceptionalism, and to present a critique of the notion that human persons stand outside the laws of creation as the final creature, entitled to control all other creatures. Ishmael identifies the human assumption of exceptionalism as the story of "Takers," those who believe that the proper human enterprise is to take land and food from all other creatures, to take more than one needs, to take it all, even at the expense of others. Against that, Ishmael observes that in the long history of creation before the human Takers become dominant, that all creatures have been essentially "Leavers," that is, they take what they need of food, but not more than they need and, consequently, leave all the rest so that it may be used by other creatures who must also eat to live. Thus the long story told and practiced by all pre-human creatures is a story of leaving, a practice of leaving and life, a leaving of creation that makes sustained, sustainable life possible for the entire creation. Only quite belatedly in the long history of creation has the narrative of the Takers become dominant. That narrative, as it is vigorously embraced and practiced, is leading, in very short order, to the destruction of the viability of creation. Ishmael articulates four things that the Takers do that jeopardizes all of creation, actions that would never occur elsewhere among nonhuman creatures:[3]

- The Takers exterminate their competitors;
- The Takers systematically destroy their competitors' food to make room for their own;
- The Takers deny their competitors access to food (in the wild the rule is: you may deny your competitors access to what you're eating, but you may not deny them access to food in general);
- Takers kill a surplus of food, but in the wild, animals never kill more than they can eat.

Ishmael formulates the "peace-keeping law" of the wild: "You may compete to the full extent of your capabilities, but you may not hunt down your competitors or destroy their food or deny them access to food. In other words, you may compete but you may not wage war."[4] Before he has finished, Ishmael affirms that Leavers have been content, for a very long time, to live "in the hands of the gods" who adequately provide food, whereas human creatures have come to know "good and evil," and so seek to secure

3. Ibid., 126.
4. Ibid., 129.

their lives beyond reliance upon the gods: "The premise of the Taker story is the world belongs to man . . . The premise of the Leaver story is man belongs to the world."[5] The Leavers make it possible for creation to go on forever, whereas the Takers pursue a policy that will bring creation to an end.

Before Quinn ends his book, he proposes, via Ishmael, that the agricultural revolution from hunting to planting, reflected in the narrative of Genesis 4, is the story of the Takers who now possess and own and produce their own food and thereby live against the law of peacemaking that makes life possible for all creatures.

The novel is, to be sure, lightly didactic. But Quinn resists decoding his story. It is clear that the Takers, the human community of exploitation and acquisitiveness, lives life against the fabric of nature and against the will of the creator. Ishmael's call for repentance, whether of Western humanity or of Enlightenment ideology, is repentance of the ideology of human exceptionalism, the recognition that humanity is subject to the same "peacekeeping laws" of the creator as are all other creatures, outside of which no sustainable life is possible.

It strikes me as peculiarly telling that Quinn has the truth of his story uttered to the human interlocutor by Ishmael, a gorilla. This comic narrative strategy asserts that Ishmael the gorilla, a hermeneutist for the nonhuman world in general, knows what his human partner learns only slowly, reluctantly, and with great obtuseness. Not too much should be made of the strategic way in which the novel works, except it cannot go unnoticed that the nonhuman agent in the narrative is the one who has wisdom about how the world works as an ordered, foodproducing system that sustains life. The nonhuman agent knows what his human counterpart does not know and does not much want to learn. We could as well take the next step for Ishmael to observe that Leavers are wise in the ways of creation and that Takers practice a foolishness that inevitably leads to death. Ishmael does everything for our subject short of using the word pair "wisdom/foolishness." Ishmael's advocacy is nicely lined out by his student's belated rejection of a familiar voice concerning the law of creation. The human partner to the learning process declares:

> Far and away the most futile admonition Christ ever offered was when he said, "Have no care for tomorrow. Don't worry about whether you're going to have something to eat. Look at the birds of

5. Ibid., 239.

the air. They neither sow nor reap nor gather into barns, but God takes perfect care of them. Don't you think he'll do the same for you?" In our culture the overwhelming answer to that question is "Hell no!" Even the most dedicated monastics saw to their sowing and reaping and gathering into barns.[6]

The speaker yearns to be out of "the hands of the gods," a yearning that is for Ishmael the ultimate foolishness.

Detachment and Objectification

The whimsical essay by which I am informed is, "Creationism and the Spirit of Nature" by Peter Gabel.[7] This paper plunges directly into the "evolution–creation" debate, though with a particular and peculiar angle of vision. The author gives primary attention to the claims, and therefore the limitations of "scientific method." Such method, he observes, proceeds by a stance of "detachment and objectification" to such "objects" in nature through a scientific range of what is knowable. Gabel suggests that such scientific method can only study the observable object and so stays on the "outside" of the object. Such method in principle cannot know anything from the "inside," and so misses out completely on whatever there might be of desire, will, or sense that can be known only intuitively and empathetically, from one knower to another knower. Thus the paper is an insistence that "scientific method" precludes knowledge about anything important that we should like to know about the "true existence" of a "living thing."

Gabel's case in point to which he refers repeatedly is the movement of a household plant toward the sunlight. Scientifically this movement is to be understood by way of a theory of photosynthesis. Against such an "external" explanation, Gabel observes that the plant's movements are "unified," a sensual unity so that one "senses in the plant, the sense of pleasure that seems to manifest in the bend of the upper stem and the stretch of the highest leaves and that seems to contrast so strikingly with the droop of plants denied access to the same sunlight."[8] The author reports that his own sense "that the meaning of the plant's living movement exceeds the photosynthesis explanation is a very strong one."[9]

6. Ibid., 228.
7. Gabel, "Creationism and the Spirit of Nature."
8. Ibid., 46.
9. Ibid.

One must, so Gabel contends, step outside the detachment and objectification of scientific method in order to embrace "the plant in an intuitive movement of comprehension from one living being to another."[10] Gabel will not go so far as to say that the plant has "consciousness" or "will," but does insist that the plant is to be seen as "beautiful and good"—as miraculously alive and "here," no less than are we.[11]

In his critique of scientific method, Gabel has no patience with or appreciation for conventional "creationism." He makes clear his disdain for conventional creationism that is allied to unworthy right-wing causes. But he allows that

> creationists have been able to touch that dimension of people's ordinary experience that sense life in all its forms as expressive of some indwelling and miraculous beauty and goodness, and that knows with a certain intuition that this indwelling presence must be at the heart of any true knowledge of the world. However absurd the strict content of their views may be, and however evil may be the association of these views with right-wing militarism and anti-communism and with a servile dependency on fundamentalist preachers who purport to speak for an authoritarian God, there is something correct and admirable in their refusal to accept the hegemony of science as a privileged source of truth.[12]

In the end, Gabel's target is not creation and evolution as such, but the way in which decisions in politics and ethics are formed among us:

> The implications of what I am saying here go much deeper than the debate between evolution and creationism because if we could succeed in freeing knowledge from the grip of science and affirm the objectivity of intuitive comprehension as the only route to understanding and communicating about the being of things, we could also begin to transform the way people think about politics and ethics, about the meaning of their own lives and the lives of others and about what kind of world we should be trying to create.[13]

Real knowing in the end is intuitive, with respect as one "living thing" relates to other "living things." It is evident that Gabel, in his rather odd

10. Ibid., 48.
11. Ibid.
12. Ibid., 52.
13. Ibid., 57.

formulation, is concerned with "real knowledge" that concerns the inscrutable character of "living things." Consequently he seeks to fend off foolish knowledge that imagines itself neutral and detached, foolish because such a stance, so prized in our culture, precludes real knowledge.

Another Way of Knowing

It is easy enough to entertain dismissal of these intellectual forays, because they lie outside established reason in our culture. Indeed, Gabel reports on such dismissive responses at the end of his article, though the responses also include some interesting affirmations. In the cases of both Quinn and Gabel, the writers reflect on the depth of creation that lies beyond scientific control. In Quinn's case, his attempt to understand creation also issues in an economic interpretation of the past in terms of Leavers and Takers. From the perspective of establishment rationality, articulation of "Leaver–Taker" on the lips of a gorilla is nonsense; and surely from that same perspective, Gabel's notion of empathetic, intuitive engagement is equally nonsense.

But, of course, in both cases the argument aims to subvert the established assumption that human persons with their much knowledge are free to act upon and, therefore, use all other creatures. In different ways, both Quinn and Gabel propose that pre-human creatures know, and what they know is congruent with the ordering of creation for life, an ordering that continues to elude human mastery. Both Gabel and Quinn ask the reader to step outside modern epistemological assumptions and to entertain the thought—imagine!!—that nonhuman creatures know, perhaps know differently, perhaps know better, but in any case know the mystery of how the world works as God's generous, food-producing creation.

As I make a transition to consider biblical texts, I note in passing that the epistemology championed differently by Quinn and Gabel is not unlike what was previously termed "primitive," "savage," or "dynamism" by historians of religion who considered the odd epistemological assumptions that seem to be reflected in the Bible. It is worth noticing, of course, that appeal to the work of Lucien Levy-Bruhl was taken to be a study in the evolution of thought toward rationality. The inescapable tone of those analyses was that this way of knowing is inadequate and inferior and it is, thankfully, only a step along the way to a more superior rationality of the modern mind.[14]

---

14. See Albright, *From Stone Age to Christianity*, 168–78; also Hahn, *Old Testament in Modern Research*, 59–74, 213–24.

It may be that we are still facing that contrast, but now we are perhaps sobered enough to entertain the thought that modern rationality cannot be so innocently championed, given the fact that it is, in Quinn's parlance, the work of "Takers," and in Gabel's categories the work of "detachment and objectification" that can never really know the inside of any living thing. It is evident that the Bible entertains another way of knowing that is not primitive or savage, but simply congruent with the character of the creation as the world over which God governs.

The Ox Knows Its Owner

The first text that I will consider is Isa 1:3:

> The ox knows its owner,
>> and the donkey its master's crib;
> but Israel does not know,
>> my people do not understand.

This verse is preceded by an announcement of a lawsuit in which witnesses are called to observe the rebellious character of Yahweh's "sons" (v. 2). In our verse, the rebelliousness of these "sons," that is, Israel, is contrasted with the ox and the donkey who are not rebellious. The point of contrast is that for both subjects of the contrast the governing verb is "know." The contrast is simple and complete: *Ox and ass know, Israel does not know (or discern)*. What the animals know is the identity of their "owner" (*ba'al*) and the place of their reliable food. One can see this pragmatic knowledge by observing such domesticated animals: at feeding time, toward dusk, they head home. They know what time it is and they know where their food is reliably provided. They know to whom they belong and on whom they can rely for food. It is likely that the usage of *ba'al* intends both to allude to the abundance of creation, and to set up a remarkable contrast between *ba'al*, a generic, non-covenantal food provider and the One to be known by Israel, the covenant Lord who presides over the food supply of the Torah community.

The appeal to such creaturely knowledge, of course, serves to accent Israel's lack of knowledge. If the verb "know" is to be taken here, as in some other contexts, as acknowledgment of sovereignty, then it is an easy turn that "not know" means a disregard of proper sovereignty, both a failure to rely upon and a failure to respond in obedience.[15] This negative nuance for Israel is the one that is important for what follows in the speeches of judgment in Isaiah. The positive dimension of knowing, here enacted by others of God's creatures, is knowledge of God's rule and God's ordering of creation for the sake of food. This is the most elemental knowledge required, a knowledge available to and practiced by all of Yahweh's creatures, with the conspicuous exception of Israel, the only creature of the creator on the horizon of this brief poetic unit who does not know.

The Stork Knows Its Times

The second text I mention is Jer 8:7:

> Even the stork in the heavens
>> knows its times;
> and the turtledove, swallow, and crane
>> observe the time of their coming;
> but my people do not know
>> the ordinance of Yahweh.

The content of the verse is closely paralleled to that of Isa 1:3. Again the contrast is between "my people" and the nonhuman creatures, conventionally translated as storks, turtledoves, swallows, and cranes. Again the contrast is a sharp one between *knowing* and *not knowing*. The birds know all they need to know; they know the seasons of the creator:

> seedtime and harvest,
> cold and heat,
> summer and winter. (Gen 8:22)

As the poetry of Isa 1:3 is verified by the regular phenomenon of cattle headed home for feeding at the right time, so the poetry of this verse is verified by the migrating patterns of birds, most spectacularly by the swallows of Capistrano. The birds know how the world is ordered by the creator, and thus they "observe the time" which is to be in sync with that ordering.

The contrast is parallel to that of Isa 1:3. "My people" is the only creature who does not know about coming and going. The preceding verses (Jer 8:4–6) have spoken of "turning" and "returning," of going away and coming

---

15. See Huffmon, "The Treaty Background of Hebrew *Yada'*"; and Huffmon and Parker, "A Further Note on the Treaty Background of Hebrew *Yada'*."

back in repentance. As the birds know, there are seasons for coming and for going; but "my people" have no sense of season or of appropriate action for a particular season in the ordering of the creator. In the second case as in the first case, Israel's capacity for "knowing" is as easy and available as it is for every other creature. Such knowing requires only to attend to the patterned life willed by the creator. To be "dumber than an ox," to know less than the flight schedule of birds, is not an act of stupidity. It is, rather, an act of deliberate recalcitrance, a defiance that sets the creature over against the creator.

Elemental Awareness

The force of these poetic images depends upon creaturely knowledge that is God-given and available to all creatures. That is the premise of being a workable creature of God. This knowledge is not "primitive" or "savage," but it is the premise of responsive creatureliness that adheres to the un-compromising reality of the creator. This is the same knowledge possessed by the "Leavers" that Quinn exposes; all creatures have access to it. With this claim, the prophetic indictment of "not knowing" becomes ominous indeed.

Now of course these poetic passages are not interested in birds or beasts of burden. These are simply foils for the indictment of "my people" who does not know. It is of immense importance, in any case, that the knowing for which Israel has a dangerous deficit is not from Torah or from Sinai revelation. This knowing is given more elementally, more bodily, more creaturely. The not knowing for which Israel is condemned is a delib-erate act of alienation from the creator, an act of autonomy and hubris that refuses to order life according to the intention of the creator, an attempt to order and control life outside "the hands of the gods."

These prophetic verses, when placed in the context of the contempo-rary proposals of Quinn and Gabel suggest that "creation theology" is not about nature worship or any of these matters that the early Barth feared. It is, rather, about the elemental awareness given to every creature, human and nonhuman, that creatures must adhere to the givens, limits, and re-quirements of the creator.

Now, of course, this alternative way of knowing has long been recog-nized in Old Testament studies. We may take William Foxwell Albright as a striking example of the way in which this alternative knowing has been widely understood in an evolutionary scheme whereby knowing has developed from the "dynamism" of primitiveness to modern rationality: "Levy-Bruhl stresses the prelogical character of primitive thought, which fails to take account of contradictions, lacks any clear concept of causal relations, for which it substitutes simple explanation by sequence, or superficial concomitance, or accidental resemblance. Fundamental to primitive thinking are also impersonality and fluidity."[16] Clearly Albright intends to show that such a way of knowing contrasts such knowing with modern knowing, even if the older knowing is not as "primitive" as had been thought. The contrast is inescapable. When placed in an evolutionary scheme as Albright does, however, the "primitive" is inferior and the modern rationality is welcomed as being superior and as the ultimate arrival in epistemology. If, however, we take the contrast of these two modes of knowledge out of an evolutionary scheme and see them as alternative choices, then we may see that the knowledge championed in these texts is a subversive alternative to autonomous rationality. It is my impression that Quinn and Gabel focus upon this subversive alternative knowing because they observe how the autonomous reason of the Takers is death-dealing. It will be an important shift in thinking about such creaturely knowing to see that it is not an inferior *way* of knowledge to be overcome but it is an alternative to be embraced, an alternative clearly championed by these two poets in a society that knew everything except whatneeds to be known about the creator.

I write this as the United States just now strides the earth with its immense, unrivaled technical capacity, sorting out every other culture according to the defining reality of U.S. military and economic power. The old truth from these poets keeps emerging again and again, how to know so much but not to know the things that make for peace (Luke 19:42). Asses and oxen show up to be fed; birds fly on schedule. But the critically competent do not know, and choose all too often another knowledge that leads to death. It occurs to me that the emergence of the knowledge of wisdom-creation is not just an interesting fresh scholarly trope in Old Testament studies. It is, rather, a resilient alternative that not all the Takers in the world can effectively obliterate. "Not knowing" has no adequate compensation in knowing everything else.

16. Albright, *From the Stone Age to Christianity*, 169.

Bibliography

Albright, William Foxwell. *From Stone Age to Christianity: Monotheism and the Historical Process*. Baltimore: Johns Hopkins University Press, 1957.

Gabel, Peter. "Creationism and the Spirit of Nature." In *The Bank Teller and Other Essays on the Politics of Meaning*, 45–67. San Francisco: Acada, 2000.

Hahn, Herbert F. *Old Testament in Modern Research: A Comprehensive Synthesis of Modern Trends in Biblical Studies*. Expanded by Horace D. Hummel. Philadelphia: Fortress, 1970.

Huffmon, Herbert B. "The Treaty Background of Hebrew *Yada'*." *BASOR* 181 (1966) 31–37.

Huffmon, Herbert B., and Simon B. Parker. "A Further Note on the Treaty Background of Hebrew *Yada'*." *BASOR* 184 (1966) 36–38.

Quinn, Daniel. *Ishmael: An Adventure of the Mind and Spirit*. New York: Bantam, 1992.

Zimmerli, Walther. "The Place and Limit of the Wisdom in the Framework of the Old Testament Theology." *Scottish Journal of Theology* 17 (1964) 146–58. Reprinted in *Studies in Andent Israelite Wisdom*, edited by James L. Crenshaw, 314–26. New York: Ktav, 1976.

three

JEREMIAH: *CREATIO IN EXTREMIS*

The book of Jeremiah offers a clear test case and model for the shift in scholarly paradigms in Old Testament study. In the "history of traditions" perspective dominated by Gerhard von Rad, the tradition of Jeremiah is firmly situated in the exodus and Sinai-covenant traditions of Moses, but with some engagement with the Davidic-messianic traditions as well.[1] This entire phase of scholarship has resulted in a lopsided emphasis upon the traditio-historical background of the book.

We may notice, however, an addendum to von Rad's perspective that has controlled Jeremiah studies. Because of the three-source theory of Bernhard Duhm and Sigmund Mowinckel, the Deuteronomic redaction of the book and the so-called Baruch document left the way open to discerning evidence of sapiential influence in the literature.[2] On the one hand, Moshe Weinfeld has urged a linkage between wisdom and the traditions of Deuteronomy.[3] On the other hand, James Muilenburg has explored the scribal role of Baruch and has linked scribal activity to the more general category of wisdom.[4] Thus it is possible to see a development in the Jeremiah traditions toward wisdom influence that in turn suggests an openness to creation. This possibility, however, has been a quite subordinate point in the

1. Von Rad, *Old Testament Theology*, 2:217 and passim.

2. The three-source theory that has dominated Jeremiah studies is now, of course, open to widespread question. See a summary of that scholarship in Childs, *Introduction to the Old Testament as Scripture*, 342–45.

3. Weinfeld, *Deuteronomy and the Deuteronomic School*.

4. Muilenburg, "Baruch the Scribe." For a more rigorous historical assessment of the scribes in the world of Jeremiah, see Dearman, "My Servants the Scribes."

interpretive models that situated Jeremiah in the Mosaic covenantal–levitical matrix reflected in the Deuteronomists and voiced in the tradition of Hosea.[5]

Creation and Chaos

The important shift in interpretive models, evidenced by the theme of this volume, permits us to pay much more sustained attention to creation themes in the tradition of Jeremiah.[6] While it is clear that "creation" is an ill-defined rubric and therefore may include many diverse elements, and while there is at the moment a temptation to pan-creationism (like an earlier pan-covenantalism), it is unmistakable that this general perspective on Yahwism pervades the book of Jeremiah, a pervasion mostly denied and kept invisible by the once dominant history-of-traditions perspective.

Leo Perdue has provided a convenient overview of "creation theology in Jeremiah" in terms of: (a) creation and history, (b) creation and the destiny of the individual, and (c) wisdom and creation.[7] Of particular interest is his discussion of "the chaos tradition" concerning the divine warrior that shows up both in the so-called Scythian Songs and in the Oracles against the Nations.[8] It is telling that this theme, especially in light of the work of Frank Cross, Patrick Miller, and Paul Hanson, can be understood in terms of "creation–chaos," whereas von Rad linked these same texts to holy war, a clear illustration of how particular methodological assumptions mandate and preclude certain readings.[9]

---

5. For the locus of Hosea (and derivatively Jeremiah) in the circles of levitical priests derived from Mosaic traditions and voiced in the Deuteronomists, see Wolff, "Hoseas geistige Heimat." It is surely more compelling to conclude that Jeremiah was nourished and evoked in these circles than to imagine that the Deuteronomic focus was artificially imposed on the tradition of Jeremiah.

6. The studies in this volume are reflective of a radically shifted paradigm in Old Testament interpretation. See Brueggemann, "The Loss and Recovery of Creation in Old Testament Theology"; and Brueggemann, "A Shifting Paradigm."

7. Perdue, *The Collapse of History*, 141–50.

8. More generally on the so-called Scythian Songs, see Childs, "The Enemy fom the North and the Chaos Tradition"; on the Oracles against the Nations, see Childs, *Introduction to the Old Testament as Scripture*, 352–53.

9. Cross, "The Divine Warrior"; Miller, *The Divine Warrior in Early Israel*; Hanson, *The Dawn of Apocalyptic*, 123–26, 182–85 and passim; von Rad, *Old Testament Theology*, 2:199.

We may list some of the rich variety of creation motifs evident in the Jeremiah traditions, in part informed by Perdue's exposition:

- An emphasis upon land can be understood in terms of the Moses–Joshua historical traditions but can also be seen as the space for life willed and maintained by the creator God (Jer 2:7; 3:19; 4:3; 33:12; 45:4)[10] and made possible by Yahweh's guarantee of fertility (8:13, 20; 22:6; 31:5).

- Fertility in turn is made possible by the assurance of rain, a matter of great significance in a marginal, arid climate (2:1–3; 3:2–3; 5:24; 14:4, 22).

- Focus upon land, fertility, and rain is also confirmed by the utilization of concrete "metaphors of nature," for example, horses and birds (8:6–7), plants and wild animals (1:11; 5:6; 12:9; 24:1), and grain, wine, and oil (31:12). Such imagery saturates the poetry.

- More generally we notice, along with Perdue, linkages to wisdom, that is, regular, orderly patterns of reality (8:7; 15:14; 17:11).

- Perhaps most interesting is the claim of 5:22 that Yahweh's ordering of the sand of the seashore creates a boundary and a limit to chaos, thus providing a safe, viable, fruitful place for human habitation.

This listing is only representative. It is sufficient nonetheless to indicate that the tradition of Jeremiah places Yahweh on a wide, panoramic screen, as wide as all creation, and situates Judah in its theo-political crisis amid the guarantees and threats that are as large as all creation. Because it is not possible to explore all such uses, I want to focus only on three cases that I take to be "limit expressions" of the "limit experiences" of Judah living in a creation that is fully dependent upon Yahweh and fully open to Yahweh's singular guarantee of life.[11]

---

10. See Brueggemann, "Israel's Sense of Place in Jeremiah"; Diepold, *Israel's Land.*

11. The terms "limit expression" and "limit experience" that are crucial to my argument are drawn from Ricoeur, "Biblical Hermeneutics."

An Unreserved Negation

In any consideration of creation themes in Jeremiah, an important reference point is 4:24–29, which is situated in a series of poetic units concerned with foreign invasion.[12] Historically this poetic unit refers to the threat of a foreign invader (apparently Babylon) who will at the behest of Yahweh terminate life in the world and, consequently, life in Jerusalem. Canonically this text and the themes it presents function as judgment in a two-stage "final form" text of judgment and hope.[13] Special attention may be paid to this text, both because it is an epitome of the ominous quality of life in jeopardy from Yahweh and because of its wondrously symmetrical mode of articulation.[14]

The poem proceeds in four parallel lines, together with a fifth line naming Yahweh as the sole agent of the dismantling of creation, even as Yahweh had been the sole agent of creation. The first four lines are introduced by ראיתי ("I looked"), the report of an observer who anticipates the destruction, accented in each line by הנה, bespeaking the surprise, intensity, and extremity of the destruction. The lines proceed from the most general (heavens and earth) to the landscape of earth (mountains and hills), to the inhabitants (human and birds), and finally to the specific land of well-being (כרמל) that Yahweh has guaranteed and that Judah now inhabits. These elements of creation are matched and trumped by the terms of negation, "waste and void" (תהו ובהו) at the outset, "quaking and moving" as signs of elemental instability, and a double negation, אין.[15] Every line except the first summarizes with "all"—all hills, all birds, all cities—nothing spared, nothing held back, nothing protected, nothing guaranteed.

It is unmistakable that the dismantling described here witnesses in calibrated ways to the creation strategy of Genesis 1. Jeremiah 4:24–26 is a step-by-step subtraction from the "very good" creation upon which Israel

12. On this larger unit of poetry, see Childs, *Introduction to the Old Testament as Scripture*, 352–53.

13. See ibid., 345–54; and more specifically, Clements, "Patterns in the Prophetic Canon."

14. Holladay (*Jeremiah 1*, 163) speaks of "the stark sublimity" of the poem. The use of the term "sublime" recalls the sense of Emmanuel Kant and Rudolf Otto that "the Sublime" is not only awesome in beauty but also profound in its threat. Thus "sublime" is exactly the correct term here.

15. Childs, "The Enemy from the North and the Chaos Tradition," has paid careful attention to the term רעש occurs in this text and links it to the ancient tradition of chaos.

has counted and in which its own life is lived. It is of course sensible to say with Perdue that such rhetoric of "the cataclysmic upheaval of nature is obvious hyperbole."[16] Such a verdict, however, misses the cumulative intent of the rhetoric, which is to imagine and invite the listener of the poem to host a scenario in which nothing reliable or life-sustaining is left. Creation theology here functions to voice a complete, unreserved, elemental negation of all that makes life livable, a negation that could hardly be uttered without such large language. Conversely, the rhetoric makes the theological point that Yahweh is fully capable of termination, and in this circumstance ready to terminate an awesome, sublime articulation of sovereignty.

Those addressed are pressed to discern themselves in a moment of radical rejection, more radical and wholesale than any "historical tradition" could possibly voice. This is the most imaginable discontinuity that could be uttered. When the text is seen as a limit articulation designed to lead Judah beyond its conventional imagination, there is nothing hyperbolic about it. This is the real thing for Yahweh the creator, the real thing for creation that has no autonomous existence, and unmistakably the real thing for Judean listeners.

Stability and Reliability

Given this intense portrayal of demolition, we cannot be emotionally or cognitively prepared for the assurance of 31:35–36, 37, which I take to be an antithesis to 4:23–26. These two brief oracles in chap. 31 appeal to the stability and reliability of creation as a ground from which to assert the stability and reliability of Yahweh's promise of durability to "the offspring" of Israel. Whereas 4:23–26 voices Yahweh's destruction of creation, these oracles assure that such demolition is precluded, prohibited, and made impossible in the economy of Yahweh.

This oracle that stands in penultimate position in "the Book of Comfort" (chs. 30–31) makes what may be regarded as the most extreme guarantee of well-being in creation theology. It is viewed by contemporary scholarship as a later part of the "rolling corpus" of the Jeremiah tradition.[17]

---

16. Perdue, *The Collapse of History*, 143.

17. On that contemporary judgment, see the commentaries of Robert Carroll, William Holladay, and William McKane. In older scholarship, Paul Volz and Wihelm Rudolph held to the early "authenticity" of the oracles.

The oracles may be treated as distinct, isolated units or as confirmation of the promise of new covenant in 31:31–34.

In any case, each oracle, termed by Herbert Huffmon as an "impossble promise," is organized around an "if" of impossibility (in each case an impossibility for creation) and taken as an assurance of the impossibility of the cessation or rejection of "the offspring" of Israel.[18] In the first oracle, the authorization formula (v. 35a) is supported by the doxology (v. 35b) and reinforced by a reiteration of the divine name (v. 35d). The doxology consists of two participial verbs, the first concerning sun, moon, and stars together with the crucial term "fixed order" (חֹק), the second concerning the sea (see Ps 146:6). The four elements of creation here mean to comprehend the entire scope of creation. The whole of v. 35 only certifies who it is who speaks, the one with power to resolve to initiate, sustain, and guarantee the created order.

It is this one who speaks the "if . . . then" of v. 36. The "if" that taken to be "not possible" is the cessation of these "fixed orders" from before the face of Yahweh.[19] On the basis of the fixed order of creation that cannot cease, the "then" is the equally impossible thought that Israel will cease; Israel is grounded in the bottom-line claim concerning the indelible sureness of creation.

The same structure pertains in the oracle of v. 37, presented as it is, sandwiched between two formulas of authorization. Here the impossible "if" is the measuring and exploration of unfathomable creation that is beyond all human measurement. It is the creation impossibility that provides the ground for the "then," the impossibility of the ending of Israel's existence. The power of these assurances, unlike either vv. 31–34 or vv. 38–40, is the wonder of the "natural order," a wonder of regularity and dependability that would seem to be nourished and noticed in something like wisdom teaching.

The juxtaposition of 4:23–26 and 31:35–37 suggests the extreme interpretive possibilities of creation theology hosted within the tradition of Jeremiah. It is likely that 4:23–26 is "authentic" to the prophetic person and is surely "early," concerned with judgment upon a recalcitrant community; it is probable that 31:35–37 is a later utterance from a subsequent

18. Huffmon, "The Impossible Word of Assurance."

19. It is perhaps not unimportant that the double use of פָּנֶה ("face") has a counterpoint in 4:26 wherein the destruction of creation is "from before Yahweh." That both the destruction and the assurance are "before Yahweh" points to the Yahwistic, theonomous focus of both realities.

generation, designed to offer hope to an exilic or postexilic community when the very existence of that community is unmistakably in jeopardy.

Thus the two texts reflect chronologically a movement from early to late, together with very different circumstances. Canonically, they move from judgment to assurance. Something like a two-stage understanding of life with Yahweh is surely indicated.[20] If, however, we take a synchronic view of the tradition and see the two accents together in the final form of the text, then an unrelieved "tension between present misery and future property" is evident in the book, as noted by Robert P. Carroll.[21] The juxtaposition of these two "limit expressions," of utter demolition (4:23–26) and total assurance (31:35–37) suggests that neither the demolition nor the assurance is the proper focus of creation theology in the tradition of Jeremiah. Rather both claims are instrumental and point beyond themselves to the one who speaks, Yahweh, the one who presides over creation and over the destiny of Judah. Thus both extremes of expression bear witness to the theological claim that finally Israel must come to terms with Yahweh upon whom its future well-being solely depends. Both the coming destruction and the subsequent assurance are functions of Yahweh's sovereign governance that Israel cannot evade and without which it cannot live.[22]

Creator, Creation, and Wisdom

In the context of these two most extreme statements, we may now consider one other recurring hymnic assertion of creation theology that will call attention to three texts (10:12; 32:17; 51:15). I take up these three texts because they roughly echo the same cadences of what must have been a more or less stylized doxological assertion. The subject of that stylized assertion is clearly creation in its linkage to the creator, and the matrix of the recurring formulation is clearly sapiential.[23]

---

20. On such a "two-stage" presentation of Judah's theological reality in the tradition of Isaiah (with special reference to Isa 8:23b), see Williamson, "First and Last in Isaiah." It is likely that such a two-stage presentation became dominant and "canonical" for the prophetic perspective in general.

21. Carroll, *Jeremiah*, 616.

22. I use the term "subsequent" because it is not possible in the tradition of Jeremiah to deny that there was a rejection in the events of 587; see Brueggemann, "A Shattered Transcendence?" The subsequent character of the assurance is more explicit in Isa 54:9 with its "never again" (עוֹד); see also Gen 9:11.

23. The intimate connection between creation and wisdom reflection is now

Thus if we are to look for the natural habitat of this rhetorical pattern, we will likely find it in wisdom materials that are at the same time instructional and liturgical. It is not our purpose to trace the antecedents of the uses of Jeremiah, except to contend that the doxological articulation is an older formulation situated outside conventional "prophetic" discourse that revolves around speeches of judgment and promise. One such reference point for such antecedent sapiential articulation is in Prov 3:19–20:

> Yahweh by wisdom founded the earth;
>> by understanding he established the heavens;
> by his knowledge the deeps broke open,
>> and the clouds drop down the dew.

This formulation begins with the naming of Yahweh and identifies three agencies whereby Yahweh creates: wisdom, understanding, and knowledge. Beyond the triad of agents, the third portion of the statement (v. 20) departs from the parallelism of the first two lines in two ways. First, the third statement of agency (knowledge) includes two objects in parallel lines (deeps, clouds), so that the match of agent and object in the first two lines (wisdom–earth, understanding–heavens) is violated. Second, the verbs in v. 20 have the created objects as their subjects, and not Yahweh, as in the first two lines. Thus the third element of the unit breaks what seems to be the natural cadence by greater variation.

This small textual unit is regarded by R. Norman Whybray as a part of a second larger expansion in the development of Proverbs 1–9.[24] More importantly, William McKane, along with Whybray, observes that the purpose of the unit is to link wisdom to Yahweh, so that Yahweh is seen to be the agent of the reliable, dazzling order of creation.[25] McKane, moreover, suggests that these verses belong to an editorial piece closely connected to Prov 8:22–31. And because Prov 8:22–31 figures large in any theological assessment of sapiential tradition, we are able to suggest that Prov 3:19–20 articulates a pivotal theological claim.

In Prov 8:22–31, wisdom is reckoned to be an intimate of Yahweh in the work of creation. In Prov 3:19–20 the same claim is made, except that "wisdom," not yet "personified," is here richly expressed by three agencies,

commonplace, as in Perdue's discussion (*The Collapse of History*). Reference may also be made to the works of von Rad and Walther Zimmerli.

24. Whybray, *Wisdom in Proverbs*, 75.

25. McKane, *Proverbs*, 296–97; Whybray, *Wisdom in Proverbs*, 75, 95–104.

wisdom and the two parallel terms. These two verses, then, make a primal statement about lived reality as creation and provide the baseline for thinking theologically and ethically about cosmic and social reality with its orderliness, its uncompromising requirements, and its unfathomable gifts.[26]

Yahweh's Reliable Attentiveness

It is clear that the Jeremiah tradition takes up this doxological, sapiential claim that redefines the world as creation and asserts the connection between Yahweh and the world through the verbs and agents of creation. It is clear that while the Jeremiah tradition recontextualizes such a sapiential formulation, it is no longer intended simply as a doxological baseline. Rather, the rhetoric is drawn into the socio-political crisis with which the Jeremiah tradition is preoccupied. The first such use of this doxological formula is found in Jer 10:12:

> It is he who made the earth by his power,
>> who established the world by his wisdom,
>> and by his understanding stretched out the heavens.

The larger unit of 10:1–16 is peculiar in its context, offering a deeply polemical and doxological contrast between the idols (who are powerless, false, and merit no attention) and Yahweh (who is incomparable, true, living, and powerful). The polemic against idols (cf. Psalms 115 and 135; Isa 44:9–20) is not usual in traditions as early as Jeremiah, and the weight of scholarly opinion has been against the "authenticity" of the passage. Be that as it may, the final assertion of v. 16 draws even the religious polemic into a Jeremianic matrix.[27]

More specifically, vv. 12–15 sharply contrasts Yahweh and the idols. In vv. 12–13, Yahweh is the creator God who works with immense power through all creation. Indeed, the large rhetorical claims here correspond to facets of the Joban speeches of the whirlwind. The counter-assertion of vv. 14–15 is a stark contrast made with an inventory of negatives: stupid,

---

26. It is clear that this articulation has close linkages to materials in Second Isaiah. It is not possible, however, to demonstrate the direction of influence.

27. One of the primary grounds for taking Jer 10:1–16 as later is the theme of the treatment of idols. Such a literary judgment based so tightly upon a view of the history of Israelite religion, however, is not necessary. Current interpretation is not inclined to hold literary judgments so closely to historical judgments, if indeed it matters much anyway about what is early and what is late.

without knowledge, shame, false, no breath, worthless, and delusion. The contrast is detailed, absolute, and sustained.

The precise doxology of v. 12 is more consistent in form than is the sapiential model cited from Prov 3:19–20. Our verse in Hebrew lacks the divine name (present in LXX as in Prov 3:19), but there can be no doubt who, in context, is asserted as the living, true God. It is this God who acts through three agents: power, wisdom, and discernment. Two of these elements are parallel to those of Prov 3:19–20, but here "power" displaces "knowledge" as the third agent. Moreover, this articulation has three verbs, of which Yahweh is the subject—"makes," "establishes," "stretched out"—so that only the middle verb (כון) is parallel to Prov 3:19–20. The structure of this verse features three well-delineated parts. The third line, unlike that of Prov 3:19–20, stays closely parallel to the first two lines and has only one object, thus yielding a triad of objects—earth, world, heavens—to stay congruent with the three verbs and three agents. The claim of the whole is that the world, and therefore the world of Israel, and therefore the world of Jeremiah's seventh-century crisis, is completely at the behest of Yahweh, who is the subject of all the verbs. It is indeed the decisive governing capacity of Yahweh that is featured, though in the poem we are given no tilt toward either demolition (as in 4:23–26) or guarantee (as in 31:35–37), for both demolition and guarantee are free choices for the living God.

It is evident that the poem, in its doxology and its polemic, takes a curious turn in v. 16. It is possible to regard this verse as an addendum for the sake of tribal chauvinism. It is also possible, however, to see v. 16 as the climactic point of the entire poem. The specialness of Israel to Yahweh is clear; but the double claim for Jacob—Yahweh as Jacob's portion, Israel as Yahweh's inheritance—is intertwined with more "creation" claims: "Yahweh of Hosts" has "formed all," thus echoing the great doxological claims linked to Yahweh's power and authority as creator.[28] The claims made for the creator in v. 16 are completely congruent with the doxology of v. 12, thus making Yahweh's attentiveness to Israel not a belated "election" but a factor in the very fabric of creation. Because the verbs of v. 12 are all positive, with no hint of negation or destruction, the purpose is to assure Israel of Yahweh's reliable attentiveness in all of his vitality and power. The poem, of course, is a bid for loyalty to Yahweh and an insistent warning against idols that perish, but the ground for appeal for loyalty to Yahweh is not threat but guarantee. The doxological affirmation of Yahweh as creator is here voiced

28. See Crenshaw, *Hymnic Affirmation of Divine Justice*.

as the ground for Israel's steadfast reliance upon Yahweh, a ground that is intrinsic to the primal work of the creator.

The Creator against the Superpower

It is discerned by scholars that 10:12–16 is reiterated in 51:15–19.[29] The entire corpus of the Oracles against the Nations (chaps. 46–51) has a problematic linkage to the Jeremiah tradition, particularly chaps. 50–51 concerning Babylon. Nonetheless, it is clear that 51:15–19 is a peculiar feature in this extended oracle.[30] The weight of the entire oracle is the devastation of Babylon; the counter-theme here is the enduring commitment of Yahweh to Israel in v. 19.

The opening verse (v. 15) reiterates 10:12. Again Yahweh's name is lacking; again three verbs with three agents and three objects are present. Together they constitute the sum of all creation. The larger unit of vv. 15–19 again divides into an affirmation of Yahweh (vv. 15–16), an attack on alternative loyalties (vv. 17–18), and an affirmation of Jacob-Israel as the peculiar object of the creator God (v. 19).

In 51:15–19 the verses of 10:12–16 are set in the oracle against Babylon. The horizon of the oracle is very large, anticipating the demolition of the hegemonic power of the time. At the threshold of the oracle, more reticent than Second Isaiah, is the anticipation of the coming Persians who will do the work of destruction. Thus in the prose of 51:11 it is the coming "Medes"; in vv. 12–14 it is the invading empire that will come with troops; and in vv. 20–23 "you" (unspecified) will fight for Israel. The title "Yahweh of Hosts," sounded in 51:19 and in 10:16, is also voiced in v. 14.

The unit makes clear that the creator God is larger, stronger, and more determined than even this awesome, brutalizing superpower. The doxological and polemical rhetoric of the oracle must find a way to affirm Yahweh as more absolute than the seemingly absolute superpower, and the only way to do that is to seize upon the creation themes of wisdom that are not tamed by historical references to Yahweh. Of course, 51:19 and 20 refer to Israel, thus drawing the doxological tradition close to the crisis of exile. All of the powers of the creator are mobilized for the sake of Israel, for Israel before the might of Babylon has no alternative way to the future.

29. See Bellis, *The Structure and Composition of Jeremiah 50:2—51:58*, 136–39.

30. Bellis regards these verses as a belated intrusion in the text.

The relationship between the uses of the creation doxology in 10:12–16 and in 51:15–19 is not obvious. In the first usage, the assurance is offered as a basis for exclusive loyalty to Yahweh against all alternative possibilities, together with a summons. In the second usage, the assurance is offered without any such summons to loyalty, as a ground of hope and a resistance against despair and docile submission to the empire. It is possible and perhaps likely that the doxology of 10:12–16 is simply taken up later and reused by a subsequent poet. Alternatively William McKane, following Bernhard Duhm, suggests that the redactors of 51:15–19 "did not know that it had appeared at chapter 10."[31] The question of the relationship between the two uses is beyond resolution. What is clear is that in making its sweeping Yahwistic claim, the tradition finds a way of pushing behind any historical possibility to the creator, who is the only source of comfort and strength, a source found by these voices to be adequate in more than one crisis.

The Creator and Possibility

A third, truncated use of the same doxological formula is found in 32:17, in the narrative that stands amid the poems of hope in the Book of Comfort (chaps. 30–31) and the collection of promises in chap. 33. Chapter 32 is organized around the narrative concerning land entitlement in vv. 1–15 that yields the reiterated summons of v. 25 and the promise of v. 44.[32] Within the specific, anticipated land transaction, the chapter offers a prayer (vv. 16–25) and an oracle (vv. 26–41) that express both the extremity of destruction and the extremity of new possibility. Given both extremities, it is asserted that "Nothing is too hard for you," first as an affirmation (v. 17) and then as a question that implies an affirmation (v. 27). This material thus ponders Yahweh's extreme possibilities in the depths of the exile, including the possibility of Yahweh abandoning his people (a termination of the assurances in 10:12; 51:15) and the possibility of Yahweh regathering his scattered people.[33] This long prose unit is indeed a limit expression required to voice the limit experience of Israel in the sixth century.

31. McKane, *Jeremiah*, 2:1309.

32. See Brueggemann, "A 'Characteristic' Reflection on What Comes Next (Jer. 32:16–44)."

33. On the category of "impossibility," see Brueggemann, "'Impossibility' and Epistemology in the Faith Tradition of Abraham and Sarah (Gen. 18:1–15)," 167–68.

I suggest that 32:17 is a pivot point in this meditation upon Yahweh's extremities: "Ah Lord Yahweh! It is you who made the heavens and the earth by your great power and by your outstretched arm! Nothing is too hard for you." This verse is uttered at the beginning of Jeremiah's prayer, which voices a recital of Israel's past with Yahweh (vv. 18–23a), a speech of judgment (vv. 23b–24), and a reiteration of Yahweh's promise (v. 25). The function of the opening doxology appears to be a motivation, linked to the promise of v. 25.[34] That is, the concrete historical promise of v. 25 would appear to be impossible, but the creator God is the one who does the impossible. The prayer reaches outside historical possibility to move Yahweh into the larger arena of the possible.

Thus creation itself is a sign and measure of Yahweh's capacity to do beyond what the world thinks is possible. In the doxological formulation, the opening is more focused and more powerful than those already cited in 10:12 and 51:15. Yahweh is addressed with the title אֲדֹנָי ("Lord"). This usage of the doxological formula is cast as a prayer; therefore, direct address is especially appropriate. The address is reinforced by the attention-getter הִנֵּה ("behold"). The substance of what is to be said to Yahweh is introduced by the emphatic pronoun אַתָּה ("you") followed by a perfect verb.[35] The doxological affirmation has only one verb and two objects, heaven and earth. Moreover, the agents (great power and outstretched arm) are different from the other uses, except that "power" is also an agent in 51:15.[36] Thus the formulation is quite different, but the structure of the utterance is close enough to be considered in the same thematic field. The point here is not simply an assurance (as in 51:15–19) or an assurance with summons (as in 10:12–16). Because of the form of address, the purpose is to remind Yahweh of his capacity to do something.

The motivation of this truncated doxology is reinforced by the second half of the sentence: Yahweh does impossibilities! The impossibility celebrated in this verse is the powerful action of the creation of heaven and earth; the impossibility in which Israel now lives is "these disasters," the

---

34. On motivation, see Miller, *They Cried to the Lord*, 114–26.

35. The lead verb in the other two uses of 10:12 and 51:15 is a participle.

36. It is worth observing that the phrase "outstretched arm" has been characteristically taken as exodus terminology. This is yet another case where the historical paradigm has dictated the terms of interpretation when, under another paradigm, the phrasing may relate to creation. Fretheim ("The Plagues as Ecological Signs of Historical Disaster") has proposed a rereading of the exodus narrative in the categories of creation. Such a rereading would, in a small detail, reassign this phrasing to creation theology.

end of Jerusalem and the ensuing exile. The impossibility anticipated here
is restoration:

> Yet you, O Lord Yahweh, have said to me, "Buy the field for money
> and get witnesses." (32:25a)

> Just as I have brought all this great disaster upon this people, so
> I will bring upon them all the good fortune that I now promise
> them. Fields shall be bought in this land . . . (32:42–43)

The impossibility for which petition is made flies in the face of the conces-
sive clause ("though") of v. 25b: "though the city has been given into the
hand of the Chaldeans." The impossibility and the petition for it constitute
a counter-reality, counter to the exile, countered only on the ground of the
power of the creator.

The rhetoric that stretches from v. 17 to v. 25 has the force of voicing
the hope of rehabilitation in the land as a miracle commensurate with the
act of creation. Appeal is made to the one as ground for the other, ground
out of which Israel hopes and out of which Yahweh may act.

Creation, Judgment, and Hope

While it is clear that the Jeremiah tradition in many incidental ways (as
mentioned above) appeals to creation thought, the most important point is
that creation themes are of structural importance to the theological accents
of judgment and hope in the final form of the text. Four conclusions may
be drawn in that regard.

(1) It is clear that the tradition of Jeremiah is familiar with and knows
how to use effectively available themes and images of creation thought. It
is now clear in biblical scholarship, as evidenced by this volume, that Old
Testament theology through the twentieth century, largely propelled by
Gerhard von Rad's determinative essay of 1936, stands in need of a major
correction. In the battle of the German Church with National Socialism,
von Rad had linked creation theology with fertility religion, as it was mani-
fested in the "Blood and Soil" ideology regnant in Germany. In response
to that crucial church crisis, von Rad drew an important theological conclusion about the Old Testament: "Our main thesis was that in genuinely

Yahwistic belief the doctrine of creation never attained to the stature of a relevant, independent doctrine. We found it invariably related, and indeed subordinated, to soteriological considerations . . . because of the exclusive commitment of Israel's faith to historical salvation, the doctrine of creation was never able to attain independent existence in its own right."[37] In retrospect it is evident that von Rad overstated the distinction between creation and soteriology.[38] And in the United States the same judgment was forcefully made by G. Ernest Wright.[39] That judgment, for several generations, has caused scholars to overlook the appeal to creation in biblical literature.

At the same time, if cautiously construed, von Rad's judgment has merit. It is clear in the texts we have considered that creation is "invariably related" to Israel's place in Yahweh's economy. It is surely true that "the doctrine of creation was never able to attain to independent existence in its own right." It is not clear, however, that such thought is subordinated to soteriology. I should argue rather that it is subordinated to the claim that Yahweh is the governor of all of reality, both what we have come to call history and what we call creation. That is, creation theology is an instance of the theonomous character and quality of all of reality, including the reality of Israel's life.

(2) In the tradition of Jeremiah, there is no doubt that the core themes are demolition and rehabilitation. Creation themes in Jeremiah, I suggest, are designed to affirm that the experience and reality of demolition, while serious, is *only penultimate*. Similarly, the prospect of return and restoration is also real and serious, but also *penultimate*. Undermining the ultimacy of both demolition and rehabilitation is the more extreme claim of Yahweh the creator, who can do the impossible by dismantling creation (and Israel's life) and who can do the equally impossible act of revamping creation (and Israel's life). All of life is referred to the creator God, who is not restrained or restricted by any "given" of either creation or history. Thus the doxologies we have cited counter the absolute autonomy of Israel the absolute despair of Israel, and the absolute hegemony of Babylon. Nothing

---

37. Von Rad, "The Theological Problem of the Old Testament Doctrine of Creation," 142.

38. It is clear that von Rad took his cue from the categories of Karl Barth. For a polemical review of Barth's categories, see Barr, *Biblical Faith and Natural Theology*. Of particular interest is Barr's assertion, "Thus the understanding of pro-Nazi theology as basically a kind of natural theology was probably a vast misdiagnosis" (112–13).

39. Wright, *The Old Testament against Its Environment*; and Wright, *God Who Acts*.

is absolute, except the "Thou" who occupies the transformative verbs of power.

(3) It is important that the theological claim not be separated from the rhetorical act. The doxologies may be about creator and creation, but they are said, sung, and spoken acts. The deabsolutizing of the penultimate realities of demolition and rehabilitation takes place through an extreme statement of wonder. The rhetoric may strike us as so familiar and conventional that we do not notice. In fact, the claims are extreme. In 4:23–26, it is extreme to say "behold" four times to dismantling. In 31:35–37, it is extreme to speak an "if–then" assurance that rates the durability of Israel with the durability of creation. It is extreme when the claim for Yahweh subverts the alternative of idols (10:1–16), when the claim of Yahweh overrides the landless present tense of the exiles (32:17), and when the claim of Yahweh trumps the hegemony of Babylon (51:15–19). It is an extremity of rhetoric in which the tradition asserts what the world cannot reasonably entertain.

The rhetoric must be so extreme, however, because the tradition offers speech that matches experience. The extremity of expression is required in order to make available the extremity of experience, which in Judah is the loss of a safe world and the prospect of a new world.[40] With this rhetoric it is possible to make available the loss and the future prospect. Such expression makes the density of the experience inescapable. The enduring effect of such rhetoric is to press the listening community to face its own lived life, to ensure Yahweh as the pivotal player in that lived life, and to certify to coming generations that lived reality presided over by Yahweh is a reliable lens through which to engage other crises that have the same world-ending and world-making scope. Indeed, it is the richness of the limit expression that causes this Jeremiah tradition to be canonically perceived as revelatory.

(4) It is important to recognize the odd, subversive world given in this extreme rhetoric. It is unmistakable that Yahweh the creator is the subject of every verb. Heaven and earth, like Israel, are always on the receiving end of that activity, always the object acted upon. The most extreme form of

40. It may be possible to suggest an analogue between the losses of sixth-century Judah and contemporary losses in the immense suffering of Auschwitz, Hiroshima, and Vietnam, to name only the most prominent examples. Robert Jay Lifton has identified "psychic numbing," that is, to cease to notice or to care, as a strategic response to evil that threatens to overwhelm. He suggests that such "psychic numbing" produces a "symbol gap," wherein there are no adequate symbols to mediate the experience. Such a situation of deficiency of speech and expression requires fresh utterances to break the numbing. By the same token, I suggest the limit expressions of the Jeremiah tradition are addressed to the limit experiences of Judah that perhaps produced such numbing.

rhetoric is that of creation, in which all imaginable reality is object. It does not surprise us, in this context, that Judah and Jerusalem are objects in the same way.

Such a view of reality contends against the conventional Enlightenment notion of autonomy that perhaps echoes the ancient anti-Yahweh claims. In a splendid articulation of the grammar of Enlightenment, Nelida Pinon urges: "You must know who is the object and who is the subject of a sentence in order to know if you are the object or subject of history. If you can't control a sentence, you don't know how to put yourself into history, to trace your own origin in the country, to vocalize, to use voice."[41] One can hear here echoes of Karl Marx's urging that human persons must become subject of their own history!

I happen to agree with that human mandate. However, the covenantal traditions of Judaism and Christianity, voiced in the magisterial I–Thou of Martin Buber and more recently in the "religion of the face" in Emmanuel Levinas, insist that below that emancipated autonomy there is an inescapable Holy Other.[42] The creation theology of Jeremiah attends to the Holy Other, who ends every dysfunctional effort at autonomy, only to authorize again an emancipated, rehabilitated history, which gives great play to the voiced subject beloved by the inscrutable Thou. It is a reality Israel mostly refuses, learning again and again that this reality is the only source of comfort and hope, a reality in which the creator offers the only possibility for creation.[43]

Bibliography

Barr, James. *Biblical Faith and Natural Theology: The Gifford Lectures for 1991*. Oxford: Clarendon, 1993.

Bellis, Alice Ogden. *The Structure and Composition of Jeremiah 50:2—51:58*. Lewiston, NY: Mellen Biblical, 1995.

Brueggemann, Walter. "A 'Characteristic' Reflection on What Comes Next (Jer. 32:16–44)." In *Prophets and Paradigms: Essays in Honor of Gene M. Tucker*, edited by Stephen Breck Reid, 16–32. JSOTSup 229. Sheffield Academic, 1996. Reprinted in Brueggemann, *The Role of Old Testament Theology in Old Testament Interpretation: And Other Essays*, edited by K. C. Hanson, 71–89. Eugene, OR: Cascade Books, 2015.

41. Quoted in Purpel, *The Moral and Spiritual Crisis in Education*, xili.

42. Buber, *I and Thou*; and Levinas, *Totality and Infinity*.

43. I am glad to join in a salute to Sib Towner, long-time friend and colleague. Sib's way in our common scholarship is deeply marked by gentleness, caring, and humaneness, a model for us in an enterprise inevitably permeated with tension and dispute.

———. "'Impossibility' and Epistemology in the Faith Tradition of Abraham and Sarah (Gen. 18:1–15)." *ZAW* 94 (1982) 615–34. Reprinted in Brueggemann, *The Psalms and the Life of Faith*, edited by Patrick D. Miller Jr., 167–88. Minneapolis: Fortress, 1995.

———. "Israel's Sense of Place in Jeremiah." In *Rhetorical Criticism: Essays in Honor of James Muilenburg*, edited by Jared J. Jackson and Martin Kessler, 149–65. Pittsburgh Theological Monograph Series 1. Pittsurgh: Pickwick Publications, 1974. Reprinted as chap. 4 below.

———. "The Loss and Recovery of Creation in Old Testament Theology." *ThTo* 53 (1996) 177–90. Reprinted in Brueggemann, *The Book that Breathes New Life: Scriptural Authority and Biblical Theology*, 83–96. Minneapolis: Fortress, 2005.

———. "A Shattered Transcendence? Exile and Restoration." In *Biblical Theology: Problems and Perspectives*, edited by Steven J. Kraftchick et al., 169–82. Nashville: Abingdon, 1995. Reprinted in Brueggemann, *The Role of Old Testament Theology in Old Testament Interpretation: And Other Essays*, edited by K. C. Hanson, 90–112. Eugene, OR: Cascade Books, 2015.

———. "A Shifting Paradigm: From 'Mighty Deeds' to 'Horizon.'" In *The Papers of the Henry Luce III Fellows in Theology*, edited by Gary H. Gilbert, 7–47. Atlanta: Scholars, 1996.

Buber, Martin. *I and Thou*. Translated by Ronald Gregor Smith. New York: Scribner, 1937.

Carroll, Robert P. *Jeremiah: A Commentary*. OTL. Philadelphia: Westminster, 1986

Childs, Brevard S. "The Enemy fom the North and the Chaos Tradition." *JBL* 78 (1959) 187–98.

———. *Introduction to the Old Testament as Scripture*. Minneapolis: Fortress, 1979.

Clements, Ronald E. "Patterns in the Prophetic Canon." In *Canon and Authority: Essays in Old Testament Religion and Theology*, edited by George W. Coats and Burke O. Long, 42–55. Philadelphia: Fortress, 1977.

Crenshaw, James L. *Hymnic Affirmation of Divine Justice: The Doxologies of Amos and Related Texts in the Old Testament*. SBLDS 24. Missoula, MT: Scholars, 1975.

Cross, Frank Moore. "The Divine Warrior." In *Canaanite Myth and Hebrew Epic: Essays in the History of the Religion of Israel*, 91–111. Cambridge: Harvard University Press, 1973.

Dearman, J. Andrew. "My Servants the Scribes: Composition and Context in Jeremiah 36." *JBL* 109 (1990) 403–21.

Diepold, Peter. *Israel's Land*. BWANT 15. Berlin: Kohlhammer, 1972.

Fretheim, Terence E. "The Plagues as Ecological Signs of Historical Disaster." *JBL* 110 (1991) 385–96.

Hanson, Paul D. *The Dawn of Apocalyptic: The Historical and Sociological Roots of Jewish Apocalyptic Eschatology*. Rev. ed. Philadelphia: Fortress, 1979.

Holladay, William L. *Jeremiah*. 2 vols. Hermeneia. Philadelphia: Fortress, 1986–89.

Huffmon, Herbert B. "The Impossible Word of Assurance: Jer. 31:34–36 (35–37)." Paper delivered at the Society of Biblical Literature meeting, New Orleans, 1996.

Levinas, Emmanuel. *Totality and Infinity: An Essay on Exteriority*. Translated by Alphonso Lingis. Pittsburgh: Duquesne University Press, 1969.

McKane, William. *A Critical and Exegetical Commentary on Jeremiah*. 2 vols. International Critical Commentary. Edinburgh: T. & T. Clark, 1986–96.

———. *Proverbs: A Commentary*. OTL. Philadelphia: Westminster, 1970.

Miller, Patrick D., Jr. *The Divine Warrior in Early Israel*. Harvard Semitic Monographs 5. Cambridge: Harvard University Press, 1973.

———. *They Cried to the Lord: The Form and Theology of Biblical Prayer*. Minneapolis: Fortress, 1994.

Muilenburg, James. "Baruch the Scribe." In *Proclmnation and the Presence: Old Testament Essays in Honour of Gwynne Henton Davies*, edited by John I. Durham and J. Roy Porter, 215–38. London: SCM, 1970.

Perdue, Leo G. *The Collapse of History: Reconstructing Old Testament Theology*. OBT. Minneapolis: Fortress, 1994. See 2nd ed.: *Reconstructing Old Testament Theology: After the Collapse of History*. OBT. Minneapolis: Fortress, 2005.

Purpel, David E. *The Moral and Spiritual Crisis in Education: A Curriculum for Justice and Compassion in Education*. Critical Studies in Education Series. New York: Bergin & Garvey, 1989.

Rad, Gerhard von. *Old Testament Theology*. Vol. 2, *The Theology of the Prophetic Traditions*. Translated by David M. G. Stalker. London: Oliver & Boyd, 1965.

———. "The Theological Problem of the Old Testament Doctrine of Creation." In *The Problem of the Hexateuch and Other Essays*, 131–43. New York: McGraw-Hill, 1966. Reprinted in *From Genesis to Chronicles: Explorations in Old Testament Theology*, edited by K. C. Hanson, 177–86. Fortress Classics in Biblical Studies. Minneapolis: Fortress, 2005.

Ricoeur, Paul. "Biblical Hermeneutics." *Semeia* 4 (1975) 107–45.

Rudolph, Wilhelm. *Jeremia*. 2nd ed. Handbuch zum Alten Testament 12. Tübingen: Mohr/Siebeck, 1958.

Volz, Paul. *Der Prophet Jeremia*. 2nd ed. Leipzig: Deichert, 1928.

Weinfeld, Moshe. *Deuteronomy and the Deuteronomic School*. 1972. Reprinted, Winona Lake, IN: Eisenbrauns, 1992.

Whybray, R. N. *Wisdom in Proverbs*. SBT 1/45. Naperville, IL: Allenson, 1965.

Williamson, Hugh G. M. "First and Last in Isaiah." In *Of Prophets' Visions and the Wisdom of Sages: Essays in Honour of R. Norman Whybray on His Seventieth Birthday*, edited by Heather A. McKay and David J. A. Clines, 95–108. JSOTSup 162. Sheffield: Sheffield Academic, 1993.

Wolff, Hans Walter. "Hoseas geistige Heimat." *TLZ* 81 (1956) 83–94.

Wright, G. Ernest. *God Who Acts: Biblical Theology as Recital*. SBT 1/8. London: SCM, 1952.

———. *The Old Testament against Its Environment*. SBT 1/2. London: SCM, 1950.

four

ISRAEL'S SENSE OF PLACE
IN JEREMIAH

It is a delight to offer this essay to James Muilenburg, the only one of his kind in our discipline. His delicate balance of rigorous objectivity and passionate subjectivity is a rare model for us. This paper, which seeks to pursue themes and methods important in his own work, is presented with the gratitude only his students can understand.

Time and Space

Recent Old Testament study, in addressing the issue of Israel's view of time and space, has tended to celebrate time and minimize space as an important faith motif.[1] This emphasis was shared not only by Bultmannian scholars[2] but also by some of Bultmann's sharpest critics, who stressed the "Mighty Deeds of God in History."[3] Such a focus was an effective one in a

---

1. The most comprehensive statement of this stance is that of Bowman, *Hebrew Thought Compared with Greek*. But a number of other scholars, including Orelli, John Marsh, H. Wheeler Robinson, have contributed to the same tendency. Muilenburg himself, in "The Biblical View of Time," 229, could write, "Of the two great peoples who have exerted a major influence upon the mind and soul of Western Man, Hellas and Israel, the one lived and throught primarily in the world of space, the other primarily in the world of time."

2. This has received its most extreme form in Fuchs and Ebeling, who regard revelation as "saving event" and that as "language event." Cf. James M. Robinson, "Hermeneutic since Barth," 57 and passim.

3. Cf. Wright, *The Old Testament and Theology*, chap. 2; and Childs, *Biblical Theology in Crisis*, chap. 2, for two reviews of that stress. Both Bultmann and the accent on

time preoccupied with meaninglessness and boredom, as the recent post-war period was perceived to be.

It is clear in more recent time that the issues of theological concern have shifted radically; instead of speaking of meaninglessness, we may better speak of rootlessness, a sense of the loss of meaningful place.[4] This shift provides an opportunity to look again at the time–space problem in Israel's faith. Without denying the importance of the time emphasis recently made, it is possible to restore a more justified balance. Israel was *par excellence* a people with a place, a land of promise, and she was intensely concerned with it.[5]

A movement may be discerned in Israel's faith that moves between *landless people yearning for land* (the fathers, the sojourn, the exile), and *landed people preserving and/or perverting their land* (monarchy and prophets, the restoration under Ezra and Nehemiah). Land (and therefore space) is an important component in Israel's faith.[6] Her faith revolved around the question of land, either a desperate yearning for it or problematic possession of it.

As Boman has written of "the uselessness of the Western concept of time"[7] for understanding Israel's notion of time, so also modern notions of space and land do not discern what Israel meant by נחלה.[8] Here I shall examine some uses in Jeremiah. Jeremiah's time, just before and just after 587, was a time when the land question was acute and urgent for Israel. For then she had to ask: How can we keep the land? Why are we losing it? How shall we live without it? How can we regain it?

Behind this exploration lies the suggestion that we cannot understand the extremity of Israel's crisis of exile (read loss of place) unless we face the *space* category in Israel's faith.

"Mighty Deeds in History," stressed timefulness as the crucial category.

4. This emphasis is reflected in Toffler's popular *Future Shock*, which is concerned with rootlessness.

5. The concern of this paper only accidentally intersects with the vigous arguments of Barr, *The Semantics of Biblical Language*; and Barr, *Biblical Words for Time*. Whereas Barr is concerned that certain words have been wrongly or over-stressed, my point is that we have simply neglected rather obvious concerns of the texts, no doubt because of our hermeneutical frame. At that point I share Barr's conclusions.

6. On land as a theological theme, see especially Wildberger, "Israel und sein Land"; Dreyfus, "Le Theme de l'heritage dans l'AT"; Horst, "Zwei Begriffe für Eigentum (Besitz)."

7. Boman, *Hebrew Thought Compared with Greek*, 129.

8. See von Rad's essays, "The Promised Land," and "There Remains Still a Rest."

Jeremiah 2:4–13

This text is easily isolated as a distinct and separate unit. Its genre is widely accepted as lawsuit.[9] Williams' observations relating it to Deuteronomy 32 both secure its genre and place it in the context of a very ancient tradition.[10] The issue of this lawsuit is: Who is to blame for loss of land—Yahweh or Israel?[11]

In this pericope, vv. 6–7 specifically concern us:

> They did not say:
> > Where is Yahweh
> > > who **brought us** up from the **land** of Egypt
> > > who **led us** in the wilderness
> > > > in a **land** of deserts and pits
> > > > in a **land** of drought and deep darkness
> > > > in a **land** that none passes through
> > > > > where no man dwells.
> > Indeed, **I brought you** to the land of bounty
> > > to eat its fruit and its good things
> > But **you came** and you defiled my **land**
> > > my inheritance you made for an abomination

Verse 6 describes Yahweeh's action governed by two participles (הַמַּעֲלֶה and הַמּוֹלִיךְ)[12] that not only express Yahweh's faithfulness but describe two *places* of Israel: a) a place of slavery, and b) the place of precariousness.

In v. 7 the rhetoric shifts and is sharpened. Verse 7a is a statement of Yahweh's innocence: "I brought you" (אָבִיא). Verse 7b is a statement of Israel's guilt: "But you came" (וַתָּבֹאוּ). With Yahweh's act, the place of slavery and the place of precariousness are now displaced by the place of well-being. The statements are clearly parallel and symmetrical, governed by the same verb. Yahweh's action leaves the land fruitful and good. Israel's action leaves it defiled and abominable.

It is striking that in this brief passage the term אֶרֶץ occurs six times, four times as negative land:

9. Huffmon, "The Covenant Lawsuit in the Prophets"; and Gese "Bemerkungen zur Sinaitradition," 151 n. 57. Gese suggests a very close parallel to Isa 1:2–3.

10. Williams, "The Fatal and Foolish Exchange."

11. It is striking that the use of lament-complaint form (as in Job, Jeremiah, Lamentations) is especially intense when the land is in jeopardy.

12. Williams, "Fatal and Foolish Exchange," 22.

- land of Egypt
- land of darkness and pits
- land of drought and deep darkness
- land where none passes through

and the contrast, two times as positive land:

- land of abundance
- my land

The contrast is complete in affirming Yahweh's fidelity. He not only leads out but also in. But v. 7b moves to a sharp climax by the use of chiasmus:

> You defiled *my land*
>> *my inheritance* you set to abomination.

It has been "land," then "my land," but now it is named and identified "my inheritance." The word pair is as striking and abrasive as can be imagined: inheritance — abomination.

The crisis of the years before and after 587 is placed in the drama of "salvation history," which is presented here presented, vv. 6–8, as a *history of land*. Israel's career with Yahweh is from place to place: from land of slavery to land of precariousness to land of well-being and now to abominable land.[13]

In this same pericope we may note the conclusion of v. 13. As he has made a dramatic contrast in v. 7, so in v. 13 the contrast is simple and total:

> fountain of living waters // cisterns hewn out for themselves

The fountain of living water, i.e. a source of fertility given and not manufactured,[14] is closely linked to the imagery of Deut 6:11:

> houses full of all good things which you did not fill,
> cisterns hewn out which you did not hew,
> vineyards and olive trees which you did not plant . . .

Thus the contrast:

---

13. The return of creation to chaos is more fully stated in 4:23–26, and earlier in the same tradition in Hos 4:3. The chaos–creation theme is important for exile and displacement as I have shown in Brueggemann, "Weariness, Exile and Chaos."

14. In an important but neglected article, Visher, "Foi et Technique," comments on Deut 11:10–15, and contrasts the land of Israel that must be worked, a contrast very similar to the one we have suggested.

in the land of abundance: חצובים אשר לא חצבת

(Deut 6:11)

in the land of defilement: לחצב להם בארות

בארת נשברים אשר לא יכלו המים

(Jer 2:13)

While the relation of Jeremiah and Deuteronomy is complex and difficult,[15] clearly the two texts speak of the same reality and they carry the same power as the previous contrast:

> The land of נחלה has cisterns you do not hew out which yield life, but
> the land of טועבה has broken cisterns you made but they hold nothing.

Jeremiah has discerned the next relocation of Israel even as her whole history is one of relocation. This relocation is dislocation. Israel now faces a future in defiled space.

Jeremiah 3:1–5, 19–25; 4:1–4

This extended poem, which now has prose elements in its midst, revolves around the motif of turn, turn away, and return, as has often been asserted.[16] Again we are concerned with the passage only in respect to our theme of land and landlessness.

The pericope clearly appeals to the older material of Deut 24:1–4. I have previously argued that the original material about marriage in Deut 24:1–4 has been extended to concern the land.[17] Whereas in Deuteronomy it is an actual marital relation that defiles the land, in Jeremiah 3 the relation of land and defilement is now through the harlotry of the entire people.

The motif occurs several times in the poem:

> Would not that land be greatly **polluted** (תחנף חנוף)
> You have played the **harlot** (זנית) wih my lovers . . .
> by the wayside you have sat awaiting lovers like an Arab in the wilderness

15. See the bibliography of Bright, *Jeremiah*, lxxi nn. 19–21; and recently Nicholson, *Preaching to the Exiles*.

16. See Muilenburg's perceptive comments, "Form Criticism and Beyond," 9–10.

17. Brueggemann, "A Form-Critical Study of the Cultic Material in Deuteronomy," 327–28.

You have *polluted* (תחניפי) the land in *your harlotry* (זנותיך)

Therefore . . . (Jer 3:1–3a)

The opening statement of v. 1 simply makes the link to the old tradition, then the theme of marital faithlessness is not mentioned until v. 20. The motifs in vv. 2–4 are very different. They include the double mention of חנף (once with infinitive absolute) and in both cases the three-fold pattern of: a) pollute, b) harlot, and c) land. The older link of harlotry and land is exploited to the full,[18] for in vv. 3–5 it is the destruction of the land in drought, which is paramount.[19]

A secondary motif is the wordplay on רע:

You have played the harlot with many lovers (רעים). (v. 1)

You have polluted the land with your harlotry and with your evils (רעתך). (v. 2c)

You have done all the evil (הרעות) that you could. (v. 5)

Thus the play on lovers and evil is clear. So also the term ארץ stands in v. 2c as expected, but it is also in v. 1c, where one expects האשה.[20] The land is the abused land. The marriage imagery is completely transformed to apply to the land. (The use of חנף, here and in v. 9, is used elsewhere in Jeremiah only in 23:9, where it also refers to land.)

In 3:1–5, the rhetorical question form is noteworthy:

Have you (*interrogative* ה) not just now called to me . . . ? (v. 4a)

Will he (*interrogative* ה) be angry forever? (v. 5a)

Will he (אם) be indignant to the end? (v. 5b)

The question pattern is utilized to ask about the father–son relation and suggests a context of familial relations, perhaps not unlike those of which

---

18. Von Rad, *Deuteronomy*, 150, argues that unchastity and defilement of land is a standard connection.

19. The cluster of notions related to rain, drought, curse, pollution, and abundance, bears investigation but lies beyond our theme. These notions have been largely ignored in the frame of Yahweh versus fertility gods. Cf. the titles expressing this stance, Wright, *The Old Testament against Its Environment*; and Habel, *Yahweh versus Baal*. More recently Harrelson, *From Fertility Cult to Worship*, has moved to a better balance as he is able to assert that "Israelite religion was also a religion of fertility" (12–13).

20. The LXX has the expected "woman," but that is likely a removal of a dramatic and unexpected "land" as the object of pollution. Cf. the point made by Martin, "The Forensic Background," 83, and his entire discussion.

Wolff and Gerstenberger have written.[21] Thus the form functions in a way most convenient to the matter under discussion, i.e., how is life to be ordered to secure well-being, when the father gives the inheritance to his son, and the son betrays the father?

This unit then has a surprising and diverse develement: a) question that appeals to old law (v. 1a); b) chiastic structure that begins with a question and ends with a corresponding declaration (v. 1b–2); c) statement of consequence resulting from the actions in vs. 2 (v. 3); and d) rhetorical qustion about father–son relation (vv. 4–5).

In terms of theme: a) v. 1a husband and wife relation; b) vv. 1b–3 violation of land; and c) vv. 4–5 father–son relation. The images of the two relationships (husband–wife in v. 1a and father–son in vv. 4–5) frame the theme of pollution of land. Clearly the issue is not simply perverted relation—as is often suggested in the stress on שׁוּב[22]—but is *loss of place.*

The poem continues in vv. 19–25 by stating Yahweh's intention:

> And I, I said,
>> How I will set you among my sons!
>> and I will give to you a pleasant *land*
>> a *heritage* of all nations most bounteous!
> And I, I said,
>> My *father* you will call me and from after me you will not turn.

The structure of this verse is controlled by the double "I said." The first announces Yahweh's intention: land for Israel. The second announces Yahweh's condition: call me "my father." The two belong together. Israel will have the land only when the land is perceived as inheritance from the father: i.e., only when Israel knows itself as heir.[23] In these motifs of נחלה and אבי, the balance of: a) eventual, relational time (אב); and b) covenantal space (נחלה) is affirmed.[24]

---

21. Wolff, *Amos' Geistige Heimat*, 7–12 [ET: *Amos, the Prophet*]; Gerstenberger, *Wesen und Herkunft.*

22. Cf. the exposition of Vischer, "Return, Rebel Sons!" which completely ignores the power of the land imagery.

23. It is striking how very differently the father–son imagery can be viewed when the balance of space and time is recovered. An alternative reading of the image is that of Wright, "How Did Early Israel Differ."

24. Not only is the Father addressed twice (vv. 4, 19), but Israel is twice called "sons" (vv. 14, 22). Thus land and father–son imagery are closely linked In the same context, note the repeated use of נעורים (vv. 4, 24, 25).

Finally, the poem concludes with an allusion to the land promise. Though only the last blessing to Abraham is mentioned, clearly the land promise is in purview.[25]

The call to turn is closely linked to care for land. In 4:1 the call for repentance is to "remove your abomination" (שִׁקּוּץ). In 3:1–2 it is called "polluted" (חָנֵף), as in 2:7, "abomination" (תּוֹעֵבָה). It is cogent to understand the removal of abomination as a restoration of נַחֲלָה. Jeremiah, seeing the Bablonian threat as Yahweh's will for loss of land, in these poems holds out hope that Israel's destiny may still be the "pleasant land, bounteous heritage, plentiful land," but he also faces the prospect that the place for Israel may be one of defiled land, of drought and death. The judgment of Yahweh in the Babylonian invasion is not perversion of a relationship or distortion of an event, but perversion of place and therefore loss of space.[26]

Jeremiah 12:7–13

Whereas 2:4–13 and 3:1–5, 19–25 hoped for rescue, with profound pathos 12:7–13 sets forth the hopelessness of Israel (and of Yahweh). The land has now been irrevocably lost. The passage is easily divided into two parts.

Images of Deserted and Perverted Land (Jer 12:7–9a)

> I have forsaken my house
>> I have abandoned **my heritage**
> I have given the beloved of my soul
>> into the hands of her enemies.
> **My heritage** has become to me like
>> a lion in the forest.
> She has lifted up her voice against me;
>> therefore I hate her.

---

25. Cf. Wolff, "The Kerygma of the Yahwist," 156. Note also the land imagery of v. 3. See my discussion of Hos 10:12, which is closely linked to this verse; Brueggemann, *Tradition for Crisis*, 80–82.

26. Note that the dependent prose passage of 3:6–10, 15–18, which promises restoration, also operates with land imagery. On the relation of the prose and poetry, cf. Nicholson, *Preaching to the Exiles*; and Miller, *Das Verhältnis Jeremias und Hesekiels sprachlich und theologisch untersucht*, 90–91.

> Is *my heritage* to me like a speckled bird of prey?
>
> Are the birds of prey against her round about?

The key term נחלה occurs three times with remarkably diverse images: a) given over to enemies, also called "delight of my life," treasured and now lost (v. 7); b) become a lion in the forest, hostile, defiant, destructive, rejecting everything Yahweh had intended (v. 8); and c) a peculiar bird, attacked by other birds (v. 9). The imagery is abrupt and inconsistent. In the first usage the heritage is simply lost, but in the second it is hostile. In the third, the imagery is unclear, but probably it is closer to the first usage. In any case, the entire review is governed by the opening verb, "I have forsaken."[27] All the trouble follows because Yahweh has left the land to its own resources, which leads to destruction and death. Again, land without father is not viable.

The imagery is reinforced by the torrent of first person pronouns: three times "my inheritance," three first person verbs, and a number of pronominal suffixes. The stunning conclusion: "therefore I hate her," is one of Jeremiah's most radical statements of a time to tear down and pluck up.[28] Yahweh has turned against his own inheritance, i.e., rejecting the promises he has made and the election he has affirmed. The language and imagery is consistently about the land, not about people.

The Destiny of the Land (Jer 12:9b–13)

> Go, assemble all the wild beasts
>> bring them to *devour*
> many shepherds have destroyed my vineyard,
>> they have tampled down *my portion*,
> they have made my pleasant *portion*
>> a desolate wilderness.

27. Cf. Muilenburg, "The Terminology of Adversity," 52–54.

28. The total rejection of what he is expected to value is perhaps illuminated by Würthwein, "Amos 5:21–27," in which the word "hate," along with others, is the antithesis of cultic acceptance by Yahweh. Cf. Rendtorff, "Priestliche Kulttheologie und prophetische Kultpolemik," for a similar point. The use of cultic terminology may suggest why polluted land is abominable, i.e., repugnant to Yahweh's presence. This is supported by the peculiar use of טמא in an earlier passage (2:7). The balance of: a) defiled place; and b) absent deity, is of course reflected in Ezekiel.

They have made it a ***desolation***:

> ***desolate*** it mourns to me.

The whole land is made ***desolate***,

> but no man lays it to heart.

Upon all the bare heights in the desert

> destroyers have come;

for the sword of Yahweh ***devours***

> > from one end of the land to the other;

> > no flesh has peace.

They have sown wheat and have reaped thorns,

> they have tired themselves out but profit nothing.

They shall be ashamed of their harvests

> because of the fierce anger of Yahweh.

This section is linked to the proceeding by the double use of my "portion" (חלק, v. 10), which echoes my "heritage." But the major note is the rich vocabulary of destruction: "devour," אכל, vv. 9, 12); "destroy," שחת (v. 10); "trample," בסס (v. 10); "desolate," שמם (vv. 10, 11);[29] "mourn," אבל (v. 11); "desert," מדבר (vv. 10, 12); "destroyers," שדד (v. 12); "anger," חרון (v. 13). The land's inescapable destiny, when Yahweh has abandoned it, is death (cf. v. 13 as failure in harvest). This poem vividly describes death at the hands of invaders. The description is introduced in v. 9a and concluded in v. 12 with the same word "devour." The first use is with "wild beasts," the final one is "sword," both characteristic curses.[30] Between these two is the powerful imagery of vineyards being trampled and destroyed, the bountiful spot being reduced to a wast, and finally in v. 13, the land is totally unproductive. The place of life is reduced to a place of death.

The entire poem is Yahweh's lament following Jeremiah's lament (vv. 1–6), though perhaps this connection is not original. Yahweh himself, according to the form, laments. But in v. 11 it is the land that mourns. Worth noting is the fact that in 12:4 the prophet uses the same language to describe the land as mourning.

Clearly Yahweh's judgment and Israel's hope concern land. The historical upheavals in the midst of Jeremiah's period are understood primarily

---

29. Cf. Muilenburg, "The Terminology of Adversity," 50–52.

30. Cf. Hillers, *Treaty-Curses*, 54–56 and passim; and Fensham, "Common Trends in Curses," 160, 166–68 and passim.

as loss of land.[31] Thus the movement is clear from vv. 7–9a, which speaks about the land being deserted and perverted, to 9b–13, which describes the reality of death and the subsequent mourning by the land. In contrast to the earlier poems we have considered, here the issue is settled, and the land is gone.[32]

Reversing the Curse

This experience of disinheritance, an obvious but neglected theme, is essential to understanding the proclamation of exilic hope. Only when the enormity of displacement is discerned is the promise of return as gripping as it is intended by the poets to be.

Jeremiah himself in a dramatic act performs a sign that ends this way:

> Houses and fields and vineyards
>> shall again be bought in the land (אֶרֶץ). (Jer 32:15)[33]

This promise, which reverses the curse (cf. Deut 28:30, 38–39; Amos 5:11; Zeph 1:13), grows out of a narrative that gives legal force to the conviction of inalienable right of inheritance.[34]

The theme of regained inheritance is more fully presented in Ezek 47:13–23, in which the return from exile is interpreted as an act of land allocation paralleling that of Joshua:

> And you shall divide it equally: I swore to give it to your fathers,
> and this land shall fall to you as your **inheritance**. (47:14)

> You shall allot it as an **inheritance** for yourselves and for the aliens
> who reside among you. (47:22a)

---

31. This is the key component in the theme of "tragic reversal" described by Gottwald, *Studies*, chap. 3.

32. Again note the derivative prose passage of 12:14–17, which speaks of hope in terms of land. On the passage, see Nicholson, *Preaching to the Exiles*, 84–88; Gottwald, *All the Kingdoms*, 294; and Herrmann, *Die Prophetischen Heilserwartungen*, 162–65. Space does not permit comment upon 16:18–21; 17:1–4; 22:28–30—all of which bear upon our theme.

33. See Fohrer, *Die symbolischen Handlungen der Propheten*, 42–44 and passim.

34. A closely paralleled text, Genesis 23, is a crucial text in P for linking that tradition to land. The structure of Genesis 23 moves from landlessness (vv. 1–4 to land (vv. 17–20), a movement structurally important to P. Cf. Brueggemann, "The Kerygma of the Priestly Writers," on the priestly tradition and land theology.

> This is the land which you shall allot as an *inheritance* among the tribes of Israel, and these are their several portions, says the Lord Yahweh. (48:29)

It is no accident that the Ezekiel tradition, which utilizes land-division as a motif of restoration, also speaks of resurrection from the dead (cf. Ezek 37:14), for the land is the essential component in the resurrection of Israel. Thus Macholz writes: "Nur in diesem Land ist die Existenz Israels für den Verfasser denkbar; auch das neue Israel kann nur existieren in diesem selben, freilich erneuerten und umgestalteten, Lande."[35]

All three exilic prophets—Jeremiah, Ezekiel, and Deutero-Isaiah—understand the inherited land to be the most visible, most significant embodiment of deliverance from exile and restoration. This balance of loss of land and gift of land provides an important model for exilic faith. Among the themes derived from and related to this model are:

1. The tradition of Jeremiah as it now stands is dominated by the motif of "building and planting, plucking up and tering down" (Jer 1:10; 12:14–17; 18:7–9; 24:6; 31:4–5, 27–28; 32:41; 42:10; 45:4), which may well be an image of loss of land and restoration of land.

2. A parallel motif is that of scattering–gathering, which has clear and obvious derivation from loss of land and regaining land (cf. Jer 23:2–3; Ezek 11:17; Isa 54:7). The motif is frequent, especially in Ezekiel.

3. through a careful analysis of vocabulary, Raitt has been able to show that rejection–election is a theme especially appropriate to Jeremiah and Ezekiel.[36] The notion of rejection–election concerns not simply Yahweh–Israel, but Yahweh-over-the-land and Israel-in-the-land.

4. The use of divorce–remarriage in both Hosea 2 and Jeremiah 3 moves back and forth between covenantal relations and placement in the land. Thus the vocabularies of abandonment (עָזַב) and harlotry, which Muilenburg has analyzed,[37] are not simply relational motifs as they have often been presented, but they concern place-

---

35. Macholz, "Noch Einmal," 349 [ET: Only in this land is Israel's existence thinkable for the author; the new Israel can also only exist in this same fully renewed and reconstituted land]. Cf. Isa 49:8 for the same motif handled differently by Deutero-Isaiah.

36. Raitt, "Function, Setting and Content in Jeremiah's Oracles of Judgment."

37. Muilenburg, "The Terminology of Adversity," 52–54.

ment in the land as the image of produce and fertility as Hosea 2 clearly indicates. That the Valley of Trouble becomes the Door of Hope (Hos 2:17 [ET 2:15]) is imagery of reentry into the land, for which the type is Joshua 7. All these models suggest that we have read space concerns as realtional concerns, and in the process we have neglected a primary dimension of the text.

Conclusion

The prominence of land as space is a central motif of biblical faith, which has been largely unexplored both by an existential and by an historical hermeneutic concerned with covenantal, relational, eventful categories. Biblical faith in the upheaval of exile returned to the basic land of promise (cf. Jer 4:1–2;[38] Ezek 20:42; Isa 51:2). In so doing, it affirmed that Yahweh wills rootage and not rootlessness for his people (or chaos; cf. Jer 4:22–26; Isa 45:18–19).

The persistent concern of biblical faith for the poor and disenfran- chised (widows, orphans, lepers, "publicans and sinners") is precisely that they have been *dis*-inherited and rendered both rootless and powerless— and Yahweh does not will it so! This central concern of biblical faith has been lost and can be rightly appreciated only when land as rootage and place is understood, when the biblical gospel is understood as Yahweh's "territorial imperative."[39]

This motif makes contact between biblical faith and contemporary so- cial and theological upheavals. The domesticated quest for "meaning" has been largely replaced by a demand for place. This is true of the Jews, who must perennially struggle with the "disenlandisment," and the problem is only more clearly focused by the modern state of Israel.[40] This is true for the

38. Wolff, "The Kerygma of the Yahwist," 156–57, has shown how this links to the older tradition.

39. Eliade, in his various writing, has described the significance and function of sa- cred space. Cf. *Cosmos and History*, 12–21; *The Sacred and the Profane*, chap. 1. Remark- ably, even Eliade (*Cosmos and History*, 102–12) overstates the case for time in Israel. Again, it is the contrast of Israel and other peoples that causes one to overlook land as place, which is so crucial for Israel's self-understanding. The crisis of exile can hardly be understood apart from this, nor is the return expressed in a different idiom.

40. This has been given various forms of expression, most passionately in the several writings of Richard Rubenstein. Cf. Jacob, "Israel History and the Church"; Neusner, *American Judaism*, 105, who uses the infelicitous term "enlandisement."

Black, who "like the Jew, has always had a land problem."[41] And it is true in a parallel way for every person who in a time of upheaval and future shock experiences rootlessness: "They will not want to play Russian Roulette with their children's schools, and they will see, one hopes, that a child is better reared in a neighborhood than in a glorified bus terminal . . . Without this early experience of territoriality it is doubtful if anyone can learn to regard the whole earth as his turf."[42]

Our hermeneutical investments influenced by salvation history or existentialist categories have led us to neglect this aspect of biblical theology. Perhaps these categories have been a reaction against the fascist tendency to equate religion and land.[43] In any case, a very different situation calls for fresh categories. Thus the point of the Jeremiah exegesis in this paper is to call attention to the blindness created by our recent hermeneutical categories, which has closed off motifs especially significant in a time of rootlessness.

The meaning of the notion of inheritance as space in the New Testament lies beyond the scope of this paper. But attention may be called to Paul's use of the motif of inheritance in Rom 8:16–17 and Gal 4:4–7. It is striking that in both cases the phrase "Abba, Father" is linked not only with sonship but with *heirdom*. The convergence of motifs is the same as in Jer 3:4, 19: "claiming the inheritance" is related to confessing the father.[44]

Even more striking is Gal 4:1–7, where the motifs of father and inheritance are joined with the notion of "fullness of time." It may be an interesting development of hermeneutical stress on time to note that the full time is the time when the son receives inheritance, i.e., it is a time for receiving space in which to live.

---

41. Williams, "Toward a Sociological Understanding," 261. Having said this, Williams quickly subordinates space to time, but his point is made.

42. Snow, *On Pilgrimage*, 38.

43. Curiously, Rubenstein uses rhetoric for "religion of the soil," not unlike that of the Hitler movement. Thus, for example, he speaks of "Israel's earth and the lost divinities of that earth," *After Auschwitz*, 70.

44. Jeremias, *Abba*, 64–67, views the matter differently, denying the tradition connection suggested here.

Bibliography

Barr, James. *Biblical Words for Time*. SBT 1/33. 1962. Reprinted, Eugene, OR: Wipf & Stock, 2009.

———. *The Semantics of Biblical Language*. 1961. Reprinted, Eugene, OR: Wipf & Stock, 2004.

Bowman, Thorlief. *Hebrew Thought Compared with Greek*. London: SCM, 1960.

Bright, John. *Jeremiah*. AB 21. Garden City, NY: Doubleday, 1965.

Brueggemann, Walter. "A Form-Critical Study of the Cultic Material in Deuteronomy." ThD diss., Union Theological Seminary, New York, 1961.

———. "The Kerygma of the Priestly Writers." *ZAW* 84 (1972) 397–414. Reprinted in Brueggemann and Wolff, *The Vitality of Old Testament Traditions*, 101–14. 2nd ed. Atlanta: John Knox, 1982.

———. *Tradition for Crisis: Hosea*. Richmond: John Knox, 1968.

———. "Weariness, Exile, and Chaos (A Motif in Royal Theology)." *CBQ* 24 (1972) 19–38.

Childs, Brevard S. *Biblical Theology in Crisis*. Philadelphia: Westminster, 1970.

Dreyfus, François-Paul. "Le Theme de l'heritage dans l'AT." *Revue des Sciences Philosophiques et Théologiqués* 42 (1958) 3–49.

Eliade, Mircea. *Cosmos and History: The Myth of the Eternal Return*. Translated by Willard R. Trask. New York: Harper, 1959.

———. *The Sacred and the Profane*. Translated by Willard R. Trask. New York: Harper, 1959.

Fensham, F. Charles. "Common Trends in Curses of the Near Eastern Treaties and *Kudurru*-Inscriptions Compared with Maledictions of Amos and Isaiah." *ZAW* 75 (1963) 155–75.

Fohrer, Georg. *Die symbolischen Handlungen der Propheten*. ATANT 54. 2nd ed. Zurich: Zwingli, 1968.

Gerstenberger, Erhard S. *Wesen und Herkunft des apodiktischen Rechts*. WMANT 20. 1965. Reprinted, Eugene, OR: Wipf & Stock, 2009.

Gese, Hartmut. "Bemerkungen zur Sinaitradition." *ZAW* 79 (1967) 137–54. Reprinted in *Vom Sinai zum Zion: Alttestamentliche Beiträge zur biblischen Theologie*, 31–48. Munich: Kaiser, 1974.

Gottwald, Norman K. *All the Kingdoms of the Earth: Israelite Prophecy and International Relations in the Ancient Near East*. 1964. Reprinted, Minneapolis: Fortress, 2014.

———. *Studies in the Book of Lamentations*. SBT 1/14. 1954. Reprinted, Eugene, OR: Wipf & Stock, 2010.

Habel, Norman. *Yahweh versus Baal*. New York: Bookman, 1964.

Herrmann, Siegfried. *Die Prophetischen Heilserwartungen im Alten Testament: Ursprung und Gestaltwandel*. BWANT 85. Stuttgart: Kohlhammer, 1965.

Hillers, Delbert R. *Treaty-Curses and the Old Testament Prophets*. Biblica et Orientalia 16. Rome: Pontifical Biblical Institute Press, 1964.

Horst, Friedrich. "Zwei Begriffe für Eigentum (Besitz)." In *Verbannung und Heimkehr: Beiträge zur Geschichte und Theologie Israels im 6. und 5. Jahrhundert v. Chr.: Wilhelm Rudolph zum 70. Geburtstage*, edited by A. Kuschke, 135–56. Tübingen: Mohr/ Siebeck, 1961.

Huffmon, Herbert B. "The Covenant Lawsuit in the Prophets." *JBL* 78 (1959) 287–89.

Jacob, Isaac H. "Israel History and the Church." *CCI Notebook*. American Jewish Congress; Commission on Community Interrelations. April 1972.

Jeremias, Joachim. *Abba: Studien zur neutestamentlichen Theologie und Zeitgeschichte*. Göttingen: Vandenhoeck & Ruprecht, 1966.

Macholz, Christian. "Noch Einmal: Planungen für den Wiederaufbau nach der Katastrophe von 587." *VT* 19 (1969) 322–52.

Martin, James D. "The Forensic Background to Jeremiah III 1." *VT* 19 (1969) 82–92.

Miller, John W. *Das Verhältnis Jeremias und Hesekiels sprachlich und theologisch Untersucht: Mit besonderer Berücksichtigung der Prosareden Jeremias*. Van Gorcum's Theologische Bibliotheek 28. Assen: Van Gorcum, 1955.

Muilenburg, James. "The Biblical View of Time." *HTR* 54 (1961) 229.

———. "Form Criticism and Beyond." *JBL* 88 (1969) 1–18.

———. "The Terminology of Adversity in Jeremiah." In *Translating and Understanding the Old Testament*, edited by Harry Thomas Frank and William L. Reed, 42–63. Nashville: Abingdon, 1970.

Neusner, Jacob. *American Judaism: Adventure in Modernity*. Englewood Cliffs, NJ: Prentice-Hall, 1972.

Nicholson, E. W. *Preaching to the Exiles: A Study of the Prose Tradition in the Book of Jeremiah*. Oxford: Blackwell, 1970.

Rad, Gerhard von. *Deuteronomy*. Translated by Dorothea Barton. OTL. Philadelphia: Westminster, 1966.

———. "The Promised Land and Yahweh's Land in the Hexateuch." In *The Problem of the Hexateuch and Other Essays*, 79–93. Translated by E. W. T. Dicken. New York: McGraw-Hill, 1966. Reprinted in *From Genesis to Chronicles: Explorations in Old Testament Theology*, edited by K. C. Hanson, 59–69. Fortress Classics in Biblical Studies. Minneapolis: Fortress, 2005.

———. "There Remains Still a Rest for the People of God." In *The Problem of the Hexateuch and Other Essays*, 94–102. Translated by E. W. T. Dicken. New York: McGraw-Hill, 1966. Reprinted in *From Genesis to Chronicles: Explorations in Old Testament Theology*, edited by K. C. Hanson, 82–88. Fortress Classics in Biblical Studies. Minneapolis: Fortress, 2005.

Raitt, Thomas. "Function, Setting and Content in Jeremiah's Oracles of Judgment." *SBL Seminar Papers* 1 (1972) 207–28.

Rendtorff, Rolf. "Priestliche Kulttheologie und prophetische Kultpolemik." *TLZ* 81 (1956) 339–42.

Robinson, James M. "Hermeneutic since Barth." In *The New Hermeneutic*, edited by James M. Robinson and John B. Cobb. New Frontiers in Theology 2. New York: Harper & Row, 1964. Reprinted in Robinson, *Language, Hermeneutic, and History*, 69–146. Eugene, OR: Cascade Books, 2008.

Rubenstein, Richard. *After Auschwitz: History, Theology, and Contemporary Judaism*. Indianapolis: Bobbs-Merrill, 1966.

Snow, John. *On Pilgrimage: Marriage in the 70s*. New York: Seabury, 1971.

Toffler, Alvin. *Future Shock*. New York: Random House, 1970.

Vischer, Wilhelm. "Foi et Technique." *Revue d'histoire et de philosophie religieuses* 44 (1964) 102–9.

———. "Return, Rebel Sons!" *Int* 8 (1954) 43–47.

Wildberger, Hans. "Israel und sein Land." *EvTh* 16 (1956) 404–22.

Williams, Prescott H. "The Fatal and the Foolish Exchange: Living Water for 'Nothings.'" *Austin Seminary Bulletin* 81 (Sept. 1965) 3–59.

Williams, Preston N. "Toward a Sociological Understanding of the Black Religious Community." *Soundings* 54 (1971) 260–70.

Wolff, Hans Walter. *Amos' Geistige Heimat.* WMANT 18. Neukirchen-Vluyn: Neukirchener, 1964.

———. *Amos the Prophet: The Man and His Background.* Translated by Foster R. McCurley. Edited by John Reumann. Philadelphia: Fortress, 1973.

———. "The Kerygma of the Yahwist." *Int* 20 (1966) 131–58. Reprinted in Walter Brueggemann and Hans Walter Wolff, *The Vitality of Old Testament Traditions*, 41–66 + 148–54. 2nd ed. Atlanta: John Knox, 1982.

Wright, G. Ernest. "How Did Early Israel Differ from Her Neighbors?" *BA* 6 (1943) 1–20.

———. *The Old Testament against Its Environment.* SBT 1/2. Naperville, IL: Allenson, 1950.

———. *The Old Testament and Theology.* New York: Harper & Row, 1969.

———. "The Terminology of Old Testament Religion and Its Significance." *Journal of Near Eastern Studies* 1 (1942) 404–14.

Würthwein, Ernst. "Amos 5:21–27." *TLZ* 72 (1947) 144–52.

five

IMAGINATION AS A MODE OF FIDELITY

Bernhard Anderson has recently published an important book on biblical interpretation, *The Living Word of the Bible*.[1] It is an important book, as is usual for him, carefully and precisely articulated. But predictably, because it is a popular book, it is largely a neglected book.

The following paper seeks to explore one theme from that book. The first chapter of Anderson's hermeneutical statement is entitled "Word of Imagination."[2] In that chapter Anderson identifies three fronts on which the question of biblical authority and interpretation is important:

1. In relation to literalists, some of whom practice "papal ecclesiasticism";

2. In relation to rigorously critical scholars who stress the human character of the text, with an acute historical sense;

3. In relaton to word-centered theologians who bracket out critical questions in relation to theological authority, a position not to be confused with literalism.

In relation to these various approaches, Anderson makes trenchant comments in two directions. First, he makes the point that good and faithful biblical interpretation must exercise *poetic sensitivity* and *artistic imagination* that lets us hear the live word of God in the text.[3] Second, he urges that we must find scholarly methods and approaches that serve and enhance such poetic and artistic imagination. Like many of us, Anderson is

---

1. Anderson, *The Living Word of the Bible*.

2. Ibid., 13–35.

3. Ibid., 29.

acutely aware that standard historical-critical methods are both important and problematic. They are important because they have liberated the Scriptures from dogmatic tyrannies, by permitting the text to be seen "in its own context" and not in the patterns of dogmatic perspective, so that all important claims are already preempted before meeting the text. But the limitations of historical-critical methods are increasingly apparent,[4] because such perspectives have not very well served the preaching task of the church. One has only to examine the arid and fragmenting offerings of the commentaries to draw such a conclusion, even when responsible methods are rigorously honored, or perhaps especially when such methods are used.

Imagination and the Articulation of Israel's Faith

Anderson's urging then is this: "The time has come for the kind of literary criticism that calls on our poetic and artistic imagination, without sacrificing the insights that historical criticism has provided."[5] That is, Anderson's proposal is that new openness for live interpretation is to be found in new method. There is a great deal to be said for that. No doubt new (for Scripture study) forms of literary criticism have provided new vitality and freedom in interpretation. But too much should not be claimed for this method either, because one can also find efforts at literary criticism that are practices of obfuscation that do not serve the live word well.

While attention should be given to the general methodological shift in the direction urged by Anderson,[6] he adds an important conclusion to his chapter on imagination. In it he makes a *theological* rather than a *methodological* statement. He links together *the practice of imagination* and *the work of the Holy Spirit.*[7] I take that to be a most important statement. Admittedly the liberating guidance of the Holy Spirit may use literary criticism, but obviously that work is not to be equated with or confined to this or any other method.

4. Those limitations are most formidably articulated by Childs, *Introduction to the Old Testament as Scripture.* See Anderson's assessment of Childs's word, "Introduction to the Old Testament as Scripture."

5. Anderson, *The Living Word of the Bible,* 29–30.

6. See Anderson's own important contributions in this regard, "From Analysis to Synthesis"; and "Tradition and Scripture in the Community of Faith." See the judicious programmatic statement of Polzin, *Moses and the Deuteronomist,* 1–24.

7. Ibid., 34–35.

Thus Anderson's urging (with which I agree) is in two parts. It is an urging about method, that a new form of literary criticism gives us the best chance to discern the vitality, richness, and power in the text. It is a theological urging that the interpreter must practice imagination that uses all methods available, but goes beyond all of them to encounter the theological claim of the text. The theological and methodological urgings are closely related to each other. But they are not to be equated. Nor is poetic freedom given by the spirit to be governed by any method. The relation of these two matters obviously will be settled in different ways by different interpreters, both in academic and ecclesiastical contexts.

Now the particular part of Anderson's provocative statement to be considered here is, *What role does imagination have in the articulation of Israel's faith?* While we would finally be concerned with our contemporary practice of imagination in the service of interpretation (as is Anderson), we may come at that contemporary question by asking how, in the process of Scripture itself, imagination is understood, practiced, and critiqued.[8] Perhaps there are clues in that ancient enterprise for our own practice of imagination.

At the outset we should seek to characterize—but not define—imagination. In this we may follow the characterization of two scholars. First, Ray Hart understands imagination as an activity:

> Wherever symbolic reference is cognitively rich, the imagination is actively at work; for imagination "cracks" the focalized boundaries of the delineated object, gaining access to a field of actuality that was, from the perspective of the closed object in rational or sensuous apprehension, merely dormant, but now is, through the active reflexivity of imagination, a vivacious stimulant to and limitant upon the will . . .[9]

> The activity of the imagination: the "loosening" of the mnemonic "given" so as to integrate its potency with expanding selfhood . . .[10]

---

8. Observe that Childs has urged that any serious theological proposal must be articulated with reference both to the academy and the believing communities; "Some Reflections on the Search for a Biblical Theology."

9. Hart, *Unfinished Man and the Imagination*, 159.

10. Ibid., 198.

> It "loosens" or "dissolves" the mnemonic given so that the potency
> of the past may fund, and be appropriated to the present.[11]

Hart uses language that is more dense than we need for our purpose. But his repeated statement will serve us well: it is a way "to loosen the givens."

Second, Tannehill characterizes the work of imagination in this way: "Imaginative shock" is to challenge old structures of thought and suggest new visions.[12] Admittedly there are complicated sociopsychological aspects to such a phenomenon as well as suble literary factors. But it will suffice for us to speak of the generation of new images/metaphors which challenge, delegitimate, deconstruct old stable realities, and that anticipate and evoke the shape of new realities. While this no doubt requires artistic sensitivity, Anderson is surely correct that such an act is "inspired," a gift of the Holy One as much as an achievement of skill. Or, said another way, such articulations are "revelatory."

יצר as Imagination

So we consider the function of imagination within Scripture as a way to find a clue for our own imaginative ways of interpreting the text. We begin with a consideration of two words that in various ways are rendered "imagination." The obvious beginning place is with יצר, which five times is used as a noun for "imagination." But we begin with the verbal form which seems to have a curious connection to the noun.

1. There is no doubt that the term is related to the "forming" which is done by a potter with clay. Thus it seems to refer to actual manual work (see, e.g., Gen 2:8; Isa 41:25; 43:21; 44:10, 21; Jer 18:2–6; 19:1, 11; Pss 2:9; 95:5; 104:26).[13] Stuhlmueller concludes: "The word יצר . . . stresses the idea of *careful workmanship*, like a potter at work, and possibly the notion of tender cultivation, like the concern of a farmer."[14]

2. But along with the material notion of "careful workmanship," a different sense can be placed on it in some texts. In Isa 43:1, 7; 45:7, 18; and Amos 4:13 two factors are common. First, it is Yahweh who does יצר.

---

11. Ibid., 200; see 246.

12. Tannehill, *The Sword of His Mouth*, 54. See the use made of this construct by Fox, "The Rhetoric of Ezekiel's Vision of the Valley of Dry Bones."

13. Cf. Stuhlmueller, *Creative Redemption in Deutero-Isaiah*, 115.

14. Ibid., 215.

Second, in each case, the verb is parallel to ברא. Now it is commonplace to say that only Yahweh can ברא, for the term ברא suggests some kind of active agent rather than physical material activity, much more sophisticated and not at all involved in actual fabrication. It seems to be an act of sheer holiness that evokes new reality. This word parallel suggests the יצר cannot only be treated simply according to the metaphor of potter. On some occasions, it would seem to have a much more playful reference in parallel to ברא, which might better be taken as to "foresee," "to form in the mind or heart," i.e. to imagine. When the verb is parallel to ברא it is fair to assume that it participates in something of the same understanding.[15]

3. This reading of the term would seem sustained by three other uses:

> Have you not heard that I determined (עשׂה) it long ago,
>> I planned (יצר) it long ago,
>> what I now bring to pass. (Isa 37:26; 2 Kgs 19:25)

> Behold I am shaping (יצר) evil against you,
>> and devising (חשׁב) a plan (חשׁב) against you. (Jer 18:11)

> I have spoken, I will bring it to pass,
>> I have purposed (יצר), I will do it (עשׂה). (Isa 46:11)

In these three uses, it is clear that Yahweh, long before historical implementation, "imagined, envisioned, conceived, determined, planned" what was to come. It is a constructive, creative act of freedom that "forms" something over against what presently exists. That is, it is a way of speaking about a newness that will assault and shatter the givens of the visible world that have been presumed. The metaphor perhaps never breaks completely free of the linkage of clay and potter, but it is equally clear that now the "forming" is not done at the potter's wheel, but in the heart or mind of the former. We have no better word for that than "imagination."

In the use of this word and related uses (especially חשׁב), we have the beginnings of a quite sophisticated psychology that Israel must articulate in

---

15. I suggest that scholars who slot יצר simply as a metaphor for working with clay have failed to understand the elastic power of metaphor. Thus, the reference to potter may be the vehicle, but a more intensive meaning pushes the term toward a very different field in relation to ברא. For a convenient summary of this characteristic of metaphor, see Trible, *God and the Rhetoric of Sexuality*, chap. 2. As we shall seek to show, taking this metaphor in its flattest possibility no doubt contributes to our misunderstanding of imagination as a legitimate human activity in the Old Testament.

its characteristically concrete modes. Anyone could see that potters "form." But it is equally clear that there is a forming that takes place prior to the work of hands with clay. That "forming" may be said to take place in the "mind" or "heart." What Israel discerns is that there is a forming that precedes at some distance the actual concrete fact. There is an anticipation or envisioning not immediate in the concrete physical act. And this previous act lives in some tension with what is visibly present. Thus the term "forming" leads to "forming" in the mind, hence imagination.

One other text is somewhat more enigmatic but makes the same point. In addressing those who have destroyed and plundered the city of Jerusalem, it is written:

> You did not look to him who did (עשׂה) it,
>
>> or have regard for him who planned (יצר) it long ago. (Isa 22:11)

That is, whoever destroys Jerusalem mistakenly does not reckon with the fact that long ago, outside the current field of event, Yahweh has had other intentions for Jerusalem that cannot be violated or nullified. Clearly the word יצר here cannot be taken concretely, but refers to the intentionality of Yahweh, or the resolve of Yahweh's heart.

This construal of the term is evident where the term occurs in parallel to חשׁב (Jer 18:11). And it is clear in the adverbial qualifiers (קדם, מרקה) from long ago (cf. Isa 22:11; 37:26; 2 Kgs 19:25) for these uses clearly place a distance between the time of imagining and the time of implementation. No such distance would be possible if the term referred only to manipulation of clay.

The metaphor still can be kept close to the work of the potter. On the one hand the potter must manipulate the clay as a physical act, as in Jeremiah 18 and 19. But obviously a good potter must be able to do more than manipulate clay. The potter must also be able to envision, to plan ahead, to foresee the shapes, to call into being in "mind's eye" what does not yet exist. That is, good potting requires imagination as well as physical skill.

4. Now on that basis, we are prepared to consider the nominal uses of our term. The most obvious uses are those in the beginning and end of the flood story (Gen 6:5; 8:21). In these the "imagination" is understood to be evil, without qualification, and the flood does not change that. It is worth noting that in 6:5, the term is used with חשׁב, so that it is "imagination of the thoughts of his heart," dearly a reference to the creative activity of the human heart to plan or envision or conceive that which is not yet visible

in the historical process. With these two texts, imagination is condemned. And undoubtedly that reading of human capacity has exercised an important influence on a negation of the aesthetic.

But we also note three other uses which are not so unambiguously negative. In David's instruction to Solomon (according to the Chronicler) it is said:

> Know the God of your father, and serve him with a whole heart and with a willing mind; for Yahweh searches all hearts and understands every plan and thought (יֵצֶר מַחֲשָׁבוֹת). (1 Chr 28:9)

Our term *ysr* again occurs with חשׁב, suggesting that it refers to the creative, constructive capacity of the human agent. And the reference to whole heart and willing mind is an affirmation that the plans and thoughts of the human person can be faithful and acceptable. Such creative intentionality can be obedient.

And in David's great prayer after the generous offering for the temple which David (and the Chronicler) regard as faithful and generous, it is requested:

> Keep forever such purposes and thoughts (יֵצֶר מַחֲשָׁבוֹת) in the hearts of your people, and direct their hearts toward you. (1 Chr 29:18)

Again יֵצֶר is linked to חשׁב and again it is treated as an arena for faithfulness.

Finally, in Deut 31:21, Moses issues a warning about covenant faithfulness as Israel is to enter the land. He says:

> For I know the purposes (יֵצֶר) which they are already forming (עשׂה), before I have brought them into the land that I swore to give.

Here it is recognized that "purposes" for the land may be wayward and disobedient. Yet clearly the voice of Moses does not presume it is necessarily so.

These five uses of the nominal form indicate that in some cases, though not all, imagination is condemned In three cases, it is risky and could be evil, but with a resolve to covenant obedience such thoughts can be faithful and obedient. Also, it is clear that in the three uses with חשׁב in Gen 6:5; 1 Chr 28:8; and 29:18, the יֵצֶר is a forming action that envisions and fashions or creates in the mind/heart something that is distinct from what is available in the "real world" of visible experience. That is, it is an act that initiates an alternative, whether for good or ill.

שרר as Disobedient Imagination

The second word for imagination is שרר, which has a much more negative connotation. Indeed, except for a usage in Deuteronomy that concerns us, it might not be involved in our question. With but two exceptions, its use is confined to the tradition of Jeremiah (Jer 3:17; 7:24; 9:12–13; 11:8; 13:10; 16:11–12; 18:12; 23:16–17). In each case Israel either chooses to live by the "stubbornness (שרר) of its own heart" (which either explicitly or implicitly is regarded as evil) or is sentenced to live by its own heart, that is, entirely by its own resources, having been abandoned by Yahweh.

In many of the uses, the negative alternative of one's own stubborn heart is contrasted with the positive alternative which could have been chosen, but has been rejected:

- They abandoned torah (9:12; 16:11).

- They abandoned Yahweh (16:11).

- They did not listen (7:24; 9:12; 11:8; 13:10; 16:12; 23:16).

- They despised the word of Yahweh (23:17).

These alternatives obviously are all in a very narrow range of covenant theology. And in each case, the negative imagination that is condemned is an assertion of autonomy which denies the covenant and the role of obedience (listening) and responsiveness to the claims of Yahweh.[16] Thus the "imagination" that is condemned is a disobedient imagination. One particular usage is of interest in light of our analysis of יצר. In 18:12, "the stubbornness of heart" is in parallel to "our plans" (חשב), which we have seen means "foresight." In v. 12, we have the parallel חשב / שרר in relation to Israel's autonomy, while in v. 11, there is the parallel יצר / חשב in relation to Yahweh's intent. Thus our term שרר is drawn into the same world of language as יצר and חשב. While Israel's own stubbornness is condemned; its practice of שרר fits our characterization as a "challenge to old structures of thought"; only in this case the old structures are the torah stipulations.

---

16. It is not accidental that "not listen" is the key indictment, for "listening is the antithesis of autonomy." Paul Ricoeur, "Naming God," 219, has a marvelous statement: "Listening excludes founding oneself." See also his comments on listening in *The Conflict of Interpretations*, 449–51.

Thus the new alternative is an unacceptable statement of independence. And this is the imagination that is condemned in the Old Testament.

Beyond the scope of Jeremiah, one of the uses is in Ps 81:12–13, a prophetic lawsuit that contains language very much like that of Jeremiah. For the rejected alternative, in addition to "not hearing," the text has לֹא אָבָה לִי, which RSV renders tersely, "would have none of me." Here שְׁרִר is parallel with יֵצֶר, "They walk in their own counsel."[17]

The final use we consider is in Deut 29:19. The text is a covenantal warning lest there be one who, when he hears the words of this sworn covenant, blesses himself in his heart, saying, "I shall be safe, though I walk in the stubbornness of my heart."

Two observations can be made. First, the *hithpa'el* "bless himself" is a striking articulation of autonomy. Such a one obviously has no need for the blessing of Yahweh. Second, the warning clearly indicates that faithful covenanting is possible, for 29:25 specifies that transgression as covenant violation. Thus in all these cases, Ps 81:12–14 and Deut 29:18–19 as well as Jeremiah, the issue is an assertion of independence that does not refer life, thought, and action to the way of Yahweh. The terms thus are not used to preclude imagination, but to preclude imagination that is not shaped in covenantal ways.

Now in an analysis of these two words, it is clear that they function primarily in distinct pieces of literature, יֵצֶר in the J narrative, the Chronicler, and positively in Second Isaiah; שְׁרִר almost exclusively in Jeremiah. The single piece of literature using both is Deuteronomy: יֵצֶר in 31:21 and שְׁרִר in 29:18–19. The convergence of the two uses requires that we look more closely at this material:

> One who, when he hears the words of this sworn covenant, blesses himself in his heart, saying, "I shall be safe though I walk in the stubbornness of my heart." (29:19)

> For I know the purposes which they are forming before I have brought them into the land I swore to give. (31:21)

---

17. Von Rad, *The Problem of the Hexateuch and Other Essays*, 23–26, has of course linked this psalm to the old credo. It becomes clear that in all of these texts dealing with the problem of an autonomy, they hold most closely to the credo–covenant claim of Yahweh's exclusive relation. The imagination that is condemned is understood to be antithetical to covenant and to the obedient hearing required by covenant.

The two uses come from different layers of the tradition. Noth may be followed in assigning our first usage (29:19) to the speeches of Deuteronomy, whereas 31:21 belongs to the introduction to the Song of Moses, which bears the mark of the Deuteronomistic historian.[18] The former is much more directly linked to the precise claims of covenant whereas the latter is more preoccupied with the dangers and temptations of the land. Because Deuteronomy usually is more positive about the prospect of obedience and the Deuteronomistic historical more aware of the cost of disobedience, we might have expected that the more negative term שרר would be used in the latter. The fact that the terms are used inversely to what we might have expected reinforces the notion that the two awarenesses of the danger of imagination move in very much the same sphere of concern.[19]

Thus they share a common notion in the primal corpus and in the derivative corpus. Both passages partake of the same motifs that are crucial to the entire *Deuteronomic* corpus. Both of them are utterly committed to covenant and to the torah of covenant. Both of them have an eye over the Jordan into the land of promise and perceive the land as a place of temptation to disobedient imagination.

And the ground for that danger is not difficult to discern. It is material independence,[20] which permits spiritual and cognitive autonomy, on which see Deut 8:17. The claims of torah are less compelling when they are not linked to issues of survival that make obedience more convincing. And the task of Deuteronomy is to make a case for obedience, including obedient imagination, in a situation suitable and tempting for an autonomous imagination.[21]

18. Noth, *The Deuteronomistic History*, 35.

19. Polzin, *Moses and the Deuteronomist*, 69–12, finds little distinction here in the various elements of these two aspects of the literature.

20. Westermann, *Elements of Old Testament Theology*, 106–8, discerns the dramatic moment in the present form of the text when material independence permits spiritual and cognitive autonomy: "they ate the produce of the land, unleavened cakes and parched grain. And the manna ceased on the morrow, when they ate of the produce of the land: and the people of Israel had manna no more, but ate of the fruit of the land of Canaan that year" (Josh 5:11–12). Westermann comments, "The bread of blessing now takes the place of the bread of saving."

21. Reference can usefully be made here to Bregman, "Religious Imagination." Bregman analyzes Calvin's statements on imagination vis-à-vis those of James Hillman. It is clear that Calvin is not resistant to imagination as such, but to autonomous imagination that takes the self as the point of reference in place of God. Now we cannot move easily and directly from this analysis of Calvin to the tradition of Deuteronomy. But the

Our analysis thus far leads to two conclusions. First, imagination is understood as exceedingly dangerous and in some cases is utterly condemned. But it is also seen to be a capacity for obedience when the "forming of an alternative future" is obedient to the claims of covenant. Second, while that agenda is found in many parts of the Old Testament, our analysis of two terms has led us especially to the tradition of Deuteronomy as a theological statement that is aware of the dangers but also is not completely closed to the possibilities of an obedient imagination.

Deuteronomy

When we consider the tradition of Deuteronomy, we are astounded at what we find. We might expect to find a restrictive obedience that is devoid of and resistant to imagination. We might expect that from the warnings and awarenesses of 29:19 and 31:21. We might expect a narrow fundamentalism of the Mosaic tradition that functions like a frightened steward who buries the trust in order to protect it (see Matt 25:24–25), simply to keep it intact. One way for Israel to have maintained its tradition in the face of the affluence and temptations in the land would have been to guard and fix the shape of the tradition to be safe for all time. (In terms of methodological implications, one may observe that this is the tendency of some literalists on the one hand who want to arrive at an unchanging meaning. On the other hand, it is also the tendency of some forms of historical-critical study that want to identify and preserve forever "the right meaning" of the text. In modern scientific form, the tendency of some unimaginative criticism is the same in its result as some literalism.) But of course Deuteronomy does no such thing. Deuteronomy is fully aware of the danger of disobedient, i.e. autonomous, imagination.

Nevertheless, it makes bold hermeneutical moves that go well beyond the old Mosaic tradition on which it is based and to which it appeals. The marvel of Deuteronomy is that while it warns against disobedient imagination, it is itself an act of radical obedient imagination. And that radicalness

---

positions are closely paralleled. Clearly what concerns the tradition of Deuteronomy is autonomy. In the land, Israel may imagine itself self-made and therefore rely on the stubbornness of one's heart, without reference to God. Thus the psycholgical base of imagination is closely linked to material reality. When material life is precarious, psychological orientation may be more focused and yielding; when material life is sure, it may be more indulgent. It is that self-indulgence that Deuteronomy seeks to preclude. And the reason is that self-indulgent imagination is conformist to the ruling powers.

is measured by its own norms of covenant. Any imaginative act in statement consonant with covenant is permitted and even welcomed.

That extraordinary quality of Deuteronomy is evident on literary grounds:[22]

1. Deuteronomy is itself a "copy" of the torah tradition (Deuteronomy 17–18). But it is surely no copy in any stenographic sense of anything we know from Moses, the book of Exodus, the Covenant Code, or anything else.[23] Of course one may hypothesize that it is a "copy" of something no longer extant. But it seems obviously the case that it is an inventive, imaginative act—a new statement "formed" in the heart/mind of these teachers and preachers, a bold act that challenges old givens. The irony is that this very tradition warns against departing to the right or the left from these commandments (Deut 5:32; 17:11, 20; 28:14; Josh 1:7). And yet, at the very moment that it issues this solemn warning, it is indeed an imaginative restatement that exercises enormous freedom and authority to match. Specifically in Deut 17:14–20, and precisely in vv. 18–20, which refers to a "second" of the tradition, the very warning about rigorous attentiveness to the commandment is in the very act a completely new articulation of commandment that can have no precedent or rootage in any older teaching.

That particular act might be a case study for us in imaginative religious teaching and a clue about imaginative scholarship. This tradition that worries about autonomy in the land and the accompanying imagination, in

---

22. This openness of a certain kind characterizes the entire tradition of Deuteronomy, even into the Deuteronomic handling of Jeremiah. It is evident there as well that the second generation of preachers to the exile exercise great imagination in letting the tradition touch new historical reality. See Nicholson, *Preaching to the Exiles*, for a balanced statement and Carroll, *From Chaos to Covenant*, for a more polemical treatment. The three texts especially identified by Wolff, "Kergygma of the Deuteronomic Historical Work," 93–100, are Deut 4:29–31; 30:1–10; and 1 Kgs 8:46–53. These three texts peculiarly give evidence of the free imagination of the tradition in meeting new challenges to the faith.

23. Of course I do not suggest that this remarkable quality is confined to the tradition of Deuteronomy, even though it is strikingly embodied there. Paul D. Hanson, "The Theological Significance of Contradiction within the Book of the Covenant," has explored the same dimension of the Book of the Covenant. He refers variously to "a dynamic of creativity and liberating, sustaining dynamic" (124, 130), "a creative, egalitarian and liberating dynamic" (129), "a dynamic which is creative, liberating and life-giving" (130). But his final statement is theologically explicit: "The ultimate referent is God who is confessed as creative, liberating, sustaining agent" (131). Harrelson, "Life, Faith and the Emergence of Tradition," who argues that there is a clear core tradition to the Old Testament and that it has a revolutionary character. *Imagination*, I suggest in agreement with Hanson, is the way in which this core exercises its *revolutionary* quality.

the moment of that worry authorizes for Israel a new institution, monarchy, which in other traditions is a way of "stubbornness of their own heart" but here is a way of not departing from the torah. And the reason this text is not disobedient imagination is that it enjoins obedience to the same God, the same perception of reality, the same social practice. That is, it is imagination faithful to and congruent with, but surely distinct from, old covenant commitments.

2. Von Rad has observed (and made a great deal of) the fact that Deuteronomy is not an address of Yahweh nor is it first of all the word of the Lord.[24] It is the word of Moses. And even if one were to reject critical theories for a later dating, we cannot on any grounds go behind the imaginative work of the person (or office) of Moses. Without being historically precise, von Rad has made a compelling case that this material is preaching or exposition, a literary residue from a regular and periodic liturgic processing of the normative memory. A liturgic processing means a combination of fidelity to the memory and imagination about an articulation that has force and relevance. The preaching of Deuteronomy is "revelatory" precisely because it is the imaginative recovery of what lies at the root of the memory: "If genuine revelation is the imaginative recovery of what lies at the root of memory, it is also an opening to what is present, yet still inchoate in one's heritage."[25] This is, I submit, what the preaching of Deuteronomy is and does. It is the imaginative recovery of the root of memory. It opens what is inchoate in the heritage. And as a result it is revelatory: it is the disclosure of what had not been seen until now as a social possibility. But we note well that for all its freedom in discerning social possibility, the power and energy are in the memory and heritage that are clearly specified.

3. Polzin, with a rather heavy theoretical frame, has shown how the tradition out of Deuteronomy is constituted to encourage a dialogue. He labels the dialogue partners the voice of "authoritarian dogmatism" and "critical traditionalism."[26] The argument Polzin mounts is persuasive, especially given the method he proposes from Voloshinov. Unfortunately, Polzin's method leads to a conclusion about the book of Deuteronomy that I believe to be excessively pejorative. He concludes that the authority

24. Von Rad, *Studies in Deuteronomy*, chaps. 1 and 2.

25. Raschke and Gregory, "Revelation, the Poetic Imagination and the Archaeology of the Feminine." Dornish, "Symbolic Systems and the Interpretation of Scripture," 6, characterizes Ricoeur's second hermeneutic as "Restorative: moving toward a recollection of the original memory of the symbol."

26. Polzin, *Moses and the Deuteronomist*, 74.

of the Mosaic voice is raised "to a position almost indistinguishable from that of the voice of God."[27] And the result is that the book of Deuteronomy (as distinct from the subsequent Deuteronomistic history) is "essentially monologic."[28] Given Polzin's method, I think that conclusion follows.

But such a view seems overly committed to a particular method and fails to note the tendency of the entire corpus. This is a tradition intended to be faithful to the memory but also *imaginative* about the new circumstance. And therefore, both "voices" (including the more "authoritarian voice") are imaginative. That is, the "old voice of Moses" is also a voice of enormous imagination, proposing the Israel a quite new discernment of the world.

4. The literary quality of Deuteronomy (and its spin-off traditions) shows the practice of imagination that breaks the givens for the sake of a freshly "formed" future. But convenantal imagination in Deuteronomy is never contained as a *literary* fact. This covenantal imagination needs also to be understood on sociological grounds. And this dimension, it seems to me, is lacking in much current reflection on imagination. That is, imagination in this tradition concerns the shape of public, visible, institutional life. Imagination as a hermeneutical practice is not simply a matter of subtlety and finesse with words. It is a use of words that function as inventive social facts. That is, it is imagination that concerns *social* possibility.

If imagination is here understood as "forming" (יצר) and "planning" (חשב) for the land (as in Deut 31:21), then what is being formed in the heart of Israel and planned for the land is an alternative way of being in the land as an intentional social community.[29] It would have been the most un-imaginative social act Israel could have committed to accept Canaan's gods and the oppressive social structures that accompany them. That would have been to retain and accept the old social givens already there. It is those that Deuteronomy condemns and prohibits and to which it offers a remarkable alternative.[30]

---

27. Ibid., 55.

28. Ibid., 72.

29. With a rather odd expression, "formed in the heart," the text combines in a fresh way two notions in a most sophisticated statement. "Formed" refers to working with clay, but "in the heart" is an imaginative forming that takes place apart from physical implementation. The metaphor thus maintains creative distance between the heart-constructing activity and the history-constructing in social practice.

30. P. D. Hanson, "The Theological Significance of Contradiction within the Book of the Covenant," 129–31, warns against treating any theological, social, or ethical system as immutable. Mottu, "Jeremiah vs. Hananiah," in a more critical way, presents Hananiah

Israel's imagination is not primarily literary or aesthetic, though it utilizes those sensitivities. It is social and sociological. It thinks in terms of the reality of community and the ways that community can reorder its public existence in different and liberating ways. I have already suggested that literary critics and sociologists of ancient Israel might usefully make common cause and must not compartmentalize their methodologies.[31] Therefore, our assessment of imagination in Deuteronomy must attend not only to the ways in which the literature *says*, but also the ways in which the words *do*, as social intervention of a most powerful and abrasive kind.

So the thesis offered here is that Deuteronomy is an act of extraordinary social imagination, for which the genre of preached law is a serviceable literary form. Gottwald's particular hypothesis[32] concerning the character and function of early Israel is of course in dispute, though I find it most compelling, given the alternatives available to us. Without settling the question of whether Yahweh is a "function" of a social experiment,[33] or even "merely" a function of a social experiment, as Gottwald's critics accuse him of suggesting, we can allow that Gottwald's general hypothesis illuminates Deuteronomy at three important points:

a. Israel, especially in the perception of Deuteronomy, is a remarkable social experiment. This is evident not only in the "sermons" of motivation but in the "legislation" offered as well.

b. The Hexateuchal tradition forms a sturdy and energizing base for that social experiment. This, I suggest, is its function even if one does not follow in detail Gottwald's understanding of its origin.

c. More than any other part of that ideological base, Deuteronomy strikes one as "originary" speech, i.e. speech which calls into being that which does not exist until the word is uttered (Rom 4:20).[34]

For now we can bracket out the many serious questions remaining in Gottwald's hypothesis. But we can suggest that Deuteronomy's preached

---

as one who "objectified and reified" a theological claim. The result is of course uncritical reactionary social practice and social policy. This lack of imagination leads to social control and oppression.

31. Brueggemann, "Israel's Social Criticism and Yahweh's Sexuality," especially the concluding comments on 764–65.

32. Gottwald, *The Tribes of Yahweh*.

33. Ibid., 611–12.

34. On originary speech, see Raschke and Gregory, "Revelation, the Poetic Imagination and the Archaeology of the Feminine," 90.

law is indeed an imagining act of envisioning a social form that is not at hand in the circumstance of Canaan and that is not available in the "old" Mosaic tradition. Deuteronomy exercises a "forming" (יצר) function in "planning/determining/proposing" a covenantal way to be in the land, a way not yet known, envisioned or evoked until Deuteronomy had its magisterial say.

Three Acts of Social Imagination

We may consider three such acts of social imagination:

1. The law of release in Deut 15:1–11 is a remarkable proposal. Obviously the notion of "release and redemption" is not confined to Deuteronomy nor does it need to be demonstrated that the proposal was actually practiced. It is enough to observe that the "legislation" is a daring thought for a social order. To be able to anticipate "there shall be no poor among you" (v. 4) in either the ancient or the modern world is almost as though one were to say, "I have a dream." Indeed, it would not take much to recast the entire piece into rhetoric like that of Martin Luther King Jr., for it is all a dreaming vision of how social criticism can be made of a hierarchical community together with an alternative proposal. This paragraph then is indeed an imaginative act if we understand that to mean breaking old givens and proposing alternative forms of existence.[35]

2. The law on kingship (Deut 17:14–20) is equally extraordinary. We have already considered the strange way in which the "copy" functions as an act of remarkable newness. Here we focus on the substantive act of imagination. This imaginative act proposes a third alternative to "no king" (Judg 8:23) and "a king like the other nations" (1 Sam 8:5, 20)—the two alternatives that dominate the discussion in 1 Samuel and which must have been the parameters of the debate.[36] But this unit takes a new way that

35. Fox, "The Rhetoric of Ezekiel's Vision of the Valley of Dry Bones," 7 and passim, has suggested that the vision of Ezek 37:1–14 seeks to give hope by creating "irrational explanation," by getting the community "to expect the unexpected, to accept the plausibility of the absurd." I suggest that the imaginative act of "release" is as implausible and unexpected as is the rising of the bones. Arendt, *The Human Condition*, 236–43, argues that forgiveness (which is linked to the year of release) is finally more radical than are the miracles. In our context, social possibility, as practiced in Deuteronomy, is more dangerously imaginative than many "religious" acts of hope. On the critical problems in social imagination, see Ricoeur, "Imagination in Discourse and in Action," 15–21.

36. See the careful summary of the debate in ancient Israel by Halpern, "The Uneasy

is without precedent anywhere in the tradition. This statement takes the political institution that is at hand, but completely transforms it, robbing it of some of its most dangerous (and most attractive and seductive) features, and bringing it to a form acceptable in covenantal categories. The law is able to see that conventional kingship presumes to be a principle of order; but when there is a practice of silver and gold and horses and wives it acts in fact for disorder. This proposal then is that the kingship be organized to work in reality for the order it claims to sponsor.

3. The little law in Deut 25:1-3 must have been an important breakthrough in the world of ancient Israel, for curbing violence in any society requires some remarkable freedom to break with harsh practices that command general assent. Taken by itself, this regulation does not seem less than barbaric. And yet, if society is organized to assault the guilty until vengeance is satisfied, then this impresses one as a first step in "prison reform" and indeed in reform of all of society toward humaneness.

There can be no doubt that these three texts are all remarkably imaginative:

- 15:1-11 a new characterization of the debt system,[37]

- 17:14-20 a transformation of the institution of monarchy,

- 25:1-3 a curb on authorized conventional violence.

The tradition is "nervous" about purposes formed for the land (31:21). And yet these laws are precisely new purposes formed for the new life in the land They are indeed acts of imagination and social construction. And one can believe that the impetus for this daring line of thought is the vision of humaneness grounded in the memory of the exodus, the reality of the covenant and finally in the sovereign will of Yahweh. But even given those groundings, this is nonetheless an act of creativity and daring. They are examples of liberated imagination in passionate service ofYahweh's sovereignty.[38]

One might wonder: How did this teaching strike its contemporaries? One can "imagine" that from two sides it appears to be the "imagination of

Compromise."

37. On the transformation of the debt system as a crucial theological act, see Belo, *A Materialist Reading of the Gospel of Mark*, 37–59.

38. These laws are examples of "redescribing" the world, as Ricoeur puts it. But such redescription concerns not simply literary expression, but concrete social practice. The law in Deuteronomy is a forming in the heart of a new social world. On new possibility wrought by imagination, see Ricoeur, "Listening to the Parables of Jesus," 245.

an evil heart." On the one hand, the old-line covenanters may have judged it to be accommodating the Canaanite practices of debt slaves and kingship, for it does take up these practices. And such an accommodation to existing practices was hardly envisioned in the initial movement of liberation. On the other hand, some may have waited eagerly to embrace Canaanite practices of wealth, power, and security, and such proposals as these are terribly "limiting." Clearly Deuteronomy is at some pains to resist the charge of autonomous imagination by the firm insistence of not departing right or left from the parameters of covenant. From what we know of the tradition, this preached law does depart from the old tradition, does act in free ways in relation to the body of the torah. But what appears to make it acceptable and finally normative is that the substance as well as the form is rigorously referred to Yahweh and the tradition of Moses.

Conclusion

Thus far we have considered *the practice of imagination* in Israel's articulation of sacred texts. We have tried to show that in the tradition of Deuteronomy (where we have been led by two word studies which overlap there), there is an awareness of the danger of imagination which is autonomous, and at the same time a vigorous practice of *emancipated imagination that is obedient*. That is how it is in the Bible itself. To take the texts most seriously is to see that they are indeed acts of imagination. It is to dishonor the texts, to flatten them either to agree with each other in conforming ways, or to reduce them to single, recoverable meanings.

With that discernment of the character of the text in view, we return to Anderson's suggestion for our own interpretive enterprise. These conclusions, which I presume to be faithful to Anderson's intent and practice, may be drawn.

1. Faithful interpretation of Scripture must be imaginative; that is, seeing the texts as powered by the revolutionary purpose of Yahweh, as evocative of new social possibility. Such a way of interpretation tries to take the text seriously according to its function in Israel, as it bears witness to this revolutionary God and as it serves as a vehicle for *this sovereignty* in terms of *social practice*.[39] To take the text as less or other than this is not faithful to the text's own intentionality.

39. I have offered an example of this interface in interpretive process in Brueggemann, "Social Criticism and Social Vision in the Deuteronomic Formula of the Judges."

Conversely, interpretation that is not attentive to this revolutionary urging is likely not to be faithful. On the one hand, interpretive postures that are "literalist" tend to flatten the hopeful, evocative force of the text as a social function. That is, the text is taken only as descriptive and not as evocative or "redescriptive." But the same charge can be made concerning much historical-critical interpretation which tends to regard the text as flat and fixed, without attention to its evocative social function. Anderson's sense of the imaginative is surely correct in seeing that one-dimensional interpretation, either literalist or "historical-critical" in that sense, is not faithful to the character and claim of the text. Either way is a means to deaden the dangerous evocation of the text.

2. Most scholarly attention is given to imaginative interpretation in terms of literary criticism that takes the text in and of itself as a single datum. This has much to commend it, and Anderson is much interested in this enterprise.[40]

3. Literary criticism that attends to the aesthetic dimension of the text must be related to *social criticism and social possibility*. That is, the word (text) is generative of an alternative world in which people live. Imaginative interpretation of the kind for which Anderson calls must be concerned with sociological analysis.[41] The text is never by itself, but is always related to a community in equilibrium or to the community in process of formation or transformation. Norman Gottwald has well articulated this in terms of the text as "narrative objectification of the superstructure."[42] However, Gottwald's tendency is to have the text *follow* the social reality. It may also

40. See most recently Anderson, "The Problem and Promise of Commentary." On 349–50, he writes concerning desirable method, that "it has an open-ended dimension which appeals to the reader's imagination." On 354, "I would expect a good commentary to help me become more of a poet in my understanding of scriptural language and the Biblical story. It is difficult for the modern mind, with its prosaic, scientific bent, to enter into the poetic and mythopoeic language of Scripture." A splendid example of the kind of interpretation offered by such literary methods is found in Clines et al., eds., *Art and Meaning: Rhetoric in Biblical Literature*. It is clear that such critical attentiveness to imagination has nothing to do with the current fad of "left brain/right brain," which tends to celebrate undisciplined fantasy and free association of ideas. See Bregman, "Religious Imagination," 37–41, for a critique of that "ideological" fad.

41. For exploration of this factor with attention to method, see the collection of essays, Culley and Overholt, eds., *Semeia 21: Anthropological Perspectives on Old Testament Prophecy*, with particular reference to the articles of Long and Wilson. Note the comment of Long: "Thus, anthropological study helps us compensate for distortions which arise from isolating religious ideology from other forms of social repression" (50).

42. Gottwald, *The Tribes of Yahweh*, 100–114.

be that the text leads and evokes social reality. In the texts cited from Deuteronomy, we dare think that the texts are anticipatory and summon Israel to a transformation of social power and social policy. And in any case for those who use the text in its canonical form, clearly the text leads social reality. If the initial preaching of Jesus in Luke 4:16–21 is reminiscent of the law of release in one of its forms,[43] it is a clear example in which text *leads* social practice and social possibility. What Gottwald does not sufficiently allow for, I suggest, is that the text may stand at the *generative beginning* as well as the ideological ending of the process of social transformation.[44]

4. Because texts that are generative initiators do not get formed in a vacuum, literary criticism can also be usefully linked to what may be called *anticipatory psychology*. Israel may have had to work with quite elementary concepts for psychology.[45] Thus, it speaks of heart in a rather undifferentiated way. But the notion of "forming in the heart" is not only bold and dangerous, but also a quite sophisticated psychological notion. It affirms that human thought is not bound by what is observable, but that the heart is capable of forming images of what could be that is not yet. The heart can make leaps in such images, even when it does not know how to get from here to there. That is, there is distance between *anticipated possibility* and *historical actuality*. And the human heart is understood to be the agent of that evoking at a distance. Indeed, the evidence is ample that God is one who images in his heart prior to his historical activity. And Israel recognizes that humankind has the same possibility. Like God, the human person is a generator of *images* that lead to *alternative acts* and *social possibilities*.

Of course Israel is aware of the danger of this capacity (Gen 6:5; 8:21). And Israel is aware that situations of prosperity and well-being may seduce Israel's heart into forming an autonomous notion of human well-being (Deut 8:17; 29:19; 31:21).

But the texts of Deuteronomy give one pause. What an incredibly generative act is imaging a social practice of release of slaves, a proposal that subverts economic vested interests. What an extraordinary invention to think about a new form of monarchy that is quite unlike every known model. And to think through the limitation of vengeance is based on the

43. On the Lukan appeal to the Jubilee law, see the comments of James A. Sanders, "Isaiah in Luke," and esp. n. 13 on the dissertation of Sharon Ringe.

44. See my review of Gottwald's work, *The Tribes of Yahweh*, in *JAAR*.

45. See the summary of the data by Johnson, *The Vitality of the Individual*, 77–84. Johnson confines his discussion to the internal life of the individual and does not probe the social significance of the personal function or organ.

insight that new ways can be found to order social passion and social power. In a variety of small moves, we are offered proposals for a genuine social *novum*. We do not know from where it comes. Anderson inclines to see in this the work of the spirit, if I rightly understand his urging (cf. Matt 16:17 on such a transcendent source of disclosure). That is, one may conclude that "flesh and blood" does not lead to such a profound proposal for the life of Israel. Or one may alternatively speak of poetic imagination, as Anderson also does. Either way, these texts are evidence of an originative generativity is what is given us in the text, to which we look for continued generativity.[46]

These two points, sociology of the new possibility and psychology of anticipation, need to be closely held together with literary ciriticism. Any one of these taken alone as a method is misleading. The text is a statement of *a generative heart* and reaches for *a social possibility*. But the sociological innovation by itself is flat, for unless there is aesthetic articulation with it, the new social possibility is readily oppressive. And an imaginative heart by itself is in a vacuum without text and without historical community, hardly an agent of power. Thus, we need methods of interpretation that take seriously the forming heart, the imaginative *text* and the emerging liberated *social possibility*.

5. But neither literary imagination, social generativity, nor a psychology of anticipation give rise to the peculiar substance of social possibility sponsored by Deuteronomy. Finally, the interpreter is driven to *the theological question*. And when we ask how to understand the new vision of social power and social possibility offered here, Deuteronomy clearly intends a social inventiveness authorized by and obedient to the sovereign will of Yahweh. Thus, the ultimate measure of every imaginative thought, imaginative text, and imaginative social possibility is how it corresponds to the character of God already disclosed in this tradition.

And we may understand that the laws on release, kingship, and vengeance are evidences of Yahweh's rule made concrete; that is, it is Yahweh who is the source of liberated Israel. Exegesis is thus translated and inadequate if it does not press this reference. All else may lead to autonomous imagination, not to bold obedience proposed in the text.

6. The interface of the claim of the text and the methods of interpretation required concerns the watershed of canon. The moment of canonization

---

46. Note that in Ricoeur's comment cited in n. 38, he still can do no better than to speak of *the heart* as the agent of new possibility.

divides the dynamics of *how the text came to be* from the dynamics of *how the text causes to be*.[47] It is hardly disputed that in the text *coming to be*, the factors of liberated social possibility, anticipatory psychology, literary finesse, and theological accountability have been operative. All of that is present in the formation of the text, and our methods reflect that the kind of interpretation for which Anderson calls, I suggest, is a recognition that these same factors are operative in the text *causing to be* in the communities that claim these texts as normative and canonical. In that way, the imaginative power that *formed the text* may be continued to be *received from the text*. But such a receiving from the text requires a mode different from the flat literalism of obscurantism or the flat historicism of rational positivism. The key to a legitimate receiving from the text is to recognize that the text belongs to its lord, or as Anderson says, "God speaks to his people today through Scripture at the point of our imagination, that is, where the 'inspired writing' meets the 'inspired reader' and becomes the 'Word of God.'"[48] Or perhaps as Ricouer says, the Poem belongs to the Poet, seen and heard, so the text continues to be a medium of *disclosure* that no method of interpretation is free to *close*.

Scholarship has focused almost exclusively on the text as *the receiving factor* at the end of the text-forming process. I suggest Anderson is calling for scholarship that views the text as *the generating factor* at the beginning of the community-forming process.

It is a delight to offer this piece in gratitude to Professor Anderson for his sensitivity to questions of method and for his unfailing attentiveness to the theological claims in the text. Hopefully, what is argued here is faithful to his lead, for so I understand and intend it.

Bibliography

Anderson, Bernhard W. "From Analysis to Synthesis: The Interpretation of Genesis 1–11." *JBL* 97 (1978) 23–29.

———. "Introduction to the Old Testament as Scripture." *ThTo* 37 (1980) 100–108.

———. *The Living Word of the Bible*. Philadelphia: Westminster, 1979.

47. The word "cause" here is of course not used mechanically, but refers to the evocative, generative power of the text. I use it because it suggests a nice contrast to the word "came." With "came to be," the text is the receiving factor at the end of the process. With "cause to be," the text is the initiating factor at the beginning of the process. Ricoeur, *The Conflict of Interpretation*, 319: "Language is less spoken *by* men than spoken *to* men."

48. Anderson, *The Living Word of the Bible*, 35.

————. "The Problem and Promise of Commentary." *Int* 36 (1982) 341–55.

————. "Tradition and Scripture in the Community of Faith," *JBL* 100 (1981) 5–21.

Arendt, Hannah A. *The Human Condition*. Charles R. Walgreen Foundation Lectures. Chicago: University of Chicago Press, 1958.

Belo, Fernando. *A Materialist Reading of the Gospel of Mark*. Translated by Matthew J. O'Connell. Maryknoll, NY: Orbis, 1981.

Bregman, Lucy. "Religious Imagination: Polytheistic Psychology Confronts Calvin." *Soundings* 63 (1980) 36–60.

Brueggemann, "Israel's Social Criticism and Yahweh's Sexuality." *JAAR Supplements* 45 (1977) 739–72.

————. Review of *The Tribes of Yahweh* by Norman K. Gottwald. *JAAR* 48 (1980) 441–51.

————. "Social Criticism and Social Vision in the Deuteronomic Formula of the Judges." In *Die Botschaft und die Boten: Festschrift für Hans Walter Wolff zum 70. Geburtstag*, edited by Jörg Jeremias and Lothar Perlitt, 101–14. Neukirchen-Vluyn: Neukirchener, 1981.

Carroll, Robert P. *From Chaos to Covenant: Prophecy in the Book of Jeremiah*. New York: Crossroad, 1981.

Childs, Brevard S. *Introduction to the Old Testament as Scripture*. Philadelphia: Fortress, 1979.

————. "Some Reflections on the Search for a Biblical Theology." *HBT* 4 (1982) 1–12.

Clines, David J. A., David M. Gunn, and Alan J. Hauser, eds. *Art and Meaning: Rhetoric in Biblical Literature*. JSOTSup 19. Sheffield: JSOT Press, 1982.

Culley, Robert C., and Thomas W. Overholt, eds. *Semeia 21: Anthropological Perspectives on Old Testament Prophecy*. 1982.

Dornish, Loretta. "Symbolic Systems and the Interpretation of Scripture: An Introduction to the Work of Paul Ricoeur." *Semeia* 4 (1975) 1–22.

Fox, Michael V. "The Rhetoric of Ezekiel's Vision of the Valley of Dry Bones." *HUCA* 51 (1980) 1–15.

Gottwald, Norman K. *The Tribes of Yahweh: A Sociology of the Religion of Liberated Israel, 1250–1050 B.C.E.* Maryknoll, NY: Orbis, 1979.

Halpern, Baruch. "The Uneasy Compromise: Israel between League and Monarchy." In *Traditions in Transformation: Turning Points in Biblical Faith*, edited by Baruch Halpern and Jon D. Levenson, 59–96. Winona Lake, IN: Eisenbrauns, 1981.

Hanson, Paul D. "The Theological Significance of Contradiction within the Book of the Covenant." In *Canon and Authority: Essays in Old Testament Religion and Theology*, edited by George W. Coats and Burke O. Long, 110–31. Philadelphia: Fortress, 1977.

Harrelson, Walter. "Life, Faith and the Emergence of Tradition." In *Tradition and Theology in the Old Testament*, edited by Douglas A. Knight, 11–30. Philadelphia: Fortress, 1977.

Hart, Ray L. *Unfinished Man and the Imagination*. New York: Herder & Herder, 1968.

Johnson, Aubrey R. *The Vitality of the Individual in the Thought of Ancient Israel*. Cardiff: University of Wales Press, 1949.

Mottu, Henry. "Jeremiah vs. Hananiah: Ideology and Truth in Old Testament Prophecy," *The Bible and Liberation*, 58–67. Radical Religious Reader. Berkeley: Community for Religious Research and Education, 1976. Reprinted in *The Bible and Liberation: Political and Social Hermeneutics*, edited by Norman K. Gottwald and Richard Horsley, 240–49. Maryknoll, NY: Orbis, 1983.

Nicholson, E. W. *Preaching to the Exiles: A Study of the Prose Tradition in the Book of Jeremiah*. Oxford: Blackwell, 1970.

Noth, Martin. *The Deuteronomistic History*. JSOTSup 15. Sheffield: JSOT Press, 1981.

Polzin, Robert. *Moses and the Deuteronomist*. New York: Seabury, 1980.

Rad, Gerhard von. *The Problem of the Hexateuch and Other Essays*. Translated by E. W. Trueman Dicken. New York: McGraw Hill, 1966. Revised and reprinted as *From Genesis to Chronicles*. Edited by K. C. Hanson, Translated by E. W. Trueman Dicken. Fortress Classics in Biblical Studies. Minneapolis: Fortress, 2005.

———. *Studies in Deuteronomy*. Translated by David Stalker. SBT 1/9. Chicago: Regnery, 1953.

Raschke Carl, and Donna Gregory. "Revelation, the Poetic Imagination and the Archaeology of the Feminine." In *The Archaeology of the Imagination*, edited by Charles E. Winquist, 89–104. JAAR Thematic Studies 48/2. Missoula, MT: Scholars, 1981.

Ricoeur, Paul. *The Conflict of Interpretations: Essays in Hermeneutics*. Edited by Don Ihde. Northwestern University Studies in Phenomenology & Existential Philosophy. Evanston, IL: Northwestern University Press, 1974.

———. "Imagination in Discourse and in Action." In *The Human Being in Action, The Irreducible Element in Man II*, edited by Anna Teresa Tymieniecka, 15–21. Analecta Husserliana 7. Boston: Reidel.

———. "Listening to the Parables of Jesus." In *The Philosophy of Paul Ricoeur: An Anthology of His Work*, edited by Charles E. Reagan and David Steward, 239–45. Boston: Beacon, 1978.

———. "Naming God." *Union Seminary Quarterly Review* 34 (1979) 215–19.

Sanders, James A. "Isaiah in Luke." *Int* 36 (1982) 150–55. Reprinted in *Luke and Scripture: The Function of Sacred Tradition in Luke–Acts*, by Craig A. Evans and James A. Sanders, 14–25. Minneapolis: Fortress, 1993.

Stuhlmueller, Carroll. *Creative Redemption in Deutero-lsaiah*. Analecta Biblica 43. Rome: Pontifical Biblical Institute, 1970.

Tannehill, Robert C. *The Sword of His Mouth*. Semeia Supplements. 1975. Reprinted, Eugene, OR: Wipf & Stock, 2003.

Trible, Phyllis. *God and the Rhetoric of Sexuality*. OBT. Philadelphia: Fortress, 1978.

Westermann, Claus. *Elements of Old Testament Theology*. Translated by Douglas W. Stott. Atlanta: John Knox, 1978.

Wolff, Hans Walter. "Kergygma of the Deuteronomic Historical Work." In The *Vitality of Old Testament Traditions*, Walter Brueggemann and Hans Walter Wolff, 83–100 + 167–71. 2nd ed. Atlanta: John Knox, 1982.

six

PSYCHOLOGICAL CRITICISM: EXPLORING THE SELF IN THE TEXT

From the beginning, the human self has been a compelling enigma for the community that produced the Bible.[1] Ancient Israel regularly asked, in narrative and liturgical texts, "What are human beings?" (Ps 8:4). Of equal importance, they asked the question with the accompanying phrase, "that you are mindful of them?"[2] The question—as well as the answer—is a theological one: the community addresses the question of the self by means of the defining reality of God. While they gave many answers to that question, Psalm 139 seems the most appropriate response to the question "What is a human?"

> For it was you who formed my inward parts;
>> you knit me together in my mother's womb.
> I praise you, for I am fearfully and wonderfully made.
>> Wonderful are your works;
> that I know very well.
>> My frame was not hidden from you,
> when I was being made in secret,
>> intricately woven in the depths of the earth.
> Your eyes beheld my unformed substance.

1. I am glad to join in salute to a valued colleague, David Peterson, from whom I have learned much and by whom I am always instructed.

2. The ancient Israelites likely asked the question with reference to males. Thus, a wooden translation of Ps 8:4 is "what is man [אֱנוֹשׁ] that you are mindful of him." In our readings. however, the term "man" must always be transposed for the sake of gender inclusion.

> In your book were written
>> all the days that were formed for me,
>> when none of them as yet existed. (Ps 139:13–16)

Verse 14 exhibits a two-fold response to the question, What is the self? the one hand, it is a response about the self: "I am fearfully and wonderfully made." But on the other hand, the lead-in phrase is indispensable: "I praise you." The self, in the horizon of this community, is always, everywhere referred to the defining reality of God, and the self cannot be pondered apart from God. Thus the question of Ps 8:4 and the affirmative response of Ps 139:13–16 situate the discussion of the self in the presence of God in a way that makes the question of the self an inescapably theological one.

From that theological beginning point, scholarship has been able discern that in the Bible the human self is presented as unitary, communal, and situated in worldly vulnerability and contingency in the presence of God.[3] Thus the following obtain. (1) The self is a single unitary agent; there is no notion of mind–body dualism. (2) The self is a member of a community and never an isolated or self-sufficient entity. (3) As both vulnerable and powerful, the human self lives in a drama set between life and death, strength and weakness. The human self waxes and wanes as the gifts of life are given or withheld, received or resisted. (4) The self is mortal and finite and subject to the vagaries of the historical process. Death is the edge of human existence, and all the rest is left to the rule of God. This "history-situated self" is thus called to freedom and responsibility in the finite zone where God has placed the self in community.

Models of Psychological Criticism

Given the centrality of "the self" in the imagination of the community that produced the biblical text, it is quite remarkable that critical study of the self in the text, that is "psychological criticism," has not, in the modem critical era, been able to arrive at a consensus with regard to its method of study nor even a consensus of perspective on the question.[4] In this regard, psychological approaches to critical study of the biblical text are unlike other

3. Among the more important and helpful studies on the dynamism of personality in the Old Testament are Johnson, *The Vitality of the Individual*; and Wolff, *Anthropology of the Old Testament*.

4. For a comprehensive review of the history of such study, see Rollins, *Soul and Psyche*; see also Kille, *Psychological Biblical Criticism*.

critical approaches. The characteristic way of critical study of the Bible is to appropriate a working method from critical scholarship in another field, then to apply that method, with necessary adjustments, to the biblical text. Such appropriation and adjustment enable critics to read the Bible "like any other book." Thus historical criticism has taken over the methods of positivistic history. Social-scientific criticism has in recent time utilized the methods of sociology and anthropological scholarship, and rhetorical criticism has followed the broad outlines of classical reading.

Perhaps psychological criticism of the Bible has not been able to agree on method or perspective precisely because the available methods from the field of psychology are quite varied, each approach following the daring work of a leading theorist. Thus the formation of "schools" of interpretation (e.g., Freudianism, Jungianism, ego psychology, object relations theory) is much more varied than we would find in historical, social-scientific, or rhetorical studies, and that difference is reflected in the interpretive practices of biblical scholars.[5] A review of the rich literature of recent decades, led most notably by Wayne Rollins, exhibits an immense plurality of practices in which numerous studies appeal to a wide variety of models and authorities in the field.[6]

In what follows, I will reflect briefly on the founding models of Sigmund Freud and Carl Jung. Then, as others have done, I will appeal to the theoretical basis that seems most congruent with the texts themselves. In moving from theory to textual specificity, we do well to remember David Jobling's caution that scholars are often tempted to let the power of the theory override the concreteness of the text itself. Jobling comments on David J. Halperin's *Seeing Ezekiel: Text and Psychology* (1993):

> I must go on to say that this book is out of touch with recent work on the psychological reading of texts, including biblical ones, and was so even at the time he published it. His aim, it seems, is to put on the couch and diagnose a real human being, Ezekiel. He simply assumes that the text of the book of Ezekiel will provide everything necessary to accomplish this task. But a great deal of history and, even more importantly, a great deal of textuality lie between us and "Ezekiel," a hypothetical person whose very existence has often been called into question. What is available for our analysis is a text, and texts are anything but transparent windows

5. On the various theories and schools of personality development, see Mitchell and Black, *Freud and Beyond*.

6. Ellens and Rollins, eds., *Psychology and the Bible* (4 vols.).

on their subject matter. In this case, moreover, we are dealing with an ancient text and a religiously canonized text. None of this need ultimately invalidate Halperin's findings, but it necessitates at least a significant reframing of them.[7]

Jobling's stricture is more broadly pertinent. There is a danger, in the eclectic enterprise of psychological criticism, to impose a psychological theory on the text in a way that overrides the specificity of the text itself and that distorts the text in order to serve the theory that an interpreter may advocate. Such a problem may be a temptation for every critical method— including imposing questions of historicity on texts!—but it is a temptation that seems peculiarly pertinent to psychological approaches. Thus while theoretical reference points are important, in the end such criticism serves well only if it permits us to read and hear the text more discerningly. My judgment is that, while biblical scholars have a wide array of resources available from this perspective, psychological criticism is still very much in its formative period and has reached neither a maturity nor a sophistication that can claim the wide engagement of scholars. We may be grateful for the bold scholars who have made these fresh beginnings in methodological exploration, but much more disciplined work remains to be done before wide assent to method can be achieved. Perhaps such an eclectic practice is inevitable, given the quite eclectic and disputatious field of personality theory in general. In the next section, I will consider the contributions of the towering figures of Freud and Jung, reflect on what I take as the most helpful interface in method among current options, and offer a textual exemplar from that perspective.

A New Era of Psychological Theory: Sigmund Freud and Carl Jung

Any proper understanding of psychological theory that may be appropriated for critical biblical study must, of course, begin where the modern study of the self begins, with Sigmund Freud and his ally and then rival, Carl Jung.

Sigmund Freud dramatically begins a new era of "the psychological." To be sure, he had antecedents, but his work is a breakthrough of stunning proportion that has become the source of all that follows, even among those

---

7. Jobling, "An Adequate Psychological Approach to the Book of Ezekiel," 204.

who depart from him or who repudiate his categories. He sought to situate the study of the self in scientific modes. For all his effort at the scientific, however, we may notice two dimensions of his work that defy the scientific. First, his shaping categories derive from foundational cultural myths that he handles imaginatively and artistically. Second, he makes clear that, for all of the objective data he offers, his own continued struggle for identity and his negotiation between Jewish legacy and Viennese culture are quite personal, defining issues for him. Freud's understanding of the psychological in modern culture is a larger-than-life personal assertion that refuses any surface reading of reality—either social or personal reality or textual reality. We may identify four dimensions of his work that pertain to our study.

First, Freud recognized and articulated the multifaceted reality of the human self, its thickness, complexity, and conflictedness that needs to be processed but could not even be fully resolved. His particular naming of that thick complexity as super-ego, ego, and id has, of course, become the assumed vocabulary of subsequent culture, both critical and popular. Freud saw, moreover, that the conflictedness remained largely hidden, because a surface equanimity is essential to managing membership in a stable (Viennese!) society. What Freud saw of selves in their thickness he also knew about texts.

Second, Freud understood the complexity and conflictedness of the self in a powerful, defining intrapersonal reality. But he also knew very well that the conflicted self does not exist in a vacuum. In fact, it has its conflictedness imposed and insisted upon by a demanding and enforcing civilization. Thus Freud's work, while particularly concerned with the personal, actually constitutes a mapping of social conformity and social dissent in a society that cannot tolerate resistance or dissent.[8] Therefore the health and emancipation of the conflicted self poses a threat to an ordered society and perhaps provides an antidote as well to a society ordered in repressive and unhealthy ways. It is on this count that Freud can appeal to the great cultural myths (e.g., Oedipus), because those myths are narrative accounts of power arrangements between society and persons in society.

Third, Freud could not have done without religion. To be sure, at a formal level he is dismissive of religion as an "illusion."[9] Given that declaration,

---

8. Freud, *Civilization and Its Discontents*.

9. See Freud, *The Future of an Illusion*. In fact, Freud's view of religion is much more complex than this title might suggest.

however, both the religious dimension of his nineteenth-century context and his own legacy as a Jew made it inevitable that he would regard the human self in religious categories. While the reduction of super-ego to social coercion dismissed the reality of God from the equation (a reduction Freud himself urged), nevertheless Freud could not escape the force of hiddenness and otherness that required symbolic articulation. As a nineteenth-century "scientist," he could not go further; however, in not going further, Freud allowed for the surging of mystery beyond human control that he located in the "unconscious." As Wayne Rollins reports, Freud himself attests to a remarkable sensation upon entering Notre Dame Cathedral and seeing Michelangelo's Moses, a sensation that surely moves into the direction of the religious.[10] It is clear that Freud was dismissive of any conventional, institutional practice or formulation of religion; he was not, however, dismissive of the reality of "other" that was beyond explanatory category.[11] Thus alongside his "scientific" commitments, the reality of "thickness" was available to him, even if in his own odd categories.

Fourth, the conflicted self, the dissent from co.nventional civilization, and the sensation of the holy all move to a final accent, namely, that Freud stands in the interpretive tradition of rabbinic Judaism. Freud is, in the end, an interpreter of the depth of the self, even as he probed into the depth of the text.

I am indebted to a remarkable study by Susan Handelman that makes a compelling case that Freud stands in continuity with the exegetical methods and interpretive assumptions of rabbinic Judaism.[12] Freud's work, like that of the rabbis, is to read and interpret texts, to find new meanings that displace old meanings, and to assert that the new meanings are not imposed but have been there in the texts all along. The work of displacement in interpretation was no doubt a way of negotiating between his two cultures, Jewish and Viennese. He was, moreover, at work on rewriting the identity of his father. The mode of interpretation that served these immediate matters was the work of displacing old interpretation through a process of recovery, reconstruction, and reappropriation. Thus *Moses and Monotheism* (which reads like wild, undisciplined speculation) is in fact an exercise in

10. Rollins, *Soul and Psyche*, 37–42.

11. It is possible that Freud might be understood according to the now popular mantra, "I am spiritual, but I am not religious." The statement generally refers to a rejection of the institutional aspects of "organized" religion with its legacy of repression and authoritarianism.

12. Handelman, *The Slayers of Moses*.

rabbinic interpretation whereby the interpretive act of patricide concerns old father and old interpretation, and the second Moses who displaces the first Egyptian Moses.[13]

Once one recognizes that *Moses and Monotheism* is not and was not intended to be a historical study but an interpretive venture, it is plain to see what Freud is doing. Handelman writes,

> And like the Rabbis, Freud insisted that he was not creating new meanings, only uncovering, like an archaeologist, what lay buried beneath. Everything is connected under the surface; the interpreter's job is to reveal, elucidate, and construct for conscious awareness those hidden unities that contain a core of definite historical truth.
>
> Interpretation is not, in the Aristotelian sense, the distinguishing of truth from falsehood, but the relationship of hidden to shown: not appearance to reality, but manifest to latent. The idiom is disguise, displacement, censorship of the superego. A dream cannot be true or false, but can only have a more or less deep meaning. Everything that logical consciousness rejects as nonsensical, useless, disconnected, contradictory, and impossible has, in fact, a meaning; and to say that dreams indeed have a meaning, Freud recognized, put him in opposition to every ruling theory. As Ricoeur puts it, Freud was the "exegete who rediscovers the logic of the illogical kingdom."[14]

The outcome of such work is the undoing of what was: "With *Moses and Monotheism*, however, the Jewish science reaches both its culmination and its undoing; it undid the Jews as the murderers of Moses; it undid Moses as an Egyptian, and it undid Freud's whole careful scientific façade."[15]

The undoing offers space for new readings and invites a proliferation of meanings; thus texts—like selves, like dreams—have many layered meanings. Freud's interpretation is an act against closed meanings of texts, just as his psychology is an act against closed selves that are so highly valued in conventional society. It is for that reason not a surprise that Handelman, after her discussion of Freud, goes on to consider Jacques Lacan, Jacques Derrida, and Harold Bloom as practitioners in the Jewish tradition of deconstruction. Old interpretation must be deconstructed in order to

13. Freud, *Moses and Monotheism*.
14. Handelman, *The Slayers of Moses*, 148.
15. Ibid., 145.

find new readings; old selves must be deconstructed to find new selves; old Moses must be deconstructed for the sake of the new Moses.

The line from Freud runs straight toward Harold Bloom and the oedipal need to displace the previous articulation by a sequence of "strong readings." Thus Freud's "Jewish method" is an invitation to readers of texts to go beyond the reductionism of closure too often proposed by conventional historical criticism.

Carl Jung is the second great founder of modern psychology and stands alongside Freud, but also over against Freud in important ways. Freud and Jung share a continual engagement with religious questions, both are attentive to the complexity of a conflicted self, and both are laboring in their scholarship to work out their own unresolved relationships with their fathers. Given the commonalities, however, Freud and Jung work very differently about the issues before them. Whereas Freud is inclined to accent disjunctive and pluralistic reality that appeals to Jewish rhetoric of confrontation, Jung reflects his Christian, Protestant nurture in a way that looks for systemic connectedness and accents the big narrative of salvation. Jung's accent is on the revelatory power of imagination, which he utilizes to identify and appropriate "archetypes" that operate in the unconscious, so that we may detect patterns of discernment and order that are reiterated form person to person. It is therefore not surprising that Jung finds evidence in the Bible for archetypes to which the text bears witness. As a result, it is the archetype, not the text, that is decisive for Jung.

I will rely on Wayne Rollins to indicate the key points in Jung's work.[16] (1) Symbols, archetypal images, and myths provide the primary points of inquiry for Jung. (2) Dreams are a primal venue for disclosures about the self. (3) Biblical personalities are studied as models and examples of the struggle for selfhood. (4) Religious phenomena in the biblical texts, mystical, sacramental, and ritual performances provide primary points of interest. (5) Jung paid attention to what he identified as the pathological dimensions of faith that concerned the "dark side" of human reality; this was matched by his interest in the therapeutic dimension of the biblical text. (6) Biblical ethics have a conflicted character. (7) Jung was attentive to the role of the reader and interpreter in rendering the biblical text. (8) Jung focused upon the origin, nature, and destiny of the human soul, so that his work is intrinsically and inescapably religious.

16. Rollins, "Jung, Analytical Psychology, and the Bible."

In sum, while Jung is enormously elusive, it is fair to say that he did not share Freud's deepest sense of human pathology. Rather, he understood that the God of the dark side is a heavy force from which the human soul can be freed for its own actualization. However, he also saw religion as a mode of nurture for the soul.[17] It is not difficult to see why Jung, in all of his elusiveness, is an attraction for religious engagement among those who prefer a "softer" sense of the psyche as a religious reality.

Special reference should be made to Jung's *Answer to Job* (1952). The book exhibits Jung's capacity to read the text carefully, but also his readiness to range widely, take in a great deal of territory, and make connections upon which critical scholarship would look askance. Before he finishes the book, Jung probes the role of Mary, the meaning of the incarnation, the importance of Sophia (that tilts toward Gnosticism), and the sweep of apocalyptic vision. For our purposes it is sufficient to see that God, in the book of Job, is presented as contradiction, as divine darkness, as an antinomy, as "total justice and also its total opposite."[18] In his articulation of original sin and salvation through incarnation, Jung clearly thinks in the broad terms of Christian theology, even if he gives that narrative his own idiosyncratic twist. But it is his particular rendering of God and the human psyche that is of note for us. First, against a common view of redemption, he proposes "reparation for a wrong done by God to man."[19] Second, about God's nature, Jung claims, "the paradoxical nature of God . . . tears him asunder into opposites and delivers him over to a seemingly insoluble conflict."[20] Third, for Jung, the self is by definition always a complexio oppositorum, and the more consciousness insists on its light nature and lays claim to moral authority, the more the self will appear as something dark and menacing.[21] The burden of religion constitutes this human predicament of a psyche rent asunder. Jung's response to this predicament is an offer of the "healing of the soul" from the wounding caused by the God of Job.

---

17. While Jung and Marx may make strange companions, it is worth noting that, in addition to his much quoted statement that religion is an "opiate," Marx also saw that religion is a powerful consolation. It is possible that his "consolation" is not so far from the "healing" that Jung attributes to religion at its best.

18. Jung, *Answer to Job*, 3, 4, 10, 15, 23.

19. Ibid., 91.

20. Ibid., 151.

21. Ibid., 133.

D. W. Winnicott and Object Relations Theory

After these comments on Freud and Jung concerning our topic of psychological criticism, I move directly to a third theorist, Donald Woods Winnicott. I do so because Winnicott, along with others who have developed
object relations theory, seems to me the theorist whose field of perception
and practice is most closely aligned with biblical rhetoric and the practice
of covenantal living. Winnicott stands in the tradition of Freud, but Freud
had understood the complexity of the human self to be an intrapersonal
unresolve. Under the influence of Harry Stack Sullivan and Melanie Klein,
Winnicott began to see that the unresolved transactions that constitute the
self are not *within the person* but are genuine *interactions between persons*.[22]
This move, it seems to me, is fundamental for an interface of psychology
with the Bible, for the Bible is relentless in its insistence upon genuine
interpersonal interaction, most especially interaction with the personal
agency of God.[23] In stressing the interpersonal, we are a long way from
Freud's internal sense of conflict and from Jung's archetypal analysis that
lacks the dynamism of the interpersonal. While Winnicott is dependent
upon his antecedents, he, along with other object relations theorists, has
moved well beyond them.[24]

Specifically, Winnicott focuses on the earliest interaction between
mother and child.[25] He believes that this dyadic interaction is the make-
or-break relationship for the health or unhealth of the child. Health for the
child (and the adult to come) depends upon a "good enough mother" who
is able to give herself over freely and fully to the child, so that the earliest

22. On the connection from Freud to Winnicott through Sullivan and Klein, see
Mitchell and Black, *Freud and Beyond*, 124–34. See also Underwood, "Winnicott's
Squiggle Game and Biblical Interpretation."

23. In Christian tradition, this interpersonal interaction comes to its remarkable
culmination in the incarnation, wherein God comes "bodied" in Nazareth form. The
Christian affirmation of incarnation is not to be reduced to philosophical categories but
has its roots in the long history of Jewish interactionism.

24. Special attention may be given to the work of Heinz Kohut. More generally, see
the discussion in Mitchell and Black, *Freud and Beyond*.

25. Winnicott characteristically speaks of "mother," but of course by such usage he
refers to whoever is the primal caregiver, which in some cases may be "father." He understands, however, that the originary physical bond of mother and child has no counterpart
with any other caregiver, so the usage of "mother" is surely correct for what he wants to
say, even if we might wish for more gender equity.

experience of the child is one of omnipotence, the sense that mother (and world) exist for the child at the behest of the child,

> The good-enough mother meets the omnipotence of the infant and to some extent makes sense of it. She does this repeatedly. A True Self begins to have life, through the strength given to the infant's weak ego by the mother's implementation of the infant's omnipotent expressions . . . It is an essential part of my theory that the True Self does not become a living reality except as a result of the mother's repeated success in meeting the infant's spontaneous gesture or sensory hallucination.[26]

As the child ages, the mother must withdraw that unconditional attentiveness so that the child can become aware that the mother has a life of her own and does not exist only for the child.

By contrast, an unhealthy child (and adult to come) will result, so concludes Winnicott, if the mother is not "good enough; that is, cannot give her full attentiveness over to the child. There may be many reasons for which the mother may be distracted or inadequate to this role. Whatever the reason, if the mother does not permit and authorize an early sense of omnipotence, the child very soon learns to hide the genuine self and to present a false self to the mother in order to receive the hoped-for responses from the mother:

> The mother who is not good enough is not able to implement the infant's omnipotence, and so she repeatedly fails to meet the infant's gesture; instead she substitutes her own gesture which is to be given sense by the compliance of the infant. Thus compliance on the part of the infant is the earliest stage of the False Self, and belongs to the mother's inability to sense her infant's needs.[27]

When this early transaction fails, the child is set on a course of false self-presentation that is practiced as dishonesty and hiding, so that the True Self is not permitted to become visible. The outcome is a compliant self who lacks "the essential critical element of creative originality."[28] While Winnicott himself was a man of deep faith, he does not, as with Freud and Jung, deal directly or explicitly with biblical material. That is, with Winnicot we do not have to contend with anything like *Moses and Monotheism* or

---

26. Winnicott, *The Maturational Processes and the Facilitating Environment*, 145.

27. Ibid.

28. Ibid., 152.

Answer to Job. What we have, rather, is a practitioner who does not impose large mythic themes (as with Freud and Jung) but who pays attention to the concreteness of interaction; he offers the best interface to the biblical characterization of life and self, because the dynamic interaction of mother and child is a close analogue of the dynamic relationship of God and Israel, God and church, God and individual person under the general rubric covenant.[29] I am not aware that Winnicott employs such terminology, but clearly he is concerned with a long-term relationship of fidelity that is marked by obligation and that has transformative power. These defining ingredients of covenant-fidelity, obligation, and transformative power are at the heart of Winnicott's theory.

In the wake of biblical testimony, Winnicott sees that the human person is constituted by a relationship. That relationship is one of mutual self-giving by the mother and eventually by the child, but it is, at the same time, an incommensurate relationship in which the mother is the defining party.[30] Mutatis mutandis, the God–other (I–Thou) relationship is, in the same way, mutual and incommensurate, a mutuality that insists on a two-way interaction, an incommensurability that requires the interaction of mutuality to be bold and courageous. It is clear that Winnicott derives his theories from Freud, but his derivative moves are in the direction of an actual relationship, so that not much energy is used on the intrapersonal and almost none at all on large mythic speculation. It all comes down to mother-child, to a relationship in which everything is at stake. The elemental question of Winnicott about the mother in relation to child is closely paralleled to the God of Israel who is "father of orphans" (Ps 68:5) and to the Christian Messiah who "will not leave you orphaned" (John 14:18).[31]

---

29. A great deal of important work remains to be done concerning the interface between the work of Winnicott and the defining categories of biblical faith. Attention may be paid, as a starting point, to Parsons, "Winnicott's Model of True and False Self Systems and Barth's Model of Sin with Application to Clinical Material."

30. Fruitful investigation may be undertaken with an interface between Winnicott's interactionism and the dialogic tradition of Jewish thought with reference to Martin Buber, Franz Rosenzweig, and, most especially, Emmanuel Levinas. Such an interface would bring the discussion to serious textual attention rather than to the wild impositions both Freud and Jung have made upon the Bible.

31. On this defining propensity in the God of biblical attestation, see Brueggemann, "Vulnerable Children, Divine Passion, and Human Obligation."

A Test-Case: Psychological Criticism and Psalm 35

From this quick consideration of three theorists, I now approach a specific text as an exercise in "psychological criticism." I will bring to the study of the text from the foregoing an awareness of a conflicted, complex self, a God who functions as complex other (dark and merciful), and the urgency of a noncompliant dialogic exchange with a dialectic of omnipotence and submissiveness. I consider Psalm 35, a lament psalm that is a venue for the sounding of many voices.[32]

I focus on a lament psalm because it is clear, given Winnicott's notion of "good enough mother" and the True Self, that Israel in its complaining, protesting addresses to Yahweh speaks the voice of a True Self, with nothing to hide or fake or hold back. Lament is an address of honesty by a courageous voice that is free enough even in the face of Yahweh. I propose that the lament is an act of omnipotence wherein the speaker assumes an initiative over against God and summons God to action and to accountability.[33] Such lament in Israel precludes excessive self-indulgence by the counterpoint of praise in which Israel repeatedly cedes initiative over to Yahweh. It is Israel's capacity for both lament and praise, for claiming and ceding, that makes possible a full, healthy interaction between a True Self and a sovereign God.[34]

32. The material that follows concerning Psalm 35 is reiterated from Brueggemann, "Dialogic Thickness in a Monologic Culture."

33. The study of the lament psalms by Lindstrom, *Suffering and Sin*, suggests that the speaker of these psalms speaks complaint and petition from a position of strength, as if the speaker had a sense of entitlement before Yahweh. Lindstrom does not speak of "entitlement" but notices that there is no confession of sin. Rather, the insistence is that God is obligated to respond to such a petition voiced in urgency.

34. The capacity to practice both lament and praise, claiming and ceding, is well characterized by Schafer, *Retelling a Life*, 94–95: "A whole person is the one who acts, the agent. A whole person acts knowingly without profound reservations about the fact of acting, and so acts with presence and personal authority and without anxiously introducing serious disclaimers . . . In sexual relations, as elsewhere, a whole person acts the role of agent while refusing to deny personhood to the sexual partner, and accepts it as a psychological fact of life that there cannot be only one whole person in the relationship . . . Guaranteeing the personal wholeness of others entails a readiness on a person's own part to serve on numerous occasions as object, ground, or milieu in relation to them, for they, too, must be given scope to exercise and confirm *their* personal agency and wholeness . . . A whole person allows the reversibility, in a relatively conflict-free fashion. He or she refrains from insisting on being only agent or object, only figure or ground, only active or passive, or only masculine or feminine, as conventionally defined. The reversibility is itself a form of action in that both refraining and allowing are actions. A whole

Psalm 35 bears all the marks of lament, according to conventional form-critical analysis. First, it features a series of petitions that reflect urgency, addressing Yahweh in the imperative mood. Verses 1–3a articulate that urgency in military figures, though the initial verb ("contend," 35:1) might suggest judicial confrontation. The second set of imperative petition is even more insistent (35:22–25). Second, the imperative petitions are matched by imprecations. The hope of the psalmist is that Yahweh will not only do good for the speaker but will retaliate against the enemy (35:4–6, 8, 26). Third, the complaint properly characterizes for Yahweh the acute jeopardy of the psalmist and the urgency of divine intervention (35:7, 11–12, 19–20). Fourth, the petition, imprecation, and complaint are supported by motivations that declare the innocence and merit of the speaker, reason enough that Yahweh should act (35:13–16). The ground for divine help is the entitlement of the speaker who has been faithful and has contributed to the well-being of the community. This entire sequence of petition, imprecation, motivation, and complaint constitutes a speech addressed to the God of the covenant who has made promises to this Israelite and who has offered sanctions that guarantee succor to those who remain faithfully in the covenant. These several components are characteristic of Israel's speech in its truth-telling mode.

The psalmist is able to articulate—that is, construct and imagine—the ongoing conversation of faith. In this rendition, the psalmist boldly speaks all of the parts to the conversation that is constitutive of faith. The capacity to line out the several elements of the conversation into a narrative whole indicates a healthy, complex self that is in touch with the many voices of the self, each of which is honored and given airtime. The psalm makes overt the ongoing multivoiced conversation of the self and, further, demonstrates that playful imagination is crucial to health and to faith. This is a daring project because the speaker ventures to anticipate what each party in the conversation may say. In the first instant, we may judge that this is an internal dialogue; that internal exchange, however, has profound implications for the external conversation that is subsequently to be enacted. We may identify five parties to the conversation that make the exchange of faith fruitfully complex. What is remarkable in this psalm is that each voice among the contesting parties is given explicit rendition.

---

person is neither threatened by reversibility nor incapable of enjoying either position in a relationship." Such reversibility is evidently Israel's way with Yahweh.

1. The psalm itself is, in the first place, *the voice of the supplicant.* That voice is, of course, the pervasive one, because the entire psalm is on the psalmist's lips. This is faith "from below" in which, for an instant, the petitioner has the upper hand and addresses Yahweh in an imperative. In such utterance there is a provisional reversal of roles: the petitioner assumes the role of senior partner in the exchange, and Yahweh is summoned to respond. The petitioner dares to instruct and command Yahweh.

2. *The second voice to this exchange is that of Yahweh,* who is given one line in the psalm. It is not, however, Yahweh who speaks. Rather it is the psalmist who proposes what Yahweh should say, thus assigning to God lines in the exchange. After the series of imperatives in 35:1–3a, the psalmist follows with yet one more, the verb "say":

> Say to my soul,
>> "I am your salvation." (35:3)

The words assigned to Yahweh are, of course, a standard salvation oracle, only not introduced by the customary "fear not." The proposed utterance is an assurance of Yahweh's attentiveness and Yahweh's presence, Yahweh's readiness and capacity to intervene transformatively in the vexed life of the speaker. It is the voice of faith that evokes the divine voice of rescue.[35] The divine response is, of course, not automatic, as is made evident in the poem of Job. It is, however, regularized enough that the psalmist dared count on it and assumed Yahweh's readiness to answer petitions. It is also possible to think that the psalm intends to head off and preclude other, less-affirmative divine responses such as those eventually offered by Yahweh to Jeremiah and to Job. The psalmist knows the utterance from Yahweh that is needed and desired and takes the initiative to assure that Yahweh speaks what is needed and not some other word that Yahweh could in freedom have uttered. The psalmist prays in uncommon confidence and with daring freedom, with a sense of entitlement that belongs to a covenantal, dialogic life.

3. In 35:9–10, the speaker quotes himself in anticipation of what he will say in the future, after deliverance by YHWH:

> All my bones shall say,
>> "O Yahweh, who is like you?
> You deliver the weak from those too strong for them,
>> the weak and needy from those who despoil them. (Ps 35:10)

---

35. On the salvation oracle as divine answer to lament, see Miller, *They Cried to the Lord,* 135–77.

The anticipated declaration of praise to Yahweh is not only to be given in words, not only by mouth, but by "all my bones," his whole being, every part of his delivered life that is now to be postured in doxology. It is, of course, obvious that his anticipated doxology is in total contrast to his present circumstance and present utterance of complaint. The speaker exhibits sufficient self-control and critical distance to imagine a situation and therefore an utterance other than his current one.

4. Claus Westermann has shown that in the psalms of complaint the relationships always form a triangle that includes, along with Yahweh and Israel, the enemy.[36] Of course, it is possible that the psalmist is simply paranoid. But such paranoia is grounded in the awareness that social life is deeply and always contested. The petitioner is at risk and without. resources; therefore, everything depends upon the intervention of Yahweh that is anticipated but not certain.

Because of that vigorous and threatening contestation in which the petitioner always finds himself, the adversary is given full play in the text. Thus, the psalm itself serves as an arena of contestation. In order to dramatize and underscore the contestation, the adversary is given full voice in the exchange of the psalm.[37] The speaker can imagine what Yahweh ought to say and will say in the future. Further, the psalmist can anticipate what he himself will say upon deliverance. So, too, the speaker is also able to imagine what the adversary might say if he were to triumph over the psalmist—a possibility that is only possible if Yahweh fails to intervene. The psalmist anticipates that in such triumph the adversary will gloat:

> They open wide their mouths against me;
>> they say, "Aha, Aha, our eyes have seen it." (Ps 35:21)

If Yahweh does not act to vindicate the psalmist, moreover, the adversaries are sure to gloat even more,

> Do not let them say to themselves,
>> "Aha, we have our heart's desire."[38]

36. Westermann, *Praise and Lament in the Psalms*, 165–213.

37. Wolff, *Das Zitat im Prophetenspruch*, has surveyed the way in which prophets in Israel can place alleged statements in the mouths of their opponents. The same rhetorical strategy recurs in the Psalter. What the adversary allegedly says is more often enacted rather than spoken.

38. This psalm evidences the thickness and dynamism of the human *nephesh*. The Hebrew term rendered in NRSV as "heart's desire" is נֶפֶשׁ. Before this verse the term is used three times in the psalm: "say to my נֶפֶשׁ" (35:3); "my נֶפֶשׁ will rejoice" (35:9);

Do not let them say,
"We have swallowed you up." (Ps 35:25)

The adversary is given a full say. But it is not the final say!

5. That imagined defeat of the speaker and of Yahweh by the adversary, however, is not the anticipated outcome of the dispute that the psalmist commends. Rather, it is anticipated that Yahweh will indeed say, "I am your salvation," and will act to make it so. Thus the psalm ends, as do many of the psalms of complaint, with an immense celebration of Yahweh's deliverance of the psalmist and the defeat of the adversary. That celebration is enacted by the psalmist in the "formula of incomparability" (35:10). Such deliverance, however, requires more than one voice of praise. The psalmist mobilizes the entire community of those who stand in solidarity with him and who hope for his acquittal (צדק, 35:27). All in that company are to exult in the vindication of their friend and so are summoned to praise. The community recognizes, in its doxology, that Yahweh is great, greater than the adversary, greater than any threat or any other deliverer. What constitutes that divine greatness, as already anticipated in the speaker's doxology in 35:10, is that Yahweh delights in the *shalom* ("well-being," 35:27) of the speaker, who is reckoned to be among the weak and needy. Yahweh not only delights in such *shalom* but also, in fact, effects shalom in a circumstance where no such well-being could have been imagined. The end result of the psalm is that the psalmist is restored to *shalom* that only Yahweh can give. By entertaining this final voice of doxological celebration, the speaker has spoken (i.e., imagined) the self upon arrival at a new condition of well-being. To be sure, that arrival is an anticipation, but the arrival is nonetheless palpable, made so by allowing yet another voice to speak.

The Self, Faith, and Dialogic Exchange

The psalmist is permitted, since it is his psalm, to manage the dialogue and place the accents where he will. The controlling capacity of the psalmist is evident in three anticipations of praise and thanks to Yahweh for saving

---

"rescue my נפש" (35:17). The נפש (i.e., the "desire") of the adversary in 35:25 is precisely to overcome the נפש of the speaker, who wants to be reassured (35:3), who anticipates praise (35:9), and who petitions for rescue (35:17). On the dynamism of the נפש, see Johnson, *The Vitality of the Individual*; and especially Wolff, *Anthropology of the Old Testament*, 10–25.

intervention. In v. 9, the anticipated formula of incomparability on the lips of the psalmist is stated.

> *Then* my soul shall rejoice in Yahweh,
>> exulting in his deliverance.

The "then" of the NRSV is only a waw conjunction in Hebrew, but it is enough to indicate that praise is withheld from Yahweh until rescue and depends upon that rescue. In v. 18, a parallel statement again withholds thanks until rescue: Then I will thank you in the great congregation; in the mighty throng I will praise you.

Here there is no indication in Hebrew at all of the "then" of the NRSV. Rather, the context justifies the usage of this coordinating adverb. The speaker is the one who will give thanks, even though the thanks in 35:18 is in the midst of the "great congregation." This anticipated thanks is the connecting point between the psalmist's praise in 35:10 and the congregation's praise in 35:27. The psalmist anticipates standing in the midst of the congregation, uttering both thanks and praise: thanks for Yahweh's deliverance from this particular threat; and generic praise of Yahweh's power to deliver. In v. 28, the "then" is again a waw conjunction in Hebrew.

> Then my tongue shall tell you of your righteousness (צֶדֶק)
>> and of your praise all day long. (Ps 35:28)

Praise concerns Yahweh's צֶדֶק, Yahweh's capacity to make things right for the speaker.

All three uses of "then" as rendered in NRSV (and I believe rightly informed by the Hebrew) withhold praise and thanks to Yahweh until deliverance is granted. In this way, assuming that Yahweh desires praise and thanks, Yahweh is at the behest of the speaker who is no easy touch but who bargains hard and holds the upper hand in the process. The psalm offers a dialogic exchange in four voices: Yahweh, the psalmist, the enemy, and the congregation—or five, if we distinguish between the present complaining voice of the psalmist and the anticipated doxological voice of the psalmist in time to come. The strategic articulation of the psalm situates the speaker and the faith of the speaker in the midst of a vigorous dialogic contestation, the place where faith is characteristically at risk and at work, the place where dialogic self-hood can arrive at an exercise of omnipotence and responsiveness.

Recovering the Complex, Dialogic Self

The capacity of biblical scholars to practice "psychological criticism" largely depends on appropriation of available personality theory. It is clear that personality theory has come a very long way from the imposition of huge mythic assumptions (that are mostly alien to the texts) toward a more modest attentiveness to the interactions that take place within the text. Psychological study of texts has often appealed to the more fantastic notions of Freud and the more speculative ideas of Jung. These studies make for interesting reading, but seldom, so it seems to me, do they illuminate the text. Thus an attempt to practice psychological criticism has produced much that strikes me as self-indulgent and misleading. I have proposed that attention be paid in particular to object relations theory because it focuses upon real human transactions marked by fidelity (and infidelity). These transactions are the nature of real life in the world, which in the Bible is broadly lined out as "covenantal fidelity" (חֶסֶד). Israel's struggle for the self is to come to terms with God and with neighbor, both "others" who are demanding and problematic as well as potentially life-giving. It is corning to terms with the other—a genuine other—that constitutes the hard work and the rich potential of the human self.

I believe that Psalm 35 permits a self that is underway in the hard negotiation with Holy Otherness that makes a True Self possible. Such a self never arrives but attends to many voices-many dimensions of self and many acknowledgements of otherness-that must be engaged in an ongoing conversation. In this case study of Psalm 35, I have not made any heavy-handed use of Winnicott, but my awareness of Winnicott has been of great heuristic value, and I would not have read the text as I have done without access to his work.

But then, as I reflected on this reading, it occurred to me that Winnicott and his many colleagues have, with varying degrees of success, only belatedly discerned what this ancient community had already recognized in full ways, that the self is complex and problematic and that the fullness of self depends upon an honored, summoned other. This biblical claim radically confronts a modern society that chooses mostly to solve its conflicts in technological ways with various forms of violence. Contemporary evidence might suggest that what is absent among us is an Other who is "good enough." For this absence, the church has much for which to answer, having denied the script of the complex, dialogic self from concrete practice. Perhaps the main work of psychological criticism is precisely to recover the wonder of this interactive practice that is so odd and so urgent in contemporary "modern" society.

Bibliography

Brueggemann, Walter. "Dialogic Thickness in a Monologic Culture." *ThTo* 64 (2007) 322–39.

———. "Vulnerable Children, Divine Passion, and Human Obligation." In *The Child in the Bible*, edited by Marcia J. Bunge et al., 399–422. Grand Rapids: Eerdmans, 2008.

Ellens, J. Harold, and Wayne G. Rollins, eds. *Psychology and the Bible: A New Way to Read the Scriptures.* 4 vols. Vol. 1, *From Freud to Kohut*; vol. 2, *From Genesis to Apocalyptic Vision*; vol. 3, *From Gospel to Gnostics*; vol. 4, *From Christ to Jesus.* London: Praeger, 2004.

Freud, Sigmund. *Civilization and Its Discontents.* Translated by Joan Riviere. London: Hogarth, 1951.

———. *The Future of an Illusion.* Translated by W. D. Robson-Scott. International Psychoanalytical Library 15. New York: Liveright, 1949.

———. *Moses and Monotheism.* Translated by Katherine Jones. New York: Knopf, 1949.

Halperin, David J. *Seeing Ezekiel: Text and Psychology.* University Park: Pennsylvania State University Press, 1993.

Handelman, Susan A. *The Slayers of Moses: The Emergence of Rabbinic Interpretation in Modern Literary Theory.* SUNY Series on Modern Jewish Literature and Culture. Albany: SUNY Press, 1982.

Jobling, David. "An Adequate Psychological Approach to the Book of Ezekiel." In *Psychology and the Bible*, Vol. 2, *From Genesis to Apocalyptic Vision*, edited by Harold J. Ellens and Wayne A. Rollins, 203–13. London: Praeger, 2004.

Johnson, Aubrey R. *The Vitality of the Individual in the Thought of Ancient Israel.* Cardiff: University of Wales Press, 1949.

Jung, Carl. *Answer to Job.* Translated by R. F. C. Hull. London: Routledge & Kegan Paul, 1979.

Kille, D. Andrew. *Psychological Biblical Criticism.* Guides to Biblical Scholarship. Minneapolis: Fortress, 2001.

Lindstrom, Fredrik. *Suffering and Sin: Interpretations of Illness in the Individual Complaint Psalms.* Coniectanea Bbiblica: Old Testament Series 37. Stockholm: Almqvist & Wiksell, 1994.

Miller, Patrick D. *They Cried to the Lord: The Form and Theology of Biblical Prayer.* Minneapolis: Fortress, 1994.

Mitchell, Stephen A., and Margaret J. Black. *Freud and Beyond: A History of Modern Psychoanalytic Thought.* New York: Basic Books, 1995.

Parsons, Marjorie. "Winnicott's Model of True and False Self Systems and Barth's Model of Sin with Application to Clinical Material." Ph.D. diss., Union Theological Seminary, New York, 1987.

Rollins, Wayne G. "Jung, Analytical Psychology, and the Bible." In *Psychology and the Bible*, Vol. 1, *From Freud to Kohut*, edited by Harold J. Ellens and Wayne A. Rollins, 89–95. London: Praeger, 2004.

————. *Soul and Psyche: The Bible in Psychological Perspective*. Minneapolis: Fortress, 1999.

Rollins, Wayne G., and D. Andrew Kille, eds. *Psychological Insight into the Bible: Texts and Readings*. Grand Rapids: Eerdrnans, 2007.

Schafer, Roy. *Retelling a Life: Narration and Dialogue in Psychoanalysis*. New York: Basic Books, 1992.

Underwood, Ralph L. "Winnicott's Squiggle Game and Biblical Interpretation." In *Psychology and the Bible*, Vol. 1, *From Freud to Kohut*, edited by Harold J. Ellens and Wayne A. Rollins, 139–51. London: Praeger, 2004.

Westermann, Claus. *Praise and Lament in the Psalms*. Translated by Keith R. Crim and Richard N. Soulen. Atlanta: John Knox, 1981.

Winnicott, D. W. *The Maturational Processes and the Facilitating Environment: Studies in the Theory of Emotional Development*. New York: International Universities Press, 1965.

Wolff. Hans Walter. *Anthropology of the Old Testament*. Translated by Margaret Kohl. Philadelphia: Fortress, 1974.

————. *Das Zitat im Prophetenspruch: Eine Studie zur prophetische Verkündigungsweise*. Munich: Kaiser, 1937. Reprinted as "Das Zitat im Prophetenspruch." In *Gesammelte Studien zum Alten Testament*, 36–129. ThBü 22. Munich: Kaiser, 1964.

seven

PSALM 37:
CONFLICT OF INTERPRETATION

In two decades of energetic activity, wisdom studies have reached some-thing of a plateau.[1] As a result of the work of Professor Whybray, along with Gerhard von Rad, James L. Crenshaw, and Roland E. Murphy (to name the most prominent), we are now able to take as a consensus a great deal concerning Israelite wisdom literature, e.g. its modes of disclosure, its assumptions about authority, its probable social contexts, its general theological intentionality, its tensions with more dominant modes of faith, and its paradoxical relation to broader wisdom traditions in the Near East.[2] The dominant wisdom literature, which functions as a normative reference point for scholarly forays concerning wisdom in other places, is found in Proverbs and Job, respectively a literature of social stability and a literature of dissonant protest.[3] Among other pieces of literature more or less related to this normative corpus, scholars have identified a fairly standard list of sapiential or instructional Psalms.[4]

1. See the recent, comprehensive review of the state of scholarship in Gammie and Perdue, eds., *The Sage in Israel and the Ancient Near East.*

2. Whybray, *The Intellectual Tradition in the Old Testament*; Whybray, *Wisdom in Proverbs*; and Whybray's survey, "The Social World of the Wisdom Writers"; von Rad, *Wisdom in Israel*; Crenshaw, *Old Testament Wisdom*; and Murphy, *Wisdom Ltterature.*

3. On the dialectic, see Perdue, "Cosmology and the Social Order in the Wisdom Tradition."

4. See Gerstenberger, "Psalms," 218–20; Kuntz, "The Canonical Wisdom Psalms of Ancient Israel"; Mowinckel, "Psalms and Wisdom"; and Murphy, "A Consideration of the Classification 'Wisdom Psalms.'"

In this paper, in the context of the scholarly consensus to which I have referred, I will consider Psalm 37, the most easily identified of the list of sapiential Psalms. I will consider it in terms of its socio-theological intentionality, and the effect of its discourse as an act of social power.[5] I will seek to show that the intention of the psalm is (perhaps deliberately) much less clear than has been most often assumed. This indeterminate quality makes the psalm surprisingly supple for interpretation, and invites conflicting readings in the face of contextual requirements, interests and possibilities.[6]

Wisdom Connections

The psalm shares the literary and theological assumptions that are regularly assigned to the earlier collections of sayings (sentences and instructions) in the book of Proverbs. That is, the psalm in its acrostic form could well be situated in the book of Proverbs itself, for it relies upon the range of claims that Zimmerli related to "creation theology,"[7] and which Koch identified as a "theory of retribution,"[8] so decisive for the oldest Proverbial wisdom. Of the many interesting and important rhetorical features of the Psalm, I will consider four:

1. Within the context of the most general sapiential theme that faithful living results in well-being (i.e. "deeds–consequence"), the most recurrent accent in this psalm is concern for land (vv. 3, 9, 11, 22, 29, 34, plus v. 18 on "inheritance"). The psalm is an instruction about how to keep the land and how to lose the land. The psalm plunges the reader immediately into practical, public, disputed matters of property, security and wealth, and therefore power. The statements about land, as we expect in such discourse, draw issues of property, security, wealth and power into the moral, theological world of faith, with specific though guarded reference to Yahweh. The psalm utilizes rhetoric that holds together material interests and

5. On the notion of socio-theology, see Neal, *A Socio-Theology of Letting Go*. More comprehensively on discourse as power, see Chopp, *The Power to Speak*.

6. The programmatic notion of conflict of interpretations is, of course, that of Ricoeur, *The Conflict of Interpretations*. Ricoeur's juxtaposition of a "hermeneutics of suspicion" and a "hermeneutics of retrieval" is closely correlated to Perdue's nice pairing of "The Paradigm of Order" and "The Paradigm of Conflict." See also Perdue, "The Social Character of Paragenesis and Paragenetic Literature," 8–12.

7. Zimmerli, "The Place and Limit of the Wisdom."

8. Koch, "Is There a Doctrine of Retribution in the Old Testament?" See the critique of Koch by Fox, *Qohelet and His Contradictions*, 125 n. 5.

transcendental claims.[9] Thus the psalm repeatedly asserts that land (and its derivative blessings and security) are not elements in sheer economic transactions, but belong to the larger fabric of communal relationships with a moral dimension, where righteousness and/or wickedness is enacted, and where Yahweh's power to give or withhold blessing is operative.[10]

This emphasis upon land is expressed in a word pair that is of peculiar interest, ירש / ברת. While the instructional theme of this psalm is hardly remarkable in a sapiential context, the use of this word pair is noteworthy. The term ירש is regularly and most often used in the land traditions that focus upon or are derived from Deuteronomy. That is, the word is most used in the "conquest traditions," which concern the seizure of land and the fulfillment of the ancestral promises.[11] Such a usage is quite remote from what seems to be the more domestic horizon of the psalm concerning the administration of property in a local community, and the difficulties of acquiring and managing landed estates.[12] The term ירש is used five times in our psalm (vv. 9, 11, 22, 29, 34). Remarkably, it is used only four times in all of Proverbs (20:13; 23:21; 30:9; 30:23).[13] In the first two uses of this latter list, the verb is used passively and negatively, "come to poverty"; that is, these uses are quite unlike the positive uses in our psalm that have the righteous person as an active subject. The verb, moreover, is not used at all in Job.

The second verb of the pair, ברת, is used five times in our psalm (vv. 9, 22, 28, 34, 38), four times in juxtaposition to ירש. (Only in v. 11 is ירש used without ברת, and only in v. 37 is ברת used without ירש.) In all five

9. On the interrelatedness of material interest and transcendental claim, see Gottwald, *The Tribes of Yahweh*, especially chap. 48 on the mutual reinforcement of "Yahwism" and "Social Egalitarianism." See ibid., 592–607, on his strictures against religious idealism that lacks self-conscious connection to material interest. Kraus (*Psalms 1–59*, 408) wants to resist an "idealist" interpretation of the psalm by insisting that the psalm is about a reaction to Yahweh, and not an "idea" about retribution. Kraus, however, stays largely in the area of piety, and does not let material interests impinge upon his reading.

10. On the interface of the economy to the larger social fabric, see Polanyi, *The Great Transformation*; and more recently Meeks, *God the Economist*.

11. For an exploration of other terms in the same semantic field, see Horst, "Zwei Begriffe für Eigentum (Besitz)."

12. That is, this psalm seems to reflect a settled economy, and does not have in purview military action, either aggressive or defensive. See below on the hypothesis of Crüsemann.

13. The last of these texts has a textual problem at the point of our term. Pertaining to our term, see McKane, *Proverbs*, 659.

uses of כרת, the verb is passive, thus refusing to identify an active agent of "cutting off." The usage of כרת is of interest for two reasons. First, it is quite uncommon to have the passive, negative verb used for such a local denial of property, for the term is most often used either for cultic excommunication (in the Priestly traditions), or as an outcome of war where the enemy is destroyed. Second, it is astonishing that the verb is used so rarely in the core sapiential literature. It occurs four times in Proverbs (2:22; 10:31; 23:18; 24:14) and not at all in Job.[14] In the uses in Proverbs, 2:22 most closely parallels the usage of our psalm, and has the most noticeable similarity between the psalm and Proverbs.[15] In 10:31 the verb is used for the "cutting off" of a perverse tongue; in 10:30, the theme of our psalm is used, but without the verb. In 23:18 and 24:14 the usage is not without linkage to the subject of our psalm (see below on אחרית), but the precise use of the verbs is not the same.

Thus, while 2:22 is a close parallel, in fact we have no other examples in the core wisdom material of the word pair, which occurs five times in our Psalm, plus two incidental uses not in a pair. I suggest that the psalm, in a most imaginative way, has taken terms from quite different language worlds to formulate a new, taut argument. The term ירש is most at home in the world of large land conquest and the term כרת is most used in terms of cultic exclusion or military defeat. Set in relation to each other, these powerful verbs make the possession of land of enormous moment, both as threat and as possibility. The repeated word pair forces the issue of land as property and security to be intimately linked to larger communal, so-ciomoral issues. The psalm redefines and recontextualizes land, and that intimate linkage is the central question in reading the Psalm. Note well that connecting land and Yahweh's righteousness is not the same as "deeds–consequence," which is a more reductionist category.

Moreover, the two verbs are each time used in an odd asymmetry. The negative verb כרת is used passively, which conforms to Koch's notion of a "sphere of destiny" in which land loss simply eventuates directly (automati-cally?) from wickedness.[16] By contrast, the positive verb ירש is an active verb, so that the righteous person is the active agent of acquiring land and generating. The psalm might have used a hiphil form or a verb like נתן in

14. The root כרת occurs in Job 31:1 and 40:28, but not in a way related to our usages.

15. Whybray (*Wisdom in Proverbs*, 40–41) regards these verses as an intrusion here, of a quite generalizing nature.

16. Koch, "Is There a Doctrine of Retribution?," 78–83 and passim.

a positive way, in order to make Yahweh's agency in giving land more visible.[17] The psalm, however, prefers to portray the positive acquiring of land as an active, accomplishment wrought through faithful living. Perhaps this contrast that correlates *positive/negative* with *active/passive* is a pedagogical strategy to emphasize that the acquisition or ownership of the land can be actively and intentionally pursued through faithful living. There is indeed something one can do to secure land, whereas the loss of land is not quite so direct.

2. The most startling statement in the psalm is the assertion of vv. 25–26, the *nun* formulation of the acrostic. As we shall see below, these two verses lend most weight to the common judgment that this psalm is the voice of a self-assured property-owning class that believes "the system works," and that is prepared to deny any evidence that might tell against this settled, stable, reliable, controllable view of social reality. The statement that "deeds–consequences" works is here fiat and without nuance, entertaining no exception or slippage. Crüsemann takes v. 25 "as typifying the older wisdom in its entirety."[18]

Such a view might be useful as an educational ploy in a very protected environment, or in the context of the very young and the very innocent (or the very devout). Such a view might even be sound piety, the kind that pervades the most innocent sapiential teaching that has as yet experienced no failure of nerve, and has not encountered any cognitive dissonance.[19] Clearly the affirmation of these verses cannot be sustained in the face of any critical social observation, but it is possible to avoid critical social observation in a protected social context.[20]

---

17. In v. 34, the role of Yahweh is made more active and explicit, but only in this one instance.

18. Crüsemann, "The Unchangeable World," 61. See also von Rad, *Wisdom in Israel*, 124–37; and Johnson, *A Morally Deep World*, 11–12, who finds the same elemental conviction in the world of Socrates, when it is asserted that "No evil can come to a good man," or can "befall the soul."

19. On cognitive dissonance, see Festinger, *A Theory of Cognitive Dissonance*, and the use made of the idea by, *When Prophecy Failed*.

20. See echoes of the same social posture in Psalm 112. Note well that such a sheltered view of reality is not merely ideological, i.e. holding to a notion, evidence notwithstanding. Such a view also requires a material arrangement, i.e. a deployment of economic-political power that assures that there will be no direct or visible contact with those who embody counter-evidence. The theory depends upon concrete social solutions and the power to sustain them.

To his credit, John Calvin, who passionately embraces the truth of scripture, finds this claim at face value too much to defend. He concedes: "It is certain that many righteous men have been reduced to beggary," and he alludes to the figure of Lazarus in Luke 16:20 as an acknowledgment of that awareness.[21] Moreover, Calvin asserts that there is "no certain rule with respect to temporal blessing." Thus Calvin deftly and tersely erodes the reliability of "deeds–consequences" as an adequate socio-theological claim, as it is undone for all of us by social reality. Calvin's acknowledgement is unflinching. His solution, however, is less daring, for he takes the affirmation of vv. 25–26 to refer to spiritual blessing, thus requiring the detachment of these verses from the materiality of the rest of the Psalm. Calvin's obvious discomfort with the verses leaves him, as it leaves any interpreter, a problem that requires comment (on which see below).

3. This psalm celebrates "the blameless" (תְּמִים v. 18; תָּם, v. 27), i.e. those who have solidarity, who bring well-being upon the community.[22] This two-fold usage of the same term is important because it brings this psalm more fully (than does יָרַשׁ / בְּרָכָה) into the orbit of sapiential vocabulary, and specifically into the problematic of Job. In v. 37 the word pair תָּם / יָשָׁר is the same one used to characterize the innocent, unperturbed Job of 1:1; 1:8; and 2:3. (See the same word pair in Prov 2:7, 21; 29:10; Ps 25:21.) The one who is "blameless and upright" is the model person of faith and righteousness, and, according to innocent wisdom, the one sure to be blessed. Thus the word pair (and the use in our psalm) points to the problem that occupies the poem of Job.

The poem of Job comes to be a battle over the actual blamelessness of Job, and over the significance of that blamelessness, once it is established. While Job is taunted by his wife for his treasured blamelessness (2:9), and is reminded that God does not care about his blamelessness (22:3), what counts most for the dramatic power of the poem is that Job refuses to give up his claim of blamelessness (cf. 12:4; 27:5; 31:6). Until the very end, Job will not relent, even though his claim requires a frontal attack on God's own "blamelessness" (9:20–22).

Thus our psalm is unflinchingly allied with and supportive of Job an claims. To be sure, neither the rhetoric nor the courage of this psalm is as far developed or as intense as is the Joban argument. But the premise is the same, and the implied struggle for moral coherence is the same. Moreover,

---

21. Calvin, *Psalms 36–92*, 39.

22. On the term, see Brueggemann, "A Neglected Sapiental Word Pair."

Prov 28:10 asserts that the blameless do inherit (נחל ה), the same verb used in Ps 37:18 with the term התמים. It is clear that our psalm is not as innocent as it first appears, but is willing to take a strong—and what turns out to be a contentious and difficult—stance as the core sapiential argument of theodicy.[23]

4. The psalm concludes with a bold assertion that, in the end, matters will be sorted out according to moral distinctions (vv. 37–40). In important ways, these verses simply reiterate the teaching of the entire psalm. The psalm does, however, look to a resolution not yet obvious or in hand. It is as though the psalm in the end concedes that the claim of vv. 25–26 is not obviously established, and so it must provide a faithful way around the problem. We may distinguish between two important concluding assertions.

First, in vv. 39–40, the rhetoric of the psalm is escalated to witness to the active, decisive intrusion of Yahweh who "helps, rescues, rescues, saves." While there have heretofore been hints of divine activity, this is a bold departure from "deeds–consequences" rhetoric; the verses stand in some tension with the rest of the psalm and more nearly cohere with Israel's "confessional" traditions. In an emergency, the psalm is pushed beyond its excessive innocence to a more vigorous theological affirmation.

Second, and for our purposes more important, vv. 37–38 twice use the term "posterity" (אחרית) to sort out the future of the blameless and the wicked. Three rhetorical points may be noted. First, the word pair "blameless, upright" is used as in Job 1:1, 8, and 2:3. This blameless-upright one is the quintessential wise person. Second, the negative passive verb, כרת, is again used, this time without being paired with ירש. Third, in these two verses, unlike vv. 39–40, there are no active verbs and no agent. Yahweh is not mentioned. These verses seem to affirm fully that the righteous person does indeed create a reliable "sphere of destiny" into the future.

What interests us most here, however, is the double use of אחרית. The psalm is willing and able to look beyond a simple moral calculation to a full, climactic reckoning ultimately wrought by God.[24] The book of Proverbs had already concluded future (Prov 14:12; 16:25; 20:21; 24:20). Two other

23. While Crenshaw shows that later, more developed wisdom teaching must address the issue of theodicy more boldly and directly, I suggest that the core options concerning theodicy are already present in the old sayings.

24. The fullest content to "ultimate reckoning" in this psalm is given by Dahood, *Psalms II*, 192–15. Dahood takes the negative judgment of v. 17 as "eschatological destroy," and the positive statement of v. 24 as "the final reward of the righteous after death." Dahood's view has not commanded very much scholarly support.

uses of אחרית in Proverbs are of particular interest. In 23:18 and 24:14, it is affirmed that the wise and righteous do indeed have a "future and hope," i.e. something yet to be received that is beyond present circumstance. Moreover, this positive affirmation in both cases makes use of the niphal of כרת, the same verb used negatively in our psalm. Thus our psalm in its conclusion is a statement of enormous confidence, well beyond the careful calculations and symmetries more easily associated with the earlier part of the psalm. It is perhaps too much to take these verses "eschatologically," but the formula of "yet a little while" in v. 10 encourages such a reading.[25]

There is of course much more to be said about the rhetoric and intentionality of this psalm. These four elements כרת / ירש concerning land, old/young, blameless, posterity—are enough to suggest that this teaching is not a bland summary of an innocuous, optimistic prudentialism. It is, rather, alert to an important intellectual dispute that admits of no easy resolution. Moreover, it is evident that the psalm is not one long, flat instruction marked by sameness and consistency. There is a variety of markers concerning abrupt rhetorical and substantive turns. These markers raise up issues, evidence tensions, lack of resolution and urgency in the ongoing conversation of practical faith. We are now ready to ask about the mode of discourse and the socio-theological intentionality of the psalm.

A First Reading: Ideology and the Status Quo

Our first reading of this psalm concerns its "ideological" support of an economic, social status quo. The preoccupation with land in this psalm assures us that the psalm is deeply embedded in and concerned for social interest. It is not neutral, disinterested, or transcendental. In order to explicate this psalm in relation to its social interest, I shall appeal to Karl Mannheim's much criticized but still useful categories of "ideology and utopia."[26]

Psalm 37 is *a powerful practice of social ideology* in the service of landed interests. The term "ideology" of course admits to two quite different readings. The earlier Marxist usage of the term, operative in Mannheim,

25. While avoiding the specific affirmation of Dahood, Calvin (*Psalms 36–92*, 51) nicely says, "It behooves us to give God time to restore to order the confused state of things."

26. In Old Testament studies, the categories of Mannheim have been most programmatically employed by Paul D. Hanson, *The Dawn of Apocalyptic*, 72 n. 45, and passim. On Mannheim, see Ricoeur, *Lectures on Ideology and Utopia*, chap. 10.

is pejorative. Thus ideology is an attempt to articulate one's social interest as social reality, or to present a part of the truth of social reality as though it were the whole. Ideology in this sense consists in deliberate deception in order to present a false, self-serving, self-justifying portrayal of reality. Mannheim uses "ideology" in this way to describe acts of social legitimation taken by those who hold power. Such legitimating acts defend and justify the status quo, so that unequal social arrangements are offered as social "givens."

A more neutral use of the term "ideology," carefully articulated by Clifford Geertz, is that it is simply a foundational articulation of the world that gives sense to experience and that permits the community to share in legitimated assumptions that permit social function.[27] In this sense, the term serves as a near synonym for theology, and contains no pejorative dimension.[28] In one usage or the other, Psalm 37 is "ideology," either legitimating inequality, or simply establishing "deeds–consequence" as a way of understanding public moral coherence.

The use of the category "ideology" for Psalm 37 was suggested to me by Otto Kaiser, in his helpful study of Job.[29] Kaiser understands ideology to be "human attempts to explain the whole or important parts of the world or life, and oo to gain compelling firm guidelines."[30] Kaiser further holds that in the early part of the sixth century BCE there was a systematic "ideologization" of faith in Judah, which produced an ethical rigorism.[31] He describes that effort in this way: "The ancient religious connection of righteousness and life was elevated to a law that allows no exceptions, and consequently the sufferings of the innocent were understood either as necessary test and purification, or must be categorically denied."[32] Kaiser then

27. Geertz, "Ideology as a Cultural System." See Ricoeur, *Lectures on Ideology and Utopia*, esp. 137–43; and Mitchell, *Iconology*, esp. Part Three. The issue of the meaning or intention of ideology turns on the issue of whether a truth claim is distortive or integrative.

28. My impression is that when used in this way by "neutral" social scientists, i.e. positivists, even the so-called neutral usage is in fact latently pejorative. Ricoeur, *Lectures on Ideology and Utopia*, 161, writes: "Because of ideology's origin in the disparaging labeling used by Napoleon against his adversaries, we must keep in mind the possibility that it is never a purely descriptive concept."

29. Kaiser, *Ideologie und Glaube*.

30. Ibid., 27.

31. Ibid., 29.

32. Ibid., 30.

proceeds to cite Psalm 1; Prov 11:21; 13:9; Gen 18:16–25, and a confession of Jeremiah as examples of the emergence of this ideology.

Kaiser's argument interests me specifically because he suggests that Psalm 37 is a primary example of this ideology.[33] (He dates the psalm to the Maccabean period, but the argument would pertain even with a somewhat earlier dating of the psalm.) Kaiser's argument concerning this psalm and others like it is that it prepares the way for the literature of Job and Ecclesiastes as it struggles precisely with this formidable ideology.[34]

Kaiser's argument is richly suggestive, though two preliminary reservations may be noted. First, Kaiser's definition of ideology makes it difficult to determine if his usage is pejorative or not. Second, his willingness to identify the time and historical context of the process of "ideologization" is not without problem, because it may indeed reflect the old (largely Christian) bias about the "decline into Judaism." My own propensity is to take a sociological rather than historical-chronological view of the process. That is, the emergence of ideology is not to be understood as a decision taken at a certain moment in Judaism, but as a characteristic tendency in every time, of those who believe they can sustain the status quo by careful attention to moral conduct, and by those who legitimate their privilege by an appeal to "transcendence."[35] While there may have been such an intense tendency in postexilic Judaism, the texts are too difficult to date and the dating largely contains a circular argument in the service of an old hypothesis about "degenerate Judaism."

That modest criticism notwithstanding, Kaiser's reading of Psalm 37 seems to me to be correct. The psalm is a bold and confident articulation of a "deeds–consequence" view of moral coherence that entertains no doubt, has no failure of nerve, and will host no exceptions.

The statements that contain our two words, ירש / כרת, make the point with clarity and without ambiguity:

> For the wicked shall be *cut off*,
>> but those who wait for the Lord shall *inherit* the land (v. 9).

---

33. Ibid., 36–39. On the burden of teaching as "order," see Van Leeuwen, "Immorality and Worldview in Proverbs 1–9."

34. Albrektson, *Studies in the Text and Theology of the Book of Lamentations*, 214–39, has set up the same problem concerning "theodic settlement" and "theodic crisis" with reference to Deuteronomy and Lamentations.

35. On this appeal to transcendence and a critique of it, see Brueggemann, "A Shape for Old Testament Theology [2 parts]."

The use of קָוָה suggests this is not confidence for what is in hand, but the reception of land is regarded as certain in time to come.[36]

> ... those blessed by the Lord shall *inherit* the land,
>> but those cursed by him shall be *cut off*. (v. 22)

Unlike vv. 9 and 10–11, this statement allows a modest place for Yahweh who is the power of blessing and of curse. But the power of blessing and curse attributed to Yahweh, in v. 21, is referred back to wickedness and righteousness, which here concern economic practices of borrowing and generosity. Thus the cause of יָרֵשׁ / כָּרַת is not the work of Yahweh, but one's own economic performance.

> ... the children of the wicked shall be *cut off*.
> The righteous shall *inherit* the land,
>> and live in it forever. (vv. 28b–29)

The statement lacks specificity, but vv. 27–28 that precede refer to evil, good and justice. Gerstenberger, in his comment on Prov 3:7, identifies this admonition as an epitome of the general perspective of wisdom.[37] It is the embrace of justice or injustice that leads to land or to land loss.

> Wait for Yahweh, and keep to his way,
>> and he will exalt you to *inherit* the land;
> you will look on the *destruction* (כָּרַת) of the wicked. (v. 34)

In this text, Yahweh has an active verb, "exalt," but again it is "hoping" and "keeping" that produce material results.

To these texts that have the word pair may be added vv. 3, 10–11, 18, and 37–38, all of which derive an assured future from a properly practiced present.

Three matters are evident in these assertions. First, they admit of no exceptions or ambiguity. The linkage of act and outcome is one-to-one. Second, the grammatical construction characteristically says nothing about how the act and the outcome are related to each other.[38] It is simply

---

36. On the concreteness of such waiting-hope, see Wolff, *Anthropology of the Old Testament*, 149–55; and Zimmerli, *Man and His Hope in the Old Testament*, ch. 3, especially p. 29.

37. Gerstenberger, *Wesen und Herkunft des 'apodiktischen Rechts,'* 49.

38. On the function of such parataxis, see Brueggemann, "The Uninflected 'Therefore' of Hos. 4.1–3."

so, taken as a premise and as a given, established through the observation of endless cases. The claim that has become "ideological" is based upon a deposit of trusted experience that is not specified or explained. What was an experienced conclusion has become a non-negotiable premise. Third, while there is no visible or explicit linkage, Yahweh hovers around these assertions in a variety of ways.

We may identify four ways in which Yahweh is regarded in these sayings on land as an outcome of conduct:

1. Only in v. 34 is Yahweh the explicit agent of inheritance.

2. In vv. 28, 29, Yahweh is the implicit subject of the acts.

3. In vv. 3 (cf. v. 4) and 9, Yahweh is the referent of the saying, but only as object, not as subject.

4. In vv. 11, 28b–29, and 37–38, Yahweh is absent, not mentioned at all.

While Yahweh is never far from the process, Yahweh's actual involvement in the process of inheriting and disinheriting is less than direct and frontal. This gingerly way with Yahweh suggests that the guaranteeing presence of *Yahweh* is indispensable for the teaching, even though the teaching is primarily preoccupied with the *land process* itself, and only then, belatedly, with its ethical-theological precondition. It is no stretch of the imagination to conclude that where Yahweh is minimally involved, the moral-theological requirements do indeed seem to be instrumental to the goal of land, precisely what an ideological statement might entail. That is, Yahweh is *useful* to the real concern.[39]

The identification of the social context and intentionality of such an ideology inevitably are to some extent circular. Though scholars are not fully agreed about the institutional context of such sayings, it is surely not too much to see that this saying reflects the perception of interest of the landed who construe and advocate certain moral-social prerequisites for acquiring and holding land.[40] The Psalm reflects a conviction that the holding of land is itself a sign of virtue as well as blessing. The presumption of

39. I have in mind the notion of "function" as Gottwald has utilized it (*The Tribes of Yahweh*, 608–21). I am of course aware of the problem of utilitarian faith. But of course this psalm and its Job-like claim are concerned precisely with the "usefulness" of Yahweh for the legitimacy and sustenance of its moral concern. On the question of the "usefulness" of faith, see Job 1:9.

40. Perdue, "Cosmology and the Social Order," 476–78, has most helpfully summarized the discussion concerning the social location of the sages.

virtue as well as blessing is the decisive ideological turn in the argument, for it introduces the category of *merit*.

The psalm not only affirms social stability and continuity, but assumes the virtue of those who enact sound stability, and seeks by its teaching to fend off the loss of property that would be tantamount to the coming of chaos. This reading of the psalm as a socially interested statement is specifically suggested by Robert Gordis and less directly by Brian Kovacs.[41] Gordis's analysis is. especially important because it is prior to and largely innocent of any theoretical, sociological reference, which was taken up in Old Testament studies well after Gordis's publication. That is, Gordis has no social theory to impose upon the text, as have later scholars (including Kovacs and Gottwald) who have become methodologically more intentional. Without appeal to any such grand theory, Gordis sees that the psalm reflects the affluent land-owner class, as does proverbial wisdom more generally. Kovacs with more methodological awareness concludes that the literature (of this proverbial kind) has a strong ideological cast.[42] In my own terms, Psalm 37 as ideology is "structure legitimating" and serves to sustain a socio-theological "orientation."[43] Verses 25–26 provide the ultimate expression of this self-assured claim that unashamedly overrides, denies and ignores social reality to the contrary. The psalm seems to have arrived at self-confidence for the owner class that this teaching is more reliable than any observable data to the contrary.[44]

41. Gordis, "The Social Background of Wisdom Literature"; Kovacs, "Is There a Class Ethic in Proverbs?" Less directly, see also Pleins, "Poverty in the Social World of the Wise"; Whybray, *Wealth and Poverty in the Book of Proverbs*; and the review article by Whybray, "Poverty, Wealth, and Point of View in Proverbs."

42. Kovacs, "Is There a Class-Ethic?," carefully nuances the class interest in the sayings, but sees that it is not blatant, but somewhat open to new experience that may cause revision in social interest.

43. On my use of these terms, see Brueggemann, "A Shape for Old Testament Theology I"; and Brueggemann, *The Message of the Psalms*, 25–49.

44. This is then what I term a "theodic settlement," i.e. an established balance between cost and benefit in terms of social power that legitimates a particular arrangement of power, and that shapes and limits social expectations. While it is usual to employ the term "theodicy" only in a crisis when social norms seem dysfunctional, in fact there can be no theodic crisis unless there is a previous consensus settlement. I take Psalm 37 to function in powerful and persuasive ways as such a settlement.

A Second Reading: Utopian

What interests me, however, is the fact that this psalm seems to receive a second, very different reading in a second, very different context. In some more contemporary liberation literature, the sorts of claims made in this psalm are taken not as congratulations for the landed, but as *a ground for hope for the landless*.[45] Moreover, the usage of v. 11 in the Sermon on the Mount (Matt 5:5) suggests a reading of the psalm very different from any socially ideological reading—a profound act of determined hope.[46] This reading takes the psalm (a) as a promise and guarantee of land for those who seem to have no means (except the claims of morality) whereby to acquire land, and therefore (b) as a critical assault on present land arrangements, which are unjust and which cannot be sustained. That is, the psalm is turned against the "wicked" who now possess the very land that has been promised to "the meek" and will indeed be given to them. In a word, what is evidently an "ideological" program of the psalm to legitimate the status quo becomes a practice of "utopia," an assurance of well-being that is certain if not yet in hand, an assurance of well-being that subvert a present ideological claims and their base in social arrangements. Frederic Jameson has subtly observed that the practice of ideology itself has inherent within it a utopian element, a yearning that the hard claims of ideology will eventuate in a well-being that is better than present, legitimate, defended, experienced reality.[47]

45. On this reading, the promise of land becomes something like a "preferential option for the poor." See Miranda, *Marx and the Bible*, 97.

46. See Ringe, *Jesus, Liberation, and the Biblical Jubilee*, 51–54; and Guelich, *The Sermon on the Mount*, 81–83, 101–2, 114. Both Ringe and Guelich link the text to Isaiah 61 and its echoes of the Jubilee, and refer to the context of Qumran. While Guelich resists a purely materialist interpretation to which Ringe is more inclined, he says of the promise of v. 11 (p. 101), "The hope of inheriting the earth is but another Old Testament expression for the initiative of God's sovereign rule in history on behalf of his own (e.g., Isa 61:7)." This latter accent is also sounded by Luz, *Matthew 1–7*, 236: "The promise of the earth makes clear that the Kingdom of Heaven also comprises a new 'this world.'"

47. Jameson, *The Political Unconscious*, 289, writes, "all class consciousness—or in other words, all ideology in the strongest sense, including the most exclusive forms of ruling class consciousness just as much as that of the oppositional or oppressed classes—is in its very nature Utopian." In speaking of the dialectic of ideology and utopia, Ricoeur, *Lectures on Ideology and Utopia*, 251, echoes Jameson: "As for myself, I assume completely the inextricable role of this utopian element, because I think that it is ultimately constitutive of any theory of ideology. It is always from the depth of a utopia that we may speak of an ideology."

Thus, in a second reading, Psalm 37 is an act of utopian hope, i.e. an affirmation about the future, even though the voice of the psalm gives no hint about how to get from here to there. That is, it is not known how the wicked will lose the land and the righteous will receive it.[48] It is only stated that it will be so. In this reading, the psalm is not a defense of present social reality, but it is an "eschatological" anticipation that things will assuredly be different:[49] The transformation of "ideology" into "utopia" in this psalm clearly requires a different reading of the text that finds in the text very different points of accent.[50]

We may identify some of the points that authorize and legitimate a second reading, and that seem to be freshly noted in this second discernment.

- The verbs to which we have referred (ירש / כרת) are characteristically imperfect and admit of a future reading. They describe what is assured, but not in hand. The word pair is anticipatory, not descriptive.

- In v. 10, the phrase עוד מעט, if not "apocalyptic," in any case anticipates a significant social inversion that is about to happen.

- The double use of אחרית in vv. 37–38 anticipates a time to come, quite in contrast to the present, a usage of אחרית echoed in Ps 73:17.

- The pervasive assault on the "wicked" suggests a present-tense time of speaking that is distressing, if not unbearable. The wicked, i.e. those who are quite unlike and in conflict with the voice of the Psalm, apparently now control the land. Thus the anticipatory stance of the psalm

48. The rhetorical elusiveness of the psalm about how the wicked will be dispossessed, in something like a parataxis, is strategically important for the affirmation of the Psalm. The revolutionary hope of the psalm knows and trusts that more is assured than is logically or technically explainable. This elusiveness is part of the subversive rhetorical strategy for avoiding socio-economic-political details to the hope, details that are bound to reduce the power of the hope and end in the "explanations" of the "ruling class."

49. "Eschatology" is admittedly a poor word for the hope of this psalm. By the term we can only mean the resolution of social conflict in the social process, never anything "beyond" the social process, which would detract from the socio-economic force of the hope.

50. This is a telling and important case of "reader-response." It is important that in the "conflict of interpretations" and the freedom of "reader response," we are not concerned with aesthetic options but with power struggles driven by competing vested interests. Goldingay, "The Dynamic Cycle of Praise and Prayer in the Psalms," has rightly seen that the same psalm can perform more than one such function and yield more than one reading. See my response: Brueggemann, "Response to John Goldingay's 'The Dynamic Cycle of Praise and Prayer.'"

is not simply an act of pious trust, though it is in part.[51] It is also an act of social criticism and social assault that means to expose present realities, and to provide the ground for questioning and dismantling the legitimacy of those who now wrongly hold the land.

- The conditions for properly and securely holding the land are serious social practices and not simply pious postures. These conditions include trust in Yahweh, doing good (v. 3), waiting for Yahweh (vv. 9, 34), meekness (v. 11), being blameless (vv. 18, 37), righteousness expressed as generosity (v. 21), and righteousness (vv. 29, 39). This entire list, when taken as a whole, proposes a radical counter-ethic, counter to those who are exploitative, greedy land-grabbers.

- The psalm advocates and proposes, according to this second reading, a radically different communal practice. These conditions are not "ideas," but are concrete social practices. Of course the mere saying of this hope for land does not turn the hope into reality. The psalm nonetheless invites and insists upon a serious adjudication of two ways in which social power is secured and in which social stability is developed and maintained. If the practice of righteousness concerns the maintenance of a viable social fabric, then the hope relates to the specifics of socio-economic practice. These real and serious preconditions for property mean that the property must be managed with reference to Yahweh and with reference to the community intended by Yahweh, clearly reference points systematically disregarded by the detached market economy practice of the wicked who believe gain is unrelated to social fabric.

- We have seen that Yahweh is only softly articulated in these affirmations. There is no doubt, however, that the reference to Yahweh, even if subdued, is decisive, as in the concluding verses (vv. 39–40). It is the interventionist, side-taking God who is decisive in the adjudication of land, property, and finally peace.

- The reference to "blamelessness" (vv. 18, 37) brings this psalm into the world of Job. There is no doubt that Job's "blamelessness" is deeply under assault in the poem of Job. Nonetheless, in more recent readings of Job, the restoration of Job (42:10–17) is taken as integral to the

51. Kraus, *Psalms 1–59*, 408, while recognizing a warm piety in the psalm, also notes the "this-worldly hope for God's intervention" that he sees resurfacing in Matt 5:5, in a way congruent with Guelich's comment on the Beatitude.

art form and to the theological intention of the final form of the text.[52] "Blamelessness" in the end is not mocked: Job may indeed serve God "for nought" (Job 1:9), but in the end he is rewarded. Thus I suggest that Psalm 37, read as social anticipation (and therefore as social criticism), is not naive and innocent about real social conflict and frustration, but in fact traces the same socio-theological dispute that is more explicit and vigorous in Job. It is the conviction of the "righteous" that they live in a world where wicked land practices cannot prevail.[53] In the meantime, the righteous (meek) must wait (vv. 9, 34). In their waiting, they must act in and for the community in ways quite contrasted with the modes of the wicked who act against the community.

I do not suggest that a *utopian reading* is a better or final reading that trumps the *ideological reading*. I suggest only that it is a second possible reading. This reading does not resolve the oddness of vv. 25–26, but surrounds and perhaps overwhelms those verses with counter claims. Even the utopian, anticipatory practice of the psalm in the end, however, will not break with the claims of vv. 25–26, which are a clear insistence upon a righteously ordered creation.[54] The anticipatory note, however, resists any chance of self-congratulations that an ideological reading of vv. 25–26 might host. That is, the anticipatory reading offers no congratulations because the gift of land is not yet in hand, and will not ever be in hand because of any virtue or merit. These verses have nothing in hand, but are a passionate hope without any hint of a failure of nerve. It is the deep expectation of these verses that the children of the righteous will not in the end be hungry

52. On the role and function of these last verses in the book of Job, see Janzen, *Job*, 261–69, and especially Clines, "Deconstructing the Book of Job." On pp. 113–14, Clines writes: "[I]t is even more disconcerting that what one hardly ever sees argued is the view that in fact the epilogue undermines the rest of the Book of Job . . . It tells us, and not at all implicitly, that the most righteous man on earth is the most wealthy . . . y ch. 42, no one, not even in heaven, is left in any doubt that it is the piety of Job, somewhat eccentrically expressed to be sure, that has led to his ultimate superlative prosperity. What the book has been doing its best to demolish, the doctrine of retribution, is on its last page triumphantly affirmed."

53. On this conviction, see my analysis of Psalm 9–10 in Brueggemann, "Psalms 9–10." I have urged that in these two Psalms, (a) Yahweh is an advocate for the poor against the rich, and (b) the Psalms are themselves an act of rhetorical, and therefore socio-political, transformation.

54. On the order of creation as an horizon for anticipatory faith, see Schmid, "Creation, Righteousness and Salvation"; and Knierim, "On the Task of Old Testament Theology."

or reduced to begging. In a world currently wicked, however, the promise and assurance are not yet kept. Thus the children of the righteous are vigorous, determined, undeterred waiting ones.[55]

A Second Context

The first, i.e. the ideological, reading of the psalm assumes and affirms a tight connection of deed and outcome, reflective of a stable, affluent society, as Gordis has shown.[56] In the first reading, the psalm "reproduces" a stable economic order that maintains economic advantage for a certain element in the community. Crüsemann concludes: "Where ownership of land is uncontested and at the same time a segmentary solidarity reigns, it will be normal to expect a correspondence between what one does and how one fares."[57]

We must now ask about a second context that has produced a second, i.e. utopian, reading of the Psalm. The proposal of a social context is always inevitably somewhat hypothetical and circular, but we may at least entertain a cogent social possibility. In his shrewd analysis of the world of Qoheleth, Crüsemann has suggested that, in the Hellenistic period, an alien state intruded upon the economy of well-established small landowners, i.e. the ones who readily trusted the ideology of "deed and consequences."[58] Thus, according to Crüsemann, the ideological crisis of Qoheleth is situated in the quite concrete social situation of small landowners. As the state preempted property and the capacity to make one's own economic decisions, the society became less and less amenable to management and control, and became increasingly an uncritical, acquisitive, currency-based society. As a result, such threatening experience made appeal to the Yahwistic tradition problematic, economic gain became primary, and despair issued in a

---

55. Notice that the affirmations are thoroughly material in their focus, not "spiritual" as in Calvin, and not pious as in Kraus.

56. Crüsemann, "The Unchangeable World," accepts the verdict of Gordis as the base line for his own conclusions. He characterizes Gordis's argument as leading to a conclusion on social location that is "unquestionably" true (58) and "irrefutable" (61). In a much earlier context, Munch, "Das Problem des Reichtums in den Psalmen 37, 49, 73," 37–40, reached the parallel conclusion that this psalm reflects a future for a *Baurnideal.*

57. Crüsemann, "The Unchangeable World," 62.

58. Crüsemann's argument is in part based on Kippenberg, *Religion und Klassenbildung im antiken Judäa,* to which I have not had access. See the critical comment of Fox, *Qohelet and His Contradictions,* 142–46.

somber reflection upon death.[59] In Crüsemann's analysis, Qoheleth reflects a growing helplessness and cynicism that seeks only "to avoid conflict," withdraw from stress, and is determined not to "get involved."[60] The urging of Qoheleth is, "One is not to be too much a *tsaddiq*."[61]

The experience of Qoheleth, reflected in the literature, is part of a context that made the old theological confidence in "deed–consequence" impossible. With the abandonment of the ideology that no longer resonated with experience, Qoheleth ends in despair.

Accepting the proposal of Kippenberg and Crüsemann,[62] I suggest that the resignation of Qoheleth marks a transition that in the end eventuated in a second, utopian reading of Psalm 37, just as the resignation of Qoheleth destroyed the first, ideological reading. In a situation of powerlessness and inability to manage or even to understand one's social setting, the new readers of the psalm will never reiterate the old ideology, but they also will not accept the resignation of Qoheleth. They will instead take the psalm as a bold anticipation that no longer trusts naively, but that moves past the sense of fatedness given in Qoheleth. In that anticipation, the reading of the psalm is no longer easily content with the status quo (how could it be!), nor resigned to the status quo (why should it be?).

Restlessness and hope are grounded in the conviction that the psalm still rings true *for the very long haul*, because of the undoubted promises of Yahweh. The grip of the wicked upon the land will soon (v. 3), in a little while (v. 10), in the end (vv. 37–38), be turned so that there will be "inheriting" and "cutting off," because the deeds–consequence linkage is not simply practical common sense, but a passionate conviction that Yahweh has ordained that the waiting, righteous ones will have the land that is rightly theirs, which has of late been seized from them. That is, the affirmation of faith that in a better time had been an easy legitimation of present-tense reality now becomes a passionate refusal to accept the fated, present-tense world of Qoheleth. In the first reading, the "meek," in their righteousness, held the land, and so could be calmly affirmative. In the second reading, however, the meek no longer have the land, or do not yet have the land,

---

59. While he does not attend much to the material dimension of the teaching, Crenshaw has probed the way in which Qoheleth finally ends in the despair of death. See Crenshaw, "The Shadow of Death in Qoheleth."and Crenshaw, *Ecclesiastes*, 23–28.

60. Crüsemann, "The Unchangeable World," 70–73.

61. Ibid., 73.

62. See Albertz, "Der sozialgeschichtliche Hintergrund und der 'Babylonischen Theodizee,'" for a social analysis of theodicy that is congruent with that of Crüsemann.

but believe that righteousness is so intrinsic to the land process that the meek will, late if not soon, receive what is rightly and surely theirs. Thus the "conflict of interpretation" yields a hermeneutical process as follows:[63]

First reading of the Psalm: Ideological description	→	loss of nerve and resignation; Qoheleth abandons the psalm	→	*Second reading of the Psalm:* Utopian redescription

This sequence is closely parallel to the dramatic sequence of the final form of the text of Job:

A first reading of Job's blamelessness (Job 1:1—2:13)	→	A dispute about Job's blamelessness (Job 3:1—42:6)	→	A restoration of Job in his blamelessness (Job 42:7-17)

Moreover, this sequence closely parallels my interpretive grid for the Psalms:

orientation → disorientation → new orientation[64]

Thus I suggest that a second reading of the psalm is generated in the same context that produced Qoheleth. Why some should read the situation through cynical abdication, and why some through determined anticipation, is not known. Partly the text invites such a second reading, partly the second readers cling to a radically revised form of the old ideology that has now become passionate hope. And partly, we do not know why faith is given as a convinced way in which to read life and text.

The second reading lives very close to the first reading in its theological premise concerning Yahweh's powerful resolve for social reality. The'intention, result and effect of this second reading, however, are quite the opposite of the first. The first reading, with self-satisfaction and self-sufficiency, celebrates a reliable present tense. The second subverts the present in its passionate embrace of a revolutionary future, a future as revolutionary as the Jubilee when the land will be given to those who have lost it.[65]

63. This interpretative grid in its many formulations is especially shaped by the work of Ricoeur. See Wallace, *The Second Naiveté*.

64. Brueggemann, "Psalms and the Life of Faith."

65. On the radicality of the Jubilee, see Ringe, *Jesus, Liberation. and the Biblical Jubilee*. But see the insistence of Mosala, *Biblical Hermeneutics and Black Theology in South Africa*, 154–89, that even in the Gospel of Luke (of all places), that radical claim has been reduced to accommodate the ruling class. Gerstenberger, *Psalms, Part I*, 160, almost inadvertently voices the double reading: "The intention is a double one: to admonish the

Conclusion

It is not surprising that the same text permits more than one reading. The text is open enough to permit more than one reading. Given our common critical propensity, we may prefer to adjudicate these competing readings in order to settle on a "true reading." All of our adjudication, however, is also context-laden. We are left to probe experientially the deeds–consequence claim of the text, whether it pertains either to present-tense possession of the land or to anticipated, promised possession of the land. Even our experiential probes, however, will be context- and interest-laden.

In our own context, an ideological-descriptive, celebrative reading might be given the Psalm, as those in the "economic West" celebrate the collapse of communist regimes in the East. Such celebration could conclude that we have "been doing something right," i.e., capitalism, which makes us "righteous" and has led to our legitimate success.[66]

Conversely, in the United States, the massive power of agribusiness continues to occupy and possess more and more land to the disadvantage of smaller farmers. An anticipatory criticism of agribusiness, as voiced for example by Wendell Berry,[67] will conclude that such indifferent, absent ownership of the land is in the long run not viable.[68] It is an exploitative practice that does damage not only to the dwellers in the land, but to the land itself. Eventually the land will be regiven to the small owner, for such large-scale acquisitiveness and greed will, soon or late, be "cut off." This anticipation is of course a refusal to accept current "economic realities," and in some sense is a hope-filled reassertion of faith that links land to virtue. In this context, an assertion of deeds-consequences performs only critical and anticipatory functions, and does not consolidate the status quo.

The maddening and inescapable reality is that these alternative readings of the same psalm continue in our own time to live in lively tension

---

faithful to keep on the right path . . . and to revive and sustain hope for a fundamental change for the better . . ."

66. This case in all its triumphalist shamelessness has been made by Fukuyama, "The End of History?"; and more fully, Fukuyama, *The End of History and the Last Man*.

67. Berry, *The Gift of Good Land*; Berry, *Home Economics*; Berry, *The Unsettling of America*.

68. The point has been most trenchantly made by Steinbeck, *The Grapes of Wrath*, 298–99, and passim. For a critical analysis of the pertinent issues in the Old Testament, see Dearman, *Property Rights in the Eighth-Century Prophets*; and Premnath, "Latifundialization and Isaiah 5.8–10."

with each other, a tension that is theologically demanding and politically urgent. In contemporaneous readings, stable wealth is justified, peasant yearning is legitimated. There is no contextless reading. Various readings may reassure or threaten. How one reads depends upon where righteousness (and therefore wisdom) are thought to be.

Bibliography

Albertz, Rainer. "Der sozialgeschichtliche Hintergrund und der 'Babylonischen Theodizee.'" In *Die Botschaft und die Boten: Festschrift für Hans Walter Wolff zum 70. Geburtstag*, edited by Jörg Jeremias and Lothar Perlitt, 349–72. Neukirchen-Vluyn: Neukirchener, 1981.

Albrektson, Bertil. *Studies in the Text and Theology of the Book of Lamentations with a Critical Edition of the Peshitta Text*. Studia theologica Lundensia 21. Lund: Gleerup, 1963.

Berry, Wendell. *The Gift of Good Land: Further Essays Cultural and Agricultural*. San Francisco: North Point, 1981.

———. *Home Economics: Fourteen Essays*. San Francisco: North Point, 1987.

———. *The Unsettling of America: Culture and Agriculture*. New York: Avon, 1977.

Brueggemann, *The Message of the Psalms: A Theological Commentary*. Minneapolis: Augsburg, 1984.

———. "A Neglected Sapiental Word Pair." *ZAW* 89 (1977) 234–58.

———. "Psalms 9–10: A Counter to Conventional Social Reality." In *The Bible and the Politics of Exegesis: Essays in Honor of Norman K. Gottwald on His Sixty-Fifth Birthday*, edited by David Jobling et al., 3–15, 297–301. Cleveland: Pilgrim, 1991. Reprinted in Brueggemann, *Social Criticism and Social Vision in Ancient Israel*. Edited by K. C. Hanson. Eugene, OR: Cascade Books, forthcoming.

———. "Psalms and the Life of Faith: A Suggested Typology of Function." *JSOT* 17 (1980) 3–32.

———. "Response to John Goldingay's 'The Dynamic Cycle of Praise and Prayer,'" *JSOT* 22 (1982) 141–42.

———. "A Shape for Old Testament Theology, I: Structure Legitimation," *CBQ* 47 (1985) 28–46. Reprinted in Brueggemann, *Old Testament Theology: Essays on Structure, Theme, and Text*, edited by Patrick D. Miller, 1–21. Minneapolis: Fortress, 1992.

———. "A Shape for Old Testament Theology, II: Embrace of Pain." *CBQ* 47 (1985) 395–415. Reprinted in Brueggemann, *Old Testament Theology: Essays on Structure, Theme, and Text*, edited by Patrick D. Miller, 22–44. Minneapolis: Fortress, 1992.

———. "The Uninflected 'Therefore' of Hos. 4.1–3." In *Reading from This Place: Social Location and Biblical Interpretation in the United States*, edited by Fernando F. Segovia and Mary Ann Tolbert. Minneapolis: Fortress, 1995.

Calvin, John. *Commentary on the Book of Psalms: Second Volume (Psalms 36–92)*. Grand Rapids: Baker, 1979

Carroll, Robert P. *When Prophecy Failed: Reactions and Responses to Failure in the Old Testament Prophetic Traditions*. London: SCM, 1979.

Clines, David J. A. "Deconstructing the Book of Job." In *What Does Eve Do to Help? and Other Readerly Questions to the Old Testament*, 106–23. JSOTSup 94. Sheffield: JSOT Press, 1990.

Chopp, Rebecca. *The Power to Speak: Feminism, Language, God*. New York: Crossroad, 1989.

Crenshaw, James L. *Ecclesiastes: A Commentary*. OTL. Philadelphia: Westminster, 1987.

———. *Old Testament Wisdom: An Introduction*. Atlanta: John Knox, 1981.

———. "The Shadow of Death in Qoheleth." In *Israelite Wisdom: Theological and Literary Essays in Honor of Samuel Terrien*, edited by John G. Gammie et al., 205–16. Homage Series. Missoula, MT: Scholars, 1978.

Crüsemann, Frank. "The Unchangeable World: The 'Crisis of Wisdom' in Qoheleth." In *God of the Lowly: Socio-Historical Interpretations of the Bible*, edited by Willy Schottroff and Wolfgang Stegemann, 57–77. Maryknoll, NY: Orbis, 1984.

Dahood, Mitchell. *Psalms II, 51–100*. AB 17. Garden City, NY: Doubleday, 1968.

Dearman, J. Andrew. *Property Rights in the Eighth-Century Prophets: The Conflict and Its Background*. SBLDS 106. Atlanta: Scholars, 1988.

Festinger, Leon. *A Theory of Cognitive Dissonance*. 1957. Reprinted, Stanford: Stanford University Press, 1962.

Fox, Michael V. *Qohelet and His Contradictions*. JSOTSup 71. Sheffield: Almond, 1989.

Fukuyama, Francis. "The End of History?" *The National Interest* (Summer 1989) 3–18.

———. *The End of History and the Last Man*. New York: Free Press, 1992.

Gammie, James G., and Leo G. Perdue, eds. *The Sage in Israel and the Ancient Near East*. Winona Lake, IN: Eisenbrarms, 1990.

Geertz, Clifford. "Ideology as a Cultural System." In *The Interpretation of Cultures: Selected Essays*, 193–233. New York: Basic Books, 1973.

Gerstenberger, Erhard S. "Psalms." In *Old Testament and Form Criticism*, edited by John H. Hayes, 179–223. Trinity University Monograph Series in Religion 2. San Antonio, TX: Trinity University Press, 1974.

———. *Psalms, Part I: With an Introduction to Cultic Poetry*. FOTL 14. Grand Rapids: Eerdmans, 1988.

———. *Wesen und Herkunft des 'apodiktischen Rechts.'* WMANT 20. 1965. Reprinted, Eugene, OR: Wipf & Stock, 2009.

Goldingay, John. "The Dynamic Cycle of Praise and Prayer in the Psalms." *JSOT* 20 (1981) 85–90.

Gordis, Robert. "The Social Background of Wisdom Literature." In *Poets, Prophets, and Sages: Essays in Biblical Interpretation*, 160–97. Bloomington: Indiana University Press, 1971.

Gottwald, Norman K. *The Tribes of Yahweh: A Sociology of the Religion of Liberated Israel, 1250–1050 B.C.E.* Maryknoll, NY: Orbis, 1979.

Guelich, Robert A. *The Sermon on the Mount: A Foundation for Understanding*. Waco, TX: Word, 1982.

Hanson, Paul D. *The Dawn of Apocalyptic: The Historical and Sociological Roots of Jewish Apocalyptic Eschatology*. Rev. ed. Philadelphia: Fortress, 1979.

Horst, Friedrich. "Zwei Begriffe für Eigentum (Besitz): נחלה und אחזה." In *Verbannung und Heimkehr: Beiträge zur Geschichte und Theologie Israels im 6. und 5. Jahrhundert v. Chr.*, edited by Arnulf Kuschke, 135–56. Tübingen: Mohr/Siebeck, 1961.

Jameson, Fredric. *The Political Unconscious: Narrative as a Socially Symbolic Act*. London: Methuen, 1981.

Janzen, J. Gerald. *Job*. Interpretation. Atlanta: John Knox, 1985.

Johnson, Lawrence E. *A Morally Deep World: An Essay on Moral Significance and Environmental Ethics*. Cambridge: Cambridge University Press, 1991.

Kaiser, Otto. *Ideologie und Glaube: Eine Gefahrdung christlichen Glaubens am alttestamentlichen Beispiel aufgezeigt*. Stuttgart: Radius, 1984.

Kippenberg, H. G. *Religion und Klassenbildung im antiken Judäa*. Studien zur Umwelt des Neuen Testaments 14. Göttingen: Vandenhoeck & Ruprecht, 1978.

Knierim, Rolf P. "On the Task of Old Testament Theology." *HBT* 6 (1984) 91–128.

———. "The Task of Old Testament Theology." In *The Task of Old Testament Theology: Method and Cases*, 1–20. Grand Rapids: Eerdmans, 1995.

Koch, Klaus. "Is There a Doctrine of Retribution in the Old Testament?" In *Theodicy in the Old Testament*, edited by James L. Crenshaw, 57–87. IRT 4. Philadelphia: Fortress, 1983

Kovacs, Brian W. "Is There a Class Ethic in Proverbs?" In *Essays in Old Testament Ethics*, edited by James L. Crenshaw and John T. Wlllis, 171–89. New York: Ktav, 1974.

Kraus, Hans-Joachim. *Psalms 1–59: A Commentary*. Translated by Hilton C. Oswald. Continental Commentaries. Minneapolis: Augsburg, 1988.

Kuntz, J. Kenneth. "The Canonical Wisdom Psalms of Ancient Israel." In *Rhetorical Criticism: Essays in Honor of James Muilenburg*, edited by Jared J. Jackson and Martin Kessler, 186–222. Pittsburgh Theological Monograph Series 1. Pittsburgh: Pickwick Publications, 1974.

Luz, Ulrich. *Matthew 1–7: A Commentary*. Translated by Wilhelm C. Linss. Continental Commentaries. Minneapolis: Augsburg, 1989. 2nd ed. *Matthew 1: A Commentary on Matthew chapter 1–7*. Translated by James E. Crouch. Hermeneia. Minneapolis: Fortress, 2007.

McKane, William. *Proverbs: A New Approach*. OTL. Philadelphia: Westminster, 1970.

Meeks, M. Douglas. *God the Economist: The Doctrine of God and Political Economy*. Minneapolis: Fortress, 1989.

Miranda, José Porfirio. *Marx and the Bible: A Critique of the Philosophy of Oppression*. Translated by John Eagleson. 1974. Reprinted, Eugene, OR: Wipf & Stock, 2004.

Mitchell, W. J. T. *Iconology: Image, Text, Ideology*. Chicago: University of Chicago Press, 1986.

Mosala, Itumelang T. *Biblical Hermeneutics and Black Theology in South Africa*. Grand Rapids: Eerdmans, 1989.

Mowinckel, Sigmund. "Psalms and Wisdom." In *Wisdom in Israel and in the Ancient Near East*, edited by Martin Noth and D. Winton Thomas, 204–24. VTSup 3. Leiden: Brill, 1955.

Munch, P. A. "Das Problem des Reichtums in den Psalmen 37, 49, 73." *ZAW* 55 (1937) 36–45.

Murphy, Roland E. "A Consideration of the Classification 'Wisdom Psalms.'" In *Congress Volume, Bonn 1962*, edited by J. A. Emerton et al., 156–67. VTSup 9. Leiden: Brill, 1983.

———. *Wisdom Ltterature: Job, Proverbs, Ruth, Canticles, Ecclesiastes and Esther*. FOTL 13. Grand Rapids: Eerdmans, 1981.

Neal, Marie Augusta. *A Socio-Theology of Letting Go: The Role of a First World Church Facing Third World Peoples*. New York: Paulist, 1977.

Perdue, Leo G. "Cosmology and the Social Order in the Wisdom Tradition." In *The Sage in Israel and the Ancient Near East,* edited by John G. Gammie and Leo G. Perdue, 457–78. Winona Lake, IN: Eisenbrarms, 1990.

———. "The Social Character of Paraenesis and Paraenetic Literature." *Semeia* 50 (1990) 5–39.

Pleins, J. David. "Poverty in the Social World of the Wise." *JSOT* 37 (1987) 61–78.

Polanyi, Karl. *The Great Transformation.* Boston: Beacon, 1957.

Premnath, D. N. "Latifundialization and Isaiah 5.8–10." *JSOT* 40 (1988) 49–60.

Rad, Gerhard von. *Wisdom in Israel.* Translated by James D. Martin. Nashville: Abingdon, 1972.

Ricoeur, Paul. *The Conflict of Interpretations.* Edited by Don Ihde. Evanston, IL: Northwestern University Press, 1974.

———. *Lectures on Ideology and Utopia.* Edited by George H. Taylor. New York: Columbia University Press, 1986.

Ringe, Sharon H. *Jesus, Liberation, and the Biblical Jubilee: Images for Ethics and Christology.* OBT. Philadelphia: Fortress, 1985.

Schmid, H. H. "Creation, Righteousness and Salvation: 'Creation Theology' as the Broad Horizon of Biblical Theology." In *Creation in the Old Testament,* edited by Bernhard W. Anderson, 102–17. IRT 6. Philadelphia: Fortress, 1984.

Steinbeck, John. *The Grapes of Wrath.* 1939. Reprinted, New York: Penguin, 1967.

Van Leeuwen, Raymond C. "Immorality and Worldview in Proverbs 1–9." *Semeia* 50 (1991) 111–44.

Wallace, Mark I. *The Second Naiveté: Barth, Ricoeur, and the New Yale Theology.* Studies in American Biblical Hermeneutics 6. Macon, GA: Mercer University Press, 1990.

Whybray, R. N. *The Intellectual Tradition in the Old Testament.* BZAW 135. Berlin: de Gruyter, 1974.

———. "Poverty, Wealth, and Point of View in Proverbs." *Expository Times* 100 (1989) 332–36.

———. "Social World of the Wisdom Writers." In *The World of Ancient Israel: Sociological, Anthropological and Political Perspectives,* edited by R. E. Clements, 227–50. Cambridge: Cambridge University Press, 1989.

———. *Wealth and Poverty in the Book of Proverbs.* JSOTSup 99. Sheffield: JSOT Press, 1990.

———. *Wisdom in Proverbs: The Concept of Wisdom in Proverbs 1–9.* SBT 1/45. London: SCM, 1965.

Wolff, Hans Walter. *Anthropology of the Old Testament.* Translated by Margaret Kohl. Philadelphia: Fortress, 1974.

Zimmerli, Walther. *Man and His Hope in the Old Testament.* SBT 2/20. Naperville, IL: Allenson, 1968.

———. "The Place and Limit of the Wisdom in the Framework of the Old Testament Theology." *Scottish Journal of Theology* 17 (1964) 146–58. Reprinted in *Studies in Ancient Israelite Wisdom,* edited by James L. Crenshaw, 314–26. Library of Biblical Studies. New York: Ktav, 1976.

eight

THE "US" OF PSALM 67

Old Testament traditions are, of course, dominated by the self-conscious, intentional self-presentation of Israel as a peculiar people in the midst of many other peoples, the existence of which is also acknowledged. That self-presentation as a peculiar people is said to have a theological grounding as the chosen people of Yahweh (as in Deut 7:6–7; 9:4–5; 14:2), an affirmation variously articulated but assumed and traded upon widely in the tradition. That theological claim, moreover, is at the same time to be understood as an instrument of social construction, no doubt fostered and enhanced through intentional social practice.[1]

Negotiating Particularity

While that special "we-ness" of Israel is deeply privileged in the Old Testament traditions, it is at the same time readily acknowledged in the tradition that Israel as a theological, socio-political community does not live in a theological or historical vacuum, and, therefore, the privileged we-ness of Israel is never permitted to become absolute, though admittedly in some readings it is treated as absolute.[2] The recognition of the existence and legitimacy of other peoples is a necessary awareness for Israel because of the

1. On the "we-ness" in ancient Israel, see Machinist, "Outsiders and Insiders"; Bush and Dekro, *Jews, Money and Social Responsibility*, 101–4; Mullen, *Narrative History and Ethnic Boundaries*; Mullen, *Ethnic Myths and Pentateuchal Foundations*. For a social-scientific approach to "we-ness," see Mennell, "The Formation of We-Images."

2. An example of absolutizing the privileged we-ness of ancient Israel is the "myth of the empty land" as a context for reception of the land of promise. See Barstad, *The Myth of the Empty Land*.

socio-political facts on the ground; it is necessary theologically because it is claimed in Israel that the God of Israel is the creator and lord of all. That recognition of other peoples on both the theological and the socio-political horizon is voiced, for example, in the blessing trajectory of the J tradition (Gen 12:3; 18:18; 22:18; 26:4; 28:14) and in the careful presentation of kinship connections in the narrative account of Deuteronomy 2.[3] Whatever may have been the facts on the ground, it is clear that in Israel's theological and liturgic traditions, the awareness of other peoples not only included acknowledgment of their existence, but also the awareness that in undeniable ways these other peoples also participated in the beneficence of Yahweh and in obligations to Yahweh, the creator God.[4]

Thus the dynamic of the Old Testament continues to negotiate the claim of particularity—a self-presentation as the peculiar people of Yahweh—together with and in tension with a larger recognition of the scope of Yahweh's governance, and therefore the theological legitimacy of other peoples as in some sense peoples of Yahweh alongside Israel. Acknowledgment of this defining and inescapable tension is variously articulated:

> It is therefore apt to note here how Rabbi Soloveitchik dealt with this topic in his essay "Confrontation." The Rav declared, in principle, for a "double confrontation." On the one hand, the people Israel must maintain its own unique and autonomous relationship with the God of Israel. On the other hand, the people Israel must take part in the "universal confrontation" of man with the cosmos, a theme developed as well in "The Lonely Man of Faith." Indeed, the Rav asserts that "the limited role" heretofore played by the Jewish people in that universal confrontation was a function of historical reality, not ideological choice; and he suggests that this phenomenon has been reversed in modern times.[5]

3. On the horizon of the J tradition, see Wolff, "The Kerygma of the Yahwist." On the theme of kinship in Deuteronomy 2, see Miller, "God's Other Stories"; and Brueggemann, *Deuteronomy*, 28–50.

4. On the latter, attention is focused upon the Noahide Laws. See Broyde, "The Obligations of Jews."

5. Blidstein, "Tikkun Olam," 19. Blidstein refers to the important article by Soloveitchik, "Confrontation." In that discussion Soloveitchik characterizes the "non-confrontational existence" of the egocentric person who is "the beauty worshipper, committed to the goods of sense and craving exclusively for boundless aesthetic experience, the voluptuary, inventing needs in order to give himself the opportunity of continual gratification, the sybarite, constantly discovering new areas where pleasure is prsued and happiness found . . ." (6). He suggests that by contrast, Jewish faith is to live a confronted life. But then he continues to say that the "confrontation" of such "confronted life" is double:

Judaism is at once both universalistic and particularistic. The very existence of two religio-legal codes of widely disparate content side by side, i.e., the Sinaitic Covenant and the Noahide code, is itself reflective, at the very minimum, of differing standards of moral and devotional responsibility. Any thinking person will perceive that the establishment of differing standards of religio-legal responsibility is either the product of capricious whem on the part of the divine lawgiver or is a correlative of disparate capacities, talents or petentials with which different peoples have been endowed or of disparate missions with which they have been charged. Any attempt to explicated the nature of Jewish responsibility vis-à-vis the nations of the world must proceed from a clear perspective of the differing roles played by Jews and the community of nations in the divine schem of creation. From this perspective is born an assessment of the nature of the human telos, that, in turn, leads to explication of the concept of *tikkun ha-olam*.[6]

The relation of the two parts of this "double confrontation" (so Soloveitchik) is differently voiced in different texts. In this essay, I will consider that bi-focal enterprise in Psalm 67, a liturgical piece that is of interest because the remarkable number of first-person plural pronouns that function in different and highly suggestive ways in the psalm.

A Formulaic Blessing

The psalm is constituted by a series of familiar and much used liturgic formulae, here brought together in a particular and suggestive configuration. The first verse is especially familiar because it is a parallel to part of the Aaronide blessing of Num 6:24–26:

> May God be gracious to us and bless us
> and make his face to shine upon us. (Ps 67:2 [ET 1])

The blessing in Numbers 6 is, of course, a priestly blessing, a pronounced upon Israel and precisely in a context of Israel's intense cultic practice of

"human beings, sharing the destiny of Adam in his general encounter with nature, and as member of a covenantal community which has preserved its identity under most unfavorable conditions, confronted by another faith community" (17). Soloveitchik critiques the tendency of the "Westernized Jews" to choose between these two encounters by attending only to the Jewish, covenantal confrontation. It is his insistence upon both confrontations that makes his articulation important for my consideration in this essay.

6. Bleich, "*Tikkun Olam*," 62.

holiness.[7] There can be no doubt that the three suffixes, "us" in v. 2 refer to Israel, and that the blessing is given in the cultic place, the place where the power of God's blessing is mot intense and conceentrated.[8]

It is to be noted, moreover, that the name of the blessing God, Yahweh—some prominent in the blessing of Numbers 6—is not uttered in the formulation of 67:2 nor anywhere in the body of the psalm that follows. The formula of benediction in v. 2 of the psalm lacks that specificity concerning the deity. This difference and absence of the tetragrammaton may reflect the character of the "Elohist" corpus in the Psalter that characteristically does not "name the name." Alternatively, it could well be that the psalm to follow from v. 2 refrains from such usage and employs a more generic reference to God that is commensurate with the more inclusive intent of the psalm. In any case, in v. 2 by itself, the anticipation of blessing is unmistakably within the scope of Israel's most common liturgic practice as the self-consciously secure people of Yahweh to whom Yahweh generously exhibits his face, presence, and blessing.

God's Way and God's Salvation

Given the intense and unmistakable focus upon Israel as recipient of God's blessing in v. 2, we are more than a little jarred by the rhetorical turn of v. 3 [ET=2], introduced by the *lamedh*. Verse 3 functions as a transition from the focus upon Israel in v. 2 to the horizon of the nations in vv. 4–6 [ET=3–5]. Verse 3 champions God's "way" and God's "salvation," terms that acutely pertain, in the first instant, precisely to Israel as in v. 2. The "way" characteristically refers to the way of Torah and "deliverance" is the substance of Israel's own memory of God's wonders expressed in doxology.[9] In this verse, however, the two terms bespeaking Israel's Torah and Israel's recue by Yahweh are linked to a second pair of terms: "earth" and "all the nations." Thus the verse oddly juxtaposes intensely Israel-referenced phenomena that constitute the data of Israel's confession of particularity to the large scope of other peoples beyond Israel. The juxtaposition inescapably

---

7. It is entirely plausible that the benediction has a pre-history in the quotidian life of Israel, but its present location makes it intensely cultic. See Levine, *Numbers 1–20*, 236–44; and Sakenfeld, "Numbers," 84–85.

8. See Westermann, *Blessing*, 103–20, on the concentration of the power of blessing in liturgical locus.

9. See Muilenburg, *The Way of Israel*.

resituates "way" and "salvation" with access now given to Torah and to rescue to those beyond the horizon of Israel itself.

The connection between the theme of "blessing" focused upon Israel in v. 2 and the theme of "deliverance" now related to the nations in v. 3 is not self-evident.[10] That connection, however, is deftly accomplished by the opening *lamedh* of v. 3, so that Yahweh's blessing of Israel (v. 2) is instrumental in exhibiting Yahweh's saving power to the nations (v. 3). The psalm begins with a characteristic Israelite formula; the accent of these two verses taken together is not upon Israel, however, but upon the nations, thus preparing us for what follows in the next verses of the psalm.

All the Nations

With the transition from Israel (v. 2) to the horizon of "all the nations" (v. 3), we are prepared for the summons to the nations in vv. 4–6 [ET=3–5]. (The *selah* at the end of v. 5 suggests a rhetorical break between v. 5 and v. 6; but the theme continues to be the same through v. 6.) It is remarkable that in these verses the term עַמִּים ("peoples") occurs five times, matched by two uses of אֻמִּים ("peoples"). The rhetorical force of these seven uses in such a brief utterance is astonishing, apparently all to be referred back to "all the nations" (כָל־גּוֹיִם) in v. 3.

This heavy cluster of nouns looking beyond Israel, moreover, is matched by a series of verbs regularly evidenced in the cohortative. In v. 4, the verbs are a double use of יָדָה, characteristically "thank," and in v. 5 we find a pair of verbs that is more comprehensive, סָמַח, רָנַן, the pair more sweepingly doxological than the preceding יָדָה, which tends to be a response to a particular divine gift.[11] The cohortative sequence is continued in v. 6, again with a double use of יָדָה provide an envelope for the other two verbs: סָמַח and רָנַן.

The distinction between the four uses of יָדָה and the two other verbs likely should not be overdrawn. Insofar as יָדָה pertains to concrete gifts from God, we may perhaps suggest a particular likage to the motif

---

10. Westermann, *What Does the Old Testament Say about God?*, decisively advanced matters when he broke open the interpretive monopoly of "history" to consider creation, themes that he then understood respectively in terms of deliverance and blessing.

11. The relationship of praise and thanks is not an easy or obvious one in the Old Testament. See the different interpretations of the relationship by Westermann, *Praise and Lament in the Psalms*, 25–30; and Guthrie, *Theology as Thanksgiving*, 12–30.

of blessing in v. 2, likely blessings of creation. At the same time, however, in v. 3 the immediate impetus for the grateful response of the nations is for the precisely covenantal matters of "way" and "deliverance," so that the traditional Israelite focus is more pertinent in v. 3 than the broader themes of creation. However that may be, it is evident that the six verbs of summons constitute a powerful rhetorical match to the seven uses of "peoples" (five plus two). It is clear that all the peoples are to respond in glad, grateful exuberance to what they have discerned God is doing in Israel. This imperative invitation is further reinforced by the double use of "all" (כל) in vv. 4 and 6, usages surely linked to "all" (כל) in v. 3.

The only departure from this repeated pattern of cohortative summons is the pause for the motivational claim in v. 5 that is introduced by כי. That motivational clause, justifying the praise of the peoples, is remarkable, for it offers an assurance to the nations that Yahweh is attentively present for the good of the nations. That assurance is voiced in a formula of equity and guidance that is no longer dependent upon the more immediate connections of God to Israel, an immediate connection to to Israel that is stil implied in v. 3. Thus the assurance to the nations in vv. 4–6 moves beyond the Israel-dependent horizon of v. 3. In vv. 4–6 the ground for praise from the nations to God is because:

- God judges the peoples in equity.[12]

- God guides the nations upon the earth.

It is clear that in both verbs (שפט and נחה) the psalm ternsfers to "all the nations" verbs that characteristically tell of God's actions in, with, and for Israel. It is, of course, primally in Israel that God "judges with equity."[13] It is in Israel that God guides and leads, and that with particular reference to the wilderness traditions. Now, however, these characteristic actions of God are committed on behalf of "the nations upon the earth." What once and characteristically was a confessional and peculiar claim of Israel for the self-consciously peculiar people of Yahweh has now become a ground for thanks, joy, and singing gladness for all peoples. To be sure, nothing is denied Israel that was claimed for Israel in v. 2; but now nothing is privileged exclusively for Israel. The psalm stops short of saying that these seven-times referenced peoples are the "chosen peoples" toward whom God acts in special ways; that claim, however, is powerfully implied in the rhetoric.

12. The text is regularly corrected to change the preposition that governs ישר (equity), and I follow that convention.

13. The phrase in the large scope of the nations is paralleled in Pss 96:10, 13; and 98:9.

The remarkable thickness of these verses is accomplished by powerful rhetorical reiteration and reinforcement:

> Let the *peoples* praise (יד״ה) you, O God;
>> let all the *peoples* praise (יד״י) you.
> Let the *nations* be glad (שׂמח) and sing for you (רנן),
>> for you judge the *peoples* with equity
>> and guide the *nations* upon the earth.
> Let the *peoples* praise (יד״ה) you, O God;
>> let all the *peoples* praise (יד״י) you.

Doxology and Benediction

The psalm concludes in vv. 7–8 [ET=6–7] with a summary statement that enunciates both a doxological affirmation (v. 7) and a benediction that echoes v. 2 though, as we shall see, with a decisive difference (v. 8).

The doxological affirmation of v. 7 begins with a claim that is surprising in two ways. First, one might expect that God would be the subject of the verb "give" (נתן) with the object "increase" (יבולה), for this claim celebrates the effect of the beneficence of the creator God. The subject, however, is not God, but ארץ, so that the earth, as blessed creation of God the creator, now has intrinsic bond to its own life and possesses the capacity to generate abundance.[14] In contrast to the theme of deliverance in v. 3, the theme of blessing announced in v. 2 and now repeated requires no direct intervention from the creator God.[15] The earth itslef has the capacity to be the effective subject of the verb of generativity.

Second, such surprising juxtaposition of verb and subject, "earth yields," moreover, is strengthened by the initial position of the noun ארץ, which calls attention to the effective agency of creation and to the scope of the blessing celebrated. The subject ארץ of the verb thus picks up the same term from v. 3 wherein God's "way" is known upon the *earth*, and

14. The celebration of the abundance of creation has led some scholars to suggest that the setting of the psalm is at harvest time, in celebration of the blessing of a good harvest. While such a connection is possible, it is hardly an obvious or necessary one.

15. that the earth itself becomes an agent of blessing means that the creation has become a "sphere of destiny," to use the phrase of Klaus Koch, "Is There a Doctrine of Retribution," though here that rhetoric is altogether celebrative and without any motif of judgment that concerns Koch's primary argument.

from v. 5 wherein God "guides . . . upon *the earth*." In these earlier uses, and now in v. 7, it is *the earth* that is the special object of God's attention, earth now invested by God with life-giving capacities. This claim for earth clearly reflects Israel's liturgic tradition of creation that celebrates that the earth itself, albeit blessed and ordained of God; the earth, infused with the blessing of the creator, can "bring forth" (יֹצֵא) (as in Gen 1:20, 24; see also Ps 65:12–13).

Finally we come to the "us" of Psalm 67 in vv. 7–8 that is the concern of this essay. The last clause of v. 7 and the first clause of v. 8 include three first-person plural pronouns:

> God, *our* God, has blessed *us*.
> May God continue to bless *us*.

These uses echo and reiterate the three-fold "us" of v. 2 that clearly referred to Israel. In vv. 7–8 the verb "bless" (בֵּרַךְ) is as in v. 2. The phrase "God, our God" matches "God" in v. 2. This God is again in the generic and without further identification, except that in v. 8, unlike v. 2, the plural pronoun attests to "our God." The first clause of v. 8 repeats the verb "bless" with the plural pronoun plus God, yet one more time. These two clauses in vv. 7 and 8 thus include three first-person plural pronouns with nothing more to limit their identity than the two-fold use of the term "bless" and the governing generic "God." Everything else is left open.

Thus we come to the question at which this essay is aimed, namely: Who is the "us" named three times in vv. 7 and 8? The first answer to be given is that the "us" in vv. 7–8, as in v. 2, is evidently Israel. This conclusion is easily based on the parallel to the obviously Israelite reference in v. 2, plus the "our" attached to "God," for Yahweh is indeed "our God" in Israel, the self-conscious community peculiarly linked to this God. This interpretation is reinforced by the recognition that v. 2 forms a rhetorical envelope with vv. 7–8, thus a characteristic feature of poetic rhetoric.

That interpretive judgment about the plural pronouns, however, is open to review. Without denying that first identification of "us" in vv. 7–8 as Israel, we may consider further that the poetry does not move directly from v. 2 to vv. 7–8. Our verdict on the pronouns in vv. 7 and 8 thus necessarily turns on: a) what happens in the intervening verses of the psalm; and b) how seriously we may take what happens in the intervening verses.

With the transitional comment of v. 3, the suggestion of v. 3 that God's "way" and God's "saving power" are known among the nations, and the cohortative invitation for the peoples to thank, rejoice, and sing because of God in vv. 4–6, we entertain the alternative judgment that the "us" of vv. 7–8 is not any longer only Israel, but now refers to many peoples who stand with and alongside Israel as the peoples whom Yahweh blesses. This would seem to be confirmed by the concluding phrase of v. 8, that "all the ends of the earth" are to fear God. This final clause of the psalm is noteworthy:

- because "all the ends of the eath" would seem to be a counterpoint to "all the nations" in v. 3 (reinforced by the "all" of vv. 4 and 6);

- because the reiteration of "earth" in v. 8, after the usages of vv. 3, 5, and 7 suggests that the scope of God's beneficent rule now extends to all creation; and

- because the verb "fear" that is characteristically an Israelite practice is now transferred to all other peoples who are to fear God even as Israel is to fear God, the notion of fear of couse pertaining to glad obedience, that is, to walking in "the way" (v. 3).

Double Confrontation

While this psalm would seem at first glance to be a collection of familiar liturgic clichés, in fact it is carefully crafted and remarkably dense and complex in its articulation. The poem moves from *Israel* in the beginning in v. 2 to the large vista of *"all peoples"* in vv. 3–6, to the *whole earth* as generative of life (vv. 7–8). The climactic statement in vv. 7b–8 does indeed look back to the acutely Israelite affirmation of v. 2, but now filtered through the larger scope of vv. 3–7a.

It would be simple enough if we could conclude that Israel's tradition of *salvation* (ישׁעה) in v. 3 is juxtaposed to the *blessing* tradition of creation in the later verses of the poem. I suggest, however, that thethemes and patterns of rhetoric are so intertwined and interlocked that they can no longer be easily separated and distinguished in that simple, now conventional fashion. That interlocking complexity of rhetoric resists the simple assignment of *salvation to Israel* and *creation (blessing) to the nations*, both by the linking of the nations to "salvation" in v. 3 and by the verbs of "thank, rejoice, sing" addressed to the nations in v. 5, verbs that characteristically relate to Israel's Yahwistic covenantal worship.

Read closely, the movement of the psalm from beginning in v. 2 through the transition in v. 3, through the full-bodied celebration with the nations in vv. 4–6, to the conclusion in vv. 7–8 is a rhetorical process whereby Israel's cherished relationship with Yahweh is here claimed as well for all the peoples who are prepared to enact these cohortative verbs. This does not, of course, diminish Israel's primal and special claim; now, however, that primal and special claim is a part of a dynamic of enlargement whereby Israel's confession of Yahweh becomes a confession made available to other peoples alongside Israel.

I was led to ponder the remarkable rhetorical drama of this psalm by the suggestive comments of Franz Rosenzweig in his exposition of the "we" of faith:

> As its beginning, the individual voices had summoned one another, antiphonally, to thanksgiving. Now they unite in the mighty unison of "we." . . . This "we" always means "all of us," or at any rate "all those of us assembled here." In fact the word "we" can consequently be understood only when accompanied by a gesture. If someone says He, I know that one person is meant, and if I hear a voice say I or Thou, I know the same even in the dark. But if someone says We, I don't know whom he means even if I see him: himself and myself; himself, myself, and any others; himself and others without me, or which others. The We per se embraces the widest conceivable circle.[16]

> The individual confronts judgment without any intermediary factor. He stands in the congregation. He says "We." But the "We" of this day [Days of Awe, New Year's Day, the Day of Atonement] are not the "We" of the people in history; the sin for which we crave forgiveness is not the sin of transgression of laws which seaparates this people from other peoples of the world. On these days, the individual in all his naked indivuality stands immediately before God . . . and so "We" in whose community the individual recognizes his sin, can be nothing less than the congregation of mankind itself. Just as the year, on these days, represents eternity, so Israel represents mankind. Israel is aware of praying "with the sinners." And—no matter what the origin of the obscure phrase may be—this means praying, in the capacity of all mankind, "with" everyone. For everyone is a sinner.[17]

Rosenzweig's passion for the great Jewish occasions of the Days of Awe, New Year's Day, and the Day of Atonement is of course powerfully Jewish.

16. Rosenzweig, *The Star of Redemption*, 236.
17. Ibid., 325.

And yet at the same time he dares to say that this "we" of the great days is not the "We" of "the people of history." That is, not Israel in its historical, confessional identity, but "nothing less than the congregation of mankind itself."

It is clear in Rosenzweig and in the psalm we have considered that the matter of praise and thanks for God's gifts is utterly and characteristically Jewish. Rosenzweig sees at the same time, however, the sweep of God's generous truth that pushes even beyond Jewishness. It is not one or the other, but both/and, both a self-conscious people peculiarly God's people and the congregation of all humankind; or as the psalm has it, both the Jewish people under God's benediction (v. 2) and all of the nations of the earth (vv. 3–6) joined together in fearful testimony before the God who evidences saving power and who causes the earth to yield its increase (vv. 7–8).

In his polemical response to Georg Pixley's exposition of the Exodus tradition, Jon Levenson is at pains to insist that the Exodus is not a generic tradition for liberation, but a particular narrative of the emancipation of Jews who were destined for the commandments of Sinai.[18] In his initial presentation, it is perhaps the case that Pixley has given ground for Levenson's judgment that in Pixley's particular rendering of the narrative that the Jewishness of the memory could disappear. In his response, Levenson insists upon the Jewishness of the tradition to the exclusion of any other usage.

I propose that Psalm 67 is an important voice in this imagining of a "double confrontation."[19] The psalm offers a reprise of Israel's peculiar linkage to God; by the time the psalm ends, however, it reckons Israel to be a part of the larger "us" that comprises the more comprehensive recipient of God's blessing, a claim that does not erode the particular "us" of the covenantal people of God. The plural pronouns of vv. 7–8 are just open enough to permit both the particularity of v. 2 and the multiple plurals of vv. 3–6, all "us" together before "our" God who is never generic but characteristically known in Israel specifically and among the nations in glad doxology, always both/and.

Bibliography

Barstad, Hans. *The Myth of the Empty Land: A Study in the History and Archaeoloogy of Judah during the "Exilic" Period.* Symbolae Osloenses 28. Oslo: Scandinavian

18. Levenson, "Exodus and Liberation." See Pixley, *On Exodus*.
19. See above on the phrasing of Rav Soloveitchik in n. 5.

University Press, 1996. Reprinted as "The Myth of the Empty Land." In *History and the Hebrew Bible*, 90–134. Forschungen zum Alten Testament 61. Tübingen: Mohr/Siebeck, 2008.

Bleich, J. David. "*Tikkun Olam*." In *Tikkun Olam: Social Responsibility in Jewish Thought and Law*, edited by David Shatz et al., 61–102. Northvale, NJ: Aronson, 1997.

Blidstein, Gerald J. "Tikkun Olam." In *Tikkun Olam: Social Responsibility in Jewish Thought and Law*, edited by David Shatz et al., 17–60. Northvale, NJ: Aronson, 1997.

Broyde, Michael J. "The Obligations of Jews to Seek Observance of Noahide Laws by Gentiles: A Theoretical Review." In *Tikkun Olam: Social Responsibility in Jewish Thought and Law*, edited by David Shatz et al., 103–43. Northvale, NJ: Aronson, 1997.

Brueggemann, Walter. *Deuteronomy*. Abingdon Old Testament Commentaries. Nashville: Abingdon, 2001.

Bush, Lawrence, and Jeffrey Dekro. *Jews, Money and Social Responsibility: Developing a "Torah of Money" for Contemporary Life*. Philadelphia: Shefa Fund, 1993.

Guthrie, Harvey H. *Theology as Thanksgiving: From Israel's Psalms to the Church's Eucharist*. New York: Seabury, 1981.

Koch, Klaus. "Is There a Doctrine of Retribution in the Old Testament?" In *Theodicy in the Old Testament*, edited by James L. Crenshaw, 57–87. IRT 4. Philadelphia: Fortress, 1983.

Levenson, Jon D. "Exodus and Liberation." In *The Hebrew Bible, the Old Testament, and Historical Criticism: Jews and Christians in Biblical Studies*, 127–59. Louisville: Westminster John Knox, 1993.

Levine, Baruch A. *Numbers 1–20*. AB 4. New York: Doubleday, 1993.

Machinist, Peter. "Outsiders and Insiders: The Biblical View of Emergent Israel and Its Context." In *The Other in Jewish Thought and History: Constructions of Jewish Culture and Identity*, edited by Laurence J. Silberstein and Robert L. Cohn, 35–60. New Perspectives on Jewish Studies. New York: New York University Press, 1994.

Mennell, Stephen. "The Formation of We-Images: A Process Theory." In *Social Theory and the Politics of Identity*, edited by Craig Calhoun, 175–97. Oxford: Blackwell, 1994.

Miller, Patrick D. "God's Other Stories: On the Margins of Deuteronomic Theology." In *Israelite Religion and Biblical Theology: Collected Essays*, 593–602. JSOTSup 267. Sheffield: Sheffield Academic, 2000.

Muilenburg, James. *The Way of Israel: Biblical Faith and Ethics*. New York: Harper, 1961.

Mullen, E. Theodore. *Ethnic Myths and Pentateuchal Foundations: A New Approach to the Formation of the Pentateuch*. Semeia Studies. Atlanta: Scholars, 1997.

———. *Narrative History and Ethnic Boundaries: The Deuteronimistic Historian and the Creation of Israelite National Identity*. Semeia Studies. Atlanta: Scholars, 1993.

Pixley, George V. *On Exodus: A Liberation Perspective*. Translated by Robert R. Barr. Maryknoll, NY: Orbis, 1987.

Rosenzweig, Franz. *The Star of Redemption*. Translated by William W. Hallo. 1971. Reprinted, Notre Dame: University of Notre Dame Press, 1985.

Sakenfeld, Katherine Doob. "Numbers." In *The Books of the Bible*, edited by Bernhard W. Anderson, 1:71–86. New York: Scribners, 1989.

Soloveitchik, Joseph B. "Confrontation." *Tradition* 6/2 (1964) 5–29.

Westermann, Claus. *Blessing in the Bible and the Life of the Church*. Translated by Keith R. Crim. OBT. Philadelphia: Fortress, 1978.

———. *Praise and Lament in the Psalms*. Translated by Translated by Keith R. Crim and Richard N. Soulen. Atlanta: John Knox, 1981.

———. *What Does the Old Testament Say about God?* Translated by Friedemann W. Golka. Atlanta: John Knox, 1979.

Wolff, Hans Walter. "The Kerygma of the Yahwist." *Int* 20 (1966) 131–58. Reprinted in Walter Brueggemann and Hans Walter Wolff, *The Vitality of Old Testament Traditions*, 41–66 + 148–54. 2nd ed. Atlanta: John Knox, 1982.

nine

AUTHORITY IN THE CHURCH

The theme of authority is a vexed one in our contemporary social setting. And our church participates fully in that vexation. Indeed, one can guess that it is the key question, both for a frightened world and for a weary church. We discover that as believers we are not immune to the problematic.

A Crisis of Authority

All around us, we are experiencing the collapse of conventional authority. We do not understand all of the reasons for this, but we need not doubt that it is happening. For good reason it makes us nervous. In my own setting, two simple examples suffice. On the one hand, within our local congregation, we are having some (heated) discussions over the prospect of an American flag in the sanctuary. It is perhaps a sign of the times that the question should even surface, for it bespeaks a mixing of authority systems. But even worse is the ground on which the issue is argued. It is hardly adequate ground to drive around churches in St. Louis and take a poll to see which churches do what.

Or on the other hand, in the civil community, our metropolitan community is under a court order about racial segregation, and the court order bites deep because it includes the suburban school districts. Now of course the issue of busing is inflammatory and disputed. But perhaps the most curious aspect is the public officials in the county and in the state—the ones who champion "law and order"—doing everything they can to erode the authority of the court to make such a decision. Of course it is not lost on such public officials that one can make a lot of political gain out of resistance to the court on this particular issue, but what an oddity that "law and order" folks should resist the court. It symbolizes the crisis of authority we are in.

So in the believing community and outside of it, we must decide how we shall respond to this crisis. In place of validated authority among us, civil or theological, we are tempted in two directions. On the one hand, we are tempted to substitute power (force) for authority. This is our temptation in the secular community. On large scale, more arms. Closer home, more police, but power is not a trade off for authority. And power is not easily translated into authority, because authority concerns legitimated power. And illegitimate power can never finally have authority. Lenski comments on this problem and the ways of working at it. He quotes Edmund Burke:

> The use of force alone is but temporary. It may subdue for a moment; but it does not remove the necessity of subduing again: and a nation is not governed which is perpetually to be conquered.

And then Lenski comments:

> Those who seize power by force find it advantageous to legitimize their rule once effective organized opposition is eliminated. Force can no longer continue to play the role it did. It can no longer function as the private resource of a special segment of the population.[1]

The recent events in Poland raise the question if brute force can be so readily legitimated as Lenski suggests.

Or we try to live unauthorized lives, lives that are not called, not summoned by anyone, not submitted to anyone. My judgment is that in our church tradition it is not the imposition of *false authority* as much as it is the seduction of *non-authority* that besets us. Through an ideological kind of psychology, the self is made into the ultimate authority that is no authority at all. And we do discern about ourselves as well as others, that lives that are not "missional", i.e., authorized beyond self, are lives without full and free identity.[2]

Examples of this abound and could be cited by any of us. A seminary student spends the summer in field education in the affluence of Aspen and Snowmass. The folks who come there come in keen expectation that this is the garden of paradise. Well, it may or may not be. But many come there

---

1. Lenski, *Power and Privilege*, 51–52.
2. See my comments in Brueggemann, "Covenanting as Human Vocation."

and find it all an empty burden; just like the place they left. Lives that are not missional are lives without full and free identity. A middle judiciary of a church has an elaborate and intense planning process. While the world around us disintegrates, the planning process yields as a major goal "increased fellowship." The settlement is for a community turned in on itself. And the end result is a community without vitality or power.

We have lost our way. We have believed the ideology of self-fulfillment and self-actualization. And it makes the church tired, because we use up our energy on ourselves, posturing or dabbling in a host of things that remain unassessed by our proper mission.

The problem of authority is a deep problem. It touches everyone. We are all seduced and domesticated by our modem world; a world that does not want to be serious about authority. It has been so long culturally since we have experienced real authority that we run either to false authority, and we find ourselves in the presence of authoritarianism; or we fear every authority, false and true, and we flee from it all and we end with autonomy. Most of us in more liberal traditions have our antennae out for every hint of authoritarianism. But we are less attentive to the alternative temptation to autonomy.[3] In the latter mode we are de-legitimated, or, if you will, illegitimate. We cannot give a reason for our life, or for our faith, or for our hope.

Facing the Author

Now how we respond to that reality matters greatly. I make a response you would expect me to make. But I want to spend some time on that expected response in the church that may contain some unexpectedness within it.

We will not become clear about *authority* until we face the *author*. Our ministry, our common life in the church, our personal lives, cannot be sorted out until we ask about the authority of Jesus. We are agreed, are we not, that we have no authority of our own. We are not self-authorized. We have no ministry of our own except the ministry of Jesus. Indeed, we have no life of our own except the one daily given, for our daily comfort is that "we belong to our faithful Savior Jesus Christ."

But that is not a conclusion to the issue. It is rather a beginning of the consideration. We are engaged in a great argument now about the authority of Jesus. We are tempted to take a mechanical, scholastic, magical view of

3. The twin seductions of authoritarianism and autonomy are well explored in Sennett, *Authority*.

the authority of Jesus. By that I mean there are false teachers in the church, both liberal and conservative, who want to settle the question of the authority of Jesus on the terms of the world. And the outcome is authority from above, i.e., authority "like a God," who can make everything right, as though Jesus were the "Almighty Shell Answer Man." And if Jesus were like that, then we really can claim the whole game as Christians. We can claim a monopoly in our society and decide everything and judge every one and have it our way. Such a view of Jesus is very poor theology, but it is marvelous for establishing social monopoly and social control.

But that is idolatry, for the Jesus of biblical faith is not like that. We cannot presume Jesus. This is obvious from the very nature of the question we are asking. He will not be pigeon-holed, either with those who hold him high by the modes of the world, or by those who melt him away to some standard pattern of savior-hood.

So consider the authority of Jesus. My purpose is not to say something new, but to remind us of what we know best and tend to forget. To recall what we know about the authority of Jesus is important in its implications for our ministry and for our common life. The authority of Jesus is an abiding dispute in the church. The Gospel of Mark is essentially a dispute about the authority of Jesus. On the whole it is clear that throughout Mark, either

a) the authority of Jesus is rejected, or

b) the authority of Jesus is accepted and wrongly understood.

So I review with you now three texts concerning Jesus' authority.

Mark 1:21–28

The first text is Mark 1:21–28. Jesus has just called the first four disciples. He is in a hurry. He goes to the synagogue and teaches. We are not told in Mark, as in the other synoptics, what he teaches. But whatever it is, it disturbs and staggers. His listeners are astonished. It is because he has authority. And there is this marvelously revealing statement:

> He taught as one who has authority, not as the scribes.

Scribes are not bad people. They are careful, clear, calculating, clear-headed. They have good memories. What they do well is to summarize and reiterate, again and again, what has been said and believed and practiced in the past. They speak what is known among us. They hold the world as a place closed and fixed and settled. Last week I talked on the phone to a student who had transferred to an eastern theological school. Nobody doubted it is a good school. He does not doubt it is a good school. That is why he transferred. And he is not sorry that he did. He said the folks are bright, work hard, teach well, think well, write well, are articulate. But they are boring, at least the ones he had met Because for the scribes, all that remains to be done is to move the pieces around. Undoubtedly the world needs scribes. But scribes have never changed anything important; have never healed anybody. Above all, scribes have never made anything new. Because they believe everything is given that will be given.

And Jesus is an utter contrast. He is not a scribe. He does not reiterate or summarize. Nor does he speak in weariness or in anger. He does not castigate. But he speaks a new word that evokes a new reality that did not exist until he spoke it (cf. Rom 4:17). Jesus' authority is that he moves out of God's gift of newness that refuses to honor the old regularities of life. Beyond that, we cannot go. But this is enough for us. Our ministry, our lives, if we have a false Jesus, are likely to be scribal, and life becomes a tired, quarrelsome holding action.

The authority of Jesus is for shattering and for making new. We who are genuine evangelicals are not strident folk who believe that Jesus easily solves it all. Nor are we tired liberals who believe there is only us. But we are folks who touch close to the fountain of God where newness is given. That is what the church sees clearly and distinctively in Jesus of Nazareth. We scarcely know how to speak about it, as Mark did not know how to speak about it, but it dismisses all our usual categories for assessing authority.

Mark 11:27–33

Mark 11:27–33 is our second text. One would think the folks in this chapter had not read chapter 1. Jesus just told his disciples about the power of faith to move mountains, i.e., to reshape the world. And the chief priests and scribes and elders who do not want the world reshaped ask him, "By what authority?" They ask. But it is clear they do not want an answer. That is how it is with us when we stand before the authority of Jesus. We want to ask, but we do not want an answer. We would rather dispute, to keep the game going. They only mean to trap Jesus. But Jesus is no fool. So he responds in kind. He will play their silly game with them. He asks them a question that they dare not answer. And so they shrewdly shut their mouths. And the conclusion comes easily to Jesus. "I won't tell you either." Jesus does not tell us about his authority.

The authority of Jesus is *inscrutable*. It must not be talked about too much. It will not be explained. It is pornographic to know too much about the sources of Jesus' power. The church loves to reflect on and dispute about his authority. On occasion we make a public spectacle of our dispute over that question. But here it is clear. His authority is not to be understood in conventional categories. It will not do to recite a creed, though creeds serve other purposes. They do not settle for us the authority question. They only announce a resolution that we have reached for the time. We should be suspicious of people who shout it too loudly and know too much.

I have a fellow pastor and friend in Missouri who regularly corresponds with me. In his heart, I suspect, he conducts heresy trials of me, though he has always treated me courteously. But I worry, because I think he knows too much about Jesus' authority. The problem for us is that Jesus' authority is not like that of the Pentagon or even a bureaucracy. It will not be quantified. He partakes of *holy hiddenness*.

Well, if it is not to be loudly asserted, what then?

First, the authority of Jesus is to be *discerned*, not proclaimed (cf. Luke 7:22). John the Baptist asks the question of authority. And Jesus will not answer. He only points to the newness among the blind, the lame, the dead, the poor. His authority is discerned wherever there are inexplicable breaks toward humanness. The authority of Jesus is not abstract or theoretical. It is concrete and specific. So the church does not speculate. We tell stories. That is how the gospel first functions, as stories of Jesus' authority.

And the other way in which the authority of Jesus is known is that it is *practiced*. It is in the doing of his will of newness that we come to know his identity as the *author* of life. And those who do not practice in obedience do not know.

Mark 15:36–39

The third text we consider is Mark 15:36–39. Here the term authority is not used. But it is the agenda. It is a scene at the cross, in the solemn stillness after the failure. Jesus uttered a loud cry and died. The curtain of the temple is torn. The others are gone. Here is left only the Roman guard. And he says: "Truly this man was a son of God." How did he decide that? On what evidence? Mark mocks the church. In Mark, the disciples, i.e., the church, never rightly understand. And after the disciples had abandoned him in his death, this outsider of a soldier knows. The contrast is sharp. The disclosure of authority is not given where we would expect it. I submit Jesus' authority is known by the soldier because of Jesus' self-giving love. It is his self-giving that tears apart the old world and makes a new one possible. It is the embrace of death in a missional way. He does not save himself. It is this that discloses his real humanity, his profound divinity, his utter authority. The soldier sees clearly that his authority is not marked by his fullness, but by his emptiness (cf. Phil 2:5–6).

So consider these three texts:

- Jesus' authority is not given to maintain the old world, but to bring in a really new one.

- Jesus' authority is not to be explained or disputed, but only discerned in the specific and practiced concreteness of caring. All the rest is inscrutable and we must leave it so.

- Jesus' authority is discerned in his emptiness and not in his fullness. And that contradicts all our other categories of authority.

As I reflect on these claims, these observations seem important:

1. This notion of authority is against all our cultural notions. Authority in our culture wants to *maintain* the world like the scribes, not speak a new one; wants to *explain* the truth, like the Pharasees, not practice it.

2. This Jesus (who is newness, inscrutable and emptied) one would not expect to make a difference. And yet we make the confession that he is finally the only one who makes a difference.

3. It becomes clear that the Jesus question is urgent. We have to reopen the agenda among us, not about Jesus, but about our relation to this newness-giving, inscrutable, empty one. Do we really belong to this one? Do we really mean to shape our life and our ministry after him? Easy answers should not be offered.

🌿

The church has never much liked the authority of Jesus. It has always wished Jesus had some other kind of authority. We have preferred that Jesus be more like all the other Messiahs who prate about.

Flinching from Jesus' Authority

Very often the church has been busy fashioning an alternative, *Ersatz Jesus*, more in keeping with the estimate we have of our own authority. The church has wished Jesus were more like the scribes; a little less newness, a little more moving of the pieces around. Less hoping, more managing. The church has wished that Jesus' authority were not so hidden in human concreteness. It is hidden there because that is the last place we expect to fmd it. If only that authority were a little clearer, a little more spectacular, a little more explainable, so that we could replicate it! The church has wished that Jesus' authority had more to do with fullness and less with emptiness. We would wish, in the words of Professor Higgins, that he "should be a little more like me."

It is written, right there in the center of Mark. Peter, who plays the role of the church in the Gospel of Mark, says that marvelous thing: "You are the Christ." You are the authorized, authorizing Messiah. And then Jesus punctures the whole thing by telling him what it means:

- "You know it means I have to die."

- "You know life comes through death."

- "You know to be with me is to be vulnerable."

And right away Peter, i.e., the church, rejects the whole program. Embracing the authority of Jesus is rather like eating tomato aspic. It looks so good, so smooth, so red. And when you bite into it, it turns your teeth. And it tastes like nothing as much as tomato aspic. Well, we are like that in the church. We have got a whole plate full of the stuff in the person of Jesus. And it turns out not to be what it had seemed, or what we had hoped. And now, we have this topic before us, because we are deciding, re-deciding what to do about him.

The church has always flinched from the authority of Jesus, not because of what would happen to *him*, but because of the clear implication of what would happen to *us*. Because we are not stupid. Our struggle with the authority of Jesus is because we are aware of our destiny with him. The peculiar authority of Jesus bespeaks a peculiar future for the church.

It would be a little encouraging to be able to say that somewhere along the way the church went astray. Then we could hope for a recovery or a restoration. But Mark insists otherwise. The church did not at some late point in the process lose its way. It resisted and wrangled and quarreled from the beginning, from the moment of being formed as church and called as disciples. Because this Jesus, this tomato aspic set before us, is a fundamental affront in the world, even that part of the world that is the church. The conflict over the authority of Jesus is not because of a misunderstanding, but because of an understanding. It is a conflict in *principle*.

Now I say this for this reason: it is important for us to recognize that the crisis of authority we presently experience is not due to our peculiar cultural setting. It may be exacerbated by our circumstance. It may take a special form of problem because of that. But the problem is not *the oddity of culture*. It is because of *the scandal of Jesus*. And the problem for us as congregations, as pastors and bishops, as believing persons is that the scandal of Jesus sets our teeth on edge and our lives at risk. And we are confronted with a way of being authorized that feels to us like we are dangerously unauthorized. We would rather have a safer badge that the world will honor. So we push and pervert and accommodate. But nothing gives. Even in the very act of accommodating and wishing for something better, we know better.

We have this call to newness that requires us to, act against all the scribal yearnings we have. We have his call to concrete acts of humaneness that requires us to resist all grandiose theoretical claims. We have this call to emptiness so that even centurians will take note, against all our lusting for fullness. The truth is, because of Jesus, the authority of the church is an insoluable crisis, and we make only provisional arrangements. So I remind you of some texts which you know very well.

Mark 6:7–13

The first text is Mark 6:7–13. Jesus sends out the twelve. This is the great missional assertion of the church in Mark. Jesus gives the church authority over unclean spirits. Now our eyes and ears have grown so conventional that we do not notice the staggering claim of this text:

1. The church is fully authorized by Jesus. There is no qualification, no explanation, no sharing with anyone else. This is it. The disciples leave with a massive and powerful mandate. They are given an unambiguous mission, to deal with *unclean spirits*. Now that leaves everything open for us, for we would all have our notions about what this means. But whatever it means, it is clear that this mission is not conventional, routine or trivial. For what scribe among us has battled an unclean spirit? Scribes do not take on unclean spirits, but at the most moths and cockroaches. Scribes have a way of

organizing the world to pretend that there is no such category as unclean spirits. And we do not notice.

The church is Jesus' mode of assaulting the principalities and powers that beset the creation, that talk us out of our identity, that seduce us into alternative modes of living. Now I will not carry that very far, because the shape of that is different for each of us. But if any of you are defeated about the Christian life, take note. We are sponsored in the world to square off against the primordial powers of evil that beset us. Of course there is no agreement among us. But when we ask what it is that keeps us and folks like us from faithful, joyous, caring humanness, this may hint at the answer.

2. Note the mandated church is to *travel light*, without visible resources. Take nothing except a staff, sign of authority. That's all. Take no bread. Do not say what shall we eat or what shall we wear? No bag, no purse, no extra clothes. The power to cope with the unclean spirits depends on being empty-handed. The power to move against the rulers of this age depends on not playing by their rules.

I had a psychiatrist once tell me: "You only have so much energy. And all the energy one uses to defend self leaves that much less for the real action." Now I suspect that the matter of traveling light is difficult because we have not much faced the issue of unclean spirits. If we are to do lesser things, then this instruction is not so urgent. But we are called to do greater things. And so the instruction about traveling light looms large. So I put the question to you, even as I myself do not want to think about it. Have you brought too much "stuff" along? And how could we as church be more resource-less? A writer in the *Christian Century* recently wrote that in mainline churches, most decisions are informed by what it would do to our pension plans. Of course. Did you bring a purse? A doctrine, a morality, a fear, an anger, a catechism, a liturgy? They render us powerless.

3. The text ends on a high note: *They did it!* They cast out the demons . . . perhaps militarism, consumerism, sexism, racism, ageism, rage that has a death grip. Demons are cast out by people who are clear about their authority and who are therefore able to travel light. They anoint the sick. And they heal them; That is, they restore them to full functioning creatureliness. I almost didn't expect this verse in Mark, because the disciples are such a blundering, incompetent lot. And aren't we yet! But here, for an instant, even in Mark, they did it. They took the mandate. They went resource-less. And the gospel had its transforming way in the world through them. We might well hold close to that text for the tough days to come.

Mark 10:35–45

Our second text is Mark 10:35–45. Jesus has just told the disciples for the third time that he must go die. It is as though he kept repeating that point because he did not think they had caught on. And of course he was right. So they were on their way to Jerusalem, to the big show-down. They were so unsuspecting. They still did not see the shape of the confrontation. They did not see how scandalous Jesus is, how much opposition he evokes, how dangerous he is, and how risky it is to be with him. They seemed to think, as we always do, that somehow, we can make Jesus fit in so there won't be so much hostility.

They are on the way. Jesus hears this noise. And he asks, "What's the problem?" The response must have shattered Jesus. He became aware at this crucial moment. His closest friends had not a clue about his authority or theirs. They were discussing thrones! We were speculating about places for us in the new age. In yet another dispute, we were disputing in the categories of the old age, as though thrones had anything to do with evangelical authority in the new age. We were engaged in doing charades about the new age according to the hopes and fears of the old categories. The church tends to think of itself as succeeding by the old norms.

Jesus winces. He says, "You have missed the point. Our agenda on this journey is not thrones. It is cups to be drunk and baptisms to be faced. It is decisions about living and dying and martyrdom and risk and not setting out." And they say, "Well, we will do that." And Jesus, (tough, authorizing Jesus) says, "Okay, you get the cup, but I still won't guarantee a throne. Because a throne is not mine to give." I don't know about you, but I would only eat tomato aspic in order to get dessert. And Jesus assures his disciples, "I am not the one who gives dessert. I only administer the aspic."

And then Jesus makes his lordly announcement about authority. Finally he gets to the subject; the thing that most interests them (and us). It is as pertinent to us as if he had announced it this morning. The world thinks authority is to be in charge, to wheel and deal. And we are all seduced into that. But we are the ones who know another way of authority; to be a servant, slave of all. It's so simple, and so obvious and yet we find ways and ways to convolute. Jesus holds out to his church a way of authority that feels to us and to the world like being unauthorized. We are authorized to be servants in the world where servants never seem to have authority.

Now I think you are like me. You live in the tricky exchange of Mark 6:7–13 and 10:35–45. On the one hand we are clear that we are mandated against unclean spirits, ready to travel light, with visions of success. But that text is eroded in our common life by this other reality about thrones that override cups and baptisms. And our sense of authority is to be double-minded; to be empty-handed and yet to be like one of the great ones who lord it over. And so we struggle and put off deciding.

Well, of course we do. There will be no resolve of that issue in this world. But I would urge that we make this struggle a public agenda in the church. We need to be clear about the real issues. Because the real issue is not strategy or lack of resources. Our strategies and resources all wait for us to face the authority of Jesus that entrusts us with an odd authority. There is a waiting to see if there will be a time when the Roman centurion, the hard ruler of this age, will observe the feeble body of the church and say, "Truly this community is the body of Christ."

Acts 3:1–10

A third text is Acts 3:1–10. You will observe that here I cheat. I had hoped to stay in Mark. But I have stepped outside Mark for the third text on the authority of the church. You know this text well, like the others. Peter and John (who together here are the church) see a lame beggar; a waiting, desperate world. The scribes are forever flipping dimes to them, because they only want to maintain the beggar, not transform the world. And Peter the bishop, the voice of the church says: "I don't have any silver or gold. I didn't bring my purse. We didn't make our budget. I am without resources, as I was commanded to be."

"But I did bring my authority." It is the authority for newness. It is the authority for a concrete act of humanness. It is authority that comes from emptiness, of being without silver and gold, without purse, without all the ways of power that this world credits. It is an authority in touch with the deep evangelical power that has been entrusted among us. It is the authority to evoke people to a new life that violates all old definitions of reality.

Peter's authorizing speech is an imperative that dares the beggar to enter the new age of well-being. And it is a verb uttered on behalf of the one who is not a scribe: "In the name of Jesus, *walk* (περιπάτει)" (v. 6). Now who could utter such a lordly word? Only the one who has no silver and gold. And all were amazed that the new age had come (v. 10).

Now that story refutes much popular religion. The "electronic church" tends to suggest that people with more silver and gold will raise more beggars to new life. Don't believe it. The power of the new age is not grounded in our fullness, but in the emptiness of Jesus. I do not speak an easy word to you about our authority.

I do not myself find it an easy word. But it is a possibility. It is a promise given to us. It requires we quit trying to talk Jesus out of his vocation of suffering, as did Peter. It is remarkable that after Peter tried to talk Jesus out of his vocation of suffering (Mark 8:32–33), Peter nonetheless joins the vocation that heals in its emptiness. And we are called to that in a world that seduces us always into fullness. I cite these texts not that we beat ourselves in guilt. But rather that together we penetrate the issues and problems and possibilities that float around in our common life. We are the ones, the very ones, the urgent ones, who could give our life in ransom (Mark 10:45). It requires we leave off our endless chatter about thrones in the next age.

🌿

Everything has pointed to this moment today, the moment of installation.[4] And I am glad to share in it, because I have been able to stay fairly close to Bob Mutton's pilgrimage. I have known him first as a rather spacy seminarian, and then as a swashbuckling youth minister. And this now is rather like "coming of age."

So the question I put today is this: what is it like to "make a bishop?" I hope you are not offended by that term, for that is what we are doing here. We avoid the term in our church, because of the ideology of freedom and autonomy in our culture. We avoid the term. But we do not escape the reality. And I am glad we do not, for the latter part of the New Testament affirms that the health of the church depends on the right kind of bishop. Now what I have to say in this moment is not unrelated to the discussions we have had earlier:

The *authority of Christ*, authorized to newness, authorized to emptiness.

---

4. This third presentation was given for the installation of Robert Mutton as an Association Minister in the Wisconsin Conference. It is therefore articulated in terms of the office of bishop. I have left it so, because I believe the office of bishop is a crucial question in our church. But beyond that, some may find the comments more pertinent, if one thinks in terms of the pastoral office, i.e., the calling of every pastor of the church. In any case, I am glad to offer these comments in celebration of Robert Mutton, whose calling as a bishop I highly prize.

The *authority of the church*, authorized to heal, authorized to travel light.

And only after we have talked about Christ and the whole church can we speak of the bishop, for the bishop receives his/her authority only from *Christ*, only by *way of the church*. All that we have said about the church is true of the bishop, called to travel light for the sake of newness, tempted as we all are to want a throne, to lord it over others.

So at the most I can pose a number of questions that are important, but should not be answered lightly or quickly:

- What kind of bishop do you call Bob to be?

- What kind of bishop are you able to be, Bob?

- What kind of church is possible here that requires and permits a certain kind of bishop?

Because the bishop exists for the sake of the church's mission.

I think there is a growing awareness in our beloved church that bishops (i.e., especially ministers of Conferences and Associations) may necessarily be skillful managers, but they must do more than manage. Bishops must be caring pastors, but they must be more than pastors. I suggest that bishops have always been needed and authorized in the church in times of stress to guide the church to a faithful confession, to keep the church from selling out. My judgment is that we are in such a time in the church, much seduced by the world around us, seduced by a successful Jesus, by consumerism, by legalism, by permissiveness, by liberalism of an ideological kind. We join up with various parties. But none of that lets us be the church. It is the bishops' task to articulate the church's identity, to locate the mission, to reassert the calling, to draw lines and make distinctions, to identify resources and locate the ways of power and energy for our common ministry.

I have fixed on Ezekiel 34, which is a remarkable statement. I got to that text by the discovery that in v. 11—which we render, "I will search out my sheep"—the Greek has, "I will ἐπισκέψομαι (*episkepsomai*)," i.e., "I will be a bishop among my people."

The text moves in two parts. First there is a sorry recital about the way this community has been exploited by false shepherds–kings–bishops:

> You eat the fat.
>> You clothe yourselves with wool.
>>> You slaughter the fatlings, but you don't feed the sheep.
>>> The weak you have not strengthened.

The crippled you have not bound up.
The lost you have not sought.

You don't value the flock. You use the flock for your own well-being, for your own agenda. It is always a temptation, for all of us. But the church does not exist for us, for the leaders, for the bureaucrats, for the managers. It exists for the faithful flock, for the sake of the mission. Ezekiel presents a sorry picture. It is a mess. The leadership has failed. So Ezekiel finds God saying:

I myself will search them out.
I will rescue.
I will bring them out.
I will gather them.
I will feed them.

It takes very little imagination to see the church is like *a scattered flock*, all over the map, no common shepherd, no single vision, no overriding purpose. And that has to do with the void of legitimate authority in a community too impressed with autonomy and authoritarianism.

But it need not be so. "I," God says, "I will be the bishop of Israel." And this is what a bishop, in the image of God, does:

I will make them lie down in safety.
I will seek the lost.
I will bring back the stray.
I will bind up the crippled.
I will strengthen the weak.
I will feed them in justice.

This awesome bishop will risk his life that the community may prosper. Now the caring of the bishop does not have to do with psychological strokes or even money. It first has to do with *nurture in evangelical faith of a radical kind*. That is how the flock is gathered, around the promises of God which matter in the ordering of our common life. Now Bob Mutton is not God. But today he is installed to continue the great tradition of "caring for the flock."

So Bob must be thinking about caring for the flock, not overwhelmed by too much program, but to focus on being a flock under the mandate of the Great Shepherd. So today let this church and this bishop consider what they are up to. Consider what kind of church it is called to be, and what kind of bishop it must have to be such a church. Certain kinds of bishops go with certain kinds of churches.

In Ezekiel 34, there is *a slovenly exploitative shepherd.* And that goes with *a scattered, hopeless flock.* Understand, I do not for a moment suggest bishops who have personally cheated the church. Rather it is when the bishop fails, the flock becomes encultureated and cannot be identified as the special flock.

But also in Ezekiel 34, it is promised that a caring bishop who exists for the sake of the flock can result in a community that is rescued, freed, strengthened, and capable of justice.

Now this new bishop, envisioned by Ezekiel, is promised to be a new David. And a new David is known by us to be Jesus Christ, the new bishop of the church, a new shepherd of the flock. So we propose today to make a bishop whose eye is fixed on the one who loves the flock and who resolves to do what must be done, to lay down his life for the flock. The well-being and faithfulness and effectiveness of the flock depends on bishops who lay down their lives for the sake of the mission.

Now I observe three things about this possibility:

1. Bob is not asked today to be utterly used up, ragged, consumed by the church. We are not talking about a bishop whose life is laid down for all the daily agendas within the flock. Bob needs space for his own humanness and his own Christianity. But we are talking about the mode and substance of his leadership. His mode has to do with the emptiness that gives him power. His substance is to be fixed on Jesus who is our shepherd.

2. We do not propose something here for the bishop that is not proposed for the whole church. It is not only the bishop but the whole church which is to practice the laying down of life for the others. All of us have become strident and full and grasping in the church. We get so removed from the realities, as the Lord of the church never does. So this new bishop might permit this church to look freshly and dangerously at our common life. It is my judgment that the time comes soon for the faithful flock to be engaged in the laying down of life, a call which will not be screened out by either our ideological conservatism or our ideological liberalism.

3. I am not speaking about a facet of life to be added to everything else, but a fundamental refocus of the church. We have perhaps been too fascinated with the ways of the world, too lustful of power, too yearning for fullness. It has come to characterize us even across

the great spectrum of our church.

And now . . . beginning again. Beginning in exile? Beginning at the null point? Beginning in reliance on the gospel? Beginning with some evangelical resolves that we do not fully trust. Beginning again as we always must, less encumbered, more resolved.

My hunch is that for our church, the times will grow more fearful. Scattered sheep and indulgent flocks will quit· early. But ours is another possibility. And what we do in this service, this celebration of broken body and poured out blood, aims at that possibility-to visit in justice, seek out, find, rescue, gather. We could together be who we are not yet, by the mercy of God. A gathered church likely will be found only where there are lean bishops.

Bibliography

Brueggemann, Walter. "Covenanting as Human Vocation." *Int* 33 (1979) 115–29.

Lenski, Gerhard. *Power and Privilege: A Theory of Social Stratification.* 1966. Reprinted, Chapel Hill: University of North Carolina Press, 1984.

Sennett, Richard. *Authority.* New York: Knopf, 1980.

ACKNOWLEDGMENTS

The essays in this volume originally appeared in the following publications. Each of the essays has been edited.

"The God of All Flesh" was originally published in *"An God Saw That It Was Good": Essays on Creation and God in Honor of Terence E. Fretheim*, edited by Frederick J. Gaiser and Mark A. Throntveit, 85–93. Word & World Supplement Series 5. Saint Paul, MN: Word & World, 2006.

"The Creatures Know" was originally published in *The Wisdom of Creation*, edited by Edward Foley and Robert Schreiter, 1–12. Collegeville, MN: Liturgical, 2004.

"Jeremiah: *Creatio in Extremis*" was originally published in *God Who Creates: Essays in Honor of W. Sibley Towner*, edited by William P. Brown and S. Dean McBride, 152–70. Grand Rapids: Eerdmans, 2000.

"Israel's Sense of Place in Jeremiah" was originally published in *Rhetorical Criticism: Essays in Honor of James Muilenburg*, edited by Jared J. Jackson and Martin Kessler, 149–65. Pittsburgh Theological Monograph Series 1. Pittsburgh: Pickwick Publications, 1974.

"Imagination as a Mode of Fidelity" was originally published in *Understanding the Word: Essays in Honor of Bernhard W. Anderson*, edited by James T. Butler, Edgar W. Conrad, and Ben C. Ollenburger, 13–35. Journal for the Study of the Old Testament Supplements 37. Sheffield: JSOT Press, 1985.

ACKNOWLEDGMENTS

"Psychological Criticism: Exploring the Self in the Text" was originally published in *Method Matters: Essays on the Interpretation of the Hebrew Bible in Honor of David L. Peterson*, edited by Joel M. LeMon and Kent Harold Richards, 213–32. Society of Biblical Literature Resources for Biblical Study 56. Atlanta: Society of Biblical Literature, 2009.

"Psalm 37: Conflict of Interpretation" was originally published in *Of Prophets' Visions and the Wisdom of Sages: Essays in Honour of R. Norman Whybray on His Seventieth Birthday*, edited by Heather A. McKay and David J. A. Clines, 229–56. Journal for the Study of the Old Testament Supplements 162. Sheffield: JSOT Press, 1985.

"The 'Us' of Psalm 67" was originally published in *Palabra, Prodigio, Poesía: In Memoriam P. Luis Alonso Schökel, S.J.*, edited by Vincente Collado Bertomeu, 233–42. Huerto de Enseñanzas (ALAS) 1. Rome: Editrice Pontificio Instituto Biblico, 2003.

"Authority in the Church" was originally published in *On the Way: The Teaching Church*, edited by Frederick R. Trost 1.2 (1982) 11–27.

NAME INDEX

SCRIPTURE INDEX

Proverbs

Ecclesiastes/Qoheleth

Isaiah

✤

NEW TESTAMENT